EIGRP Network Design Solutions

Ivan Pepelnjak

CISCO SYSTEMS

CISCO PRESS®

Cisco Press
201 West 103rd Street
Indianapolis, IN 46290 USA

EIGRP Network Design Solutions

Ivan Pepelnjak

Copyright © 2000 Cisco Press

Cisco Press logo is a trademark of Cisco Systems, Inc.

Published by:
Cisco Press
201 West 103rd Street
Indianapolis, IN 46290 USA

Printed in the United States of America   2 3 4 5 6 7 8 9 0

Library of Congress Cataloging-in-Publication Number: 99-61718

ISBN: 1-57870-165-1

Warning and Disclaimer

This book is designed to provide information about EIGRP Network Design Solutions. Every effort has been made to make this book as complete and as accurate as possible, but no warranty or fitness is implied.

The information is provided on an "as is" basis. The author, Cisco Press, and Cisco Systems, Inc., shall have neither liability nor responsibility to any person or entity with respect to any loss or damages arising from the information contained in this book or from the use of the discs or programs that may accompany it.

The opinions expressed in this book belong to the author and are not necessarily those of Cisco Systems, Inc.

Trademark Acknowledgments

All terms mentioned in this book that are known to be trademarks or service marks have been appropriately capitalized. Cisco Press or Cisco Systems, Inc. cannot attest to the accuracy of this information. Use of a term in this book should not be regarded as affecting the validity of any trademark or service mark.

Feedback Information

At Cisco Press, our goal is to create in-depth technical books of the highest quality and value. Each book is crafted with care and precision, undergoing rigorous development that involves the unique expertise of members from the professional technical community.

Readers' feedback is a natural continuation of this process. If you have any comments regarding how we could improve the quality of this book, or otherwise alter it to better suit your needs, you can contact us through e-mail at ciscopress@mcp.com. Please make sure to include the book title and ISBN in your message.

We greatly appreciate your assistance.

Publisher	John Wait
Executive Editor	Alicia Buckley
Cisco Systems Program Manager	Jim LeValley
Managing Editor	Patrick Kanouse
Acquisitions Editor	Tracy Hughes
	Brett Bartow
Development Editor	Allison Beaumont Johnson
Project Editor	Dayna Isley
Copy Editor	Sydney Jones
Technical Editors	Don Slice
	Russ White
Publishing Coordinator	Amy Lewis
Book Designer	Regina Rexrode
Cover Designer	Louisa Klucznik
Proofreader	Bob LaRoche
Production Team	Argosy
Indexer	Cheryl Lenser

CISCO SYSTEMS

Corporate Headquarters
Cisco Systems, Inc.
170 West Tasman Drive
San Jose, CA 95134-1706
USA
http://www.cisco.com
Tel: 408 526-4000
  800 553-NETS (6387)
Fax: 408 526-4100

European Headquarters
Cisco Systems Europe s.a.r.l.
Parc Evolic, Batiment L1/L2
16 Avenue du Quebec
Villebon, BP 706
91961 Courtaboeuf Cedex
France
http://www-europe.cisco.com
Tel: 33 1 69 18 61 00
Fax: 33 1 69 28 83 26

**Americas
Headquarters**
Cisco Systems, Inc.
170 West Tasman Drive
San Jose, CA 95134-1706
USA
http://www.cisco.com
Tel: 408 526-7660
Fax: 408 527-0883

Asia Headquarters
Nihon Cisco Systems K.K.
Fuji Building, 9th Floor
3-2-3 Marunouchi
Chiyoda-ku, Tokyo 100
Japan
http://www.cisco.com
Tel: 81 3 5219 6250
Fax: 81 3 5219 6001

Cisco Systems has more than 200 offices in the following countries. Addresses, phone numbers, and fax numbers are listed on the Cisco Connection Online Web site at http://www.cisco.com/offices.

Argentina • Australia • Austria • Belgium • Brazil • Canada • Chile • China • Colombia • Costa Rica • Croatia • Czech Republic • Denmark • Dubai, UAE Finland • France • Germany • Greece • Hong Kong • Hungary • India • Indonesia • Ireland • Israel • Italy • Japan • Korea • Luxembourg • Malaysia Mexico • The Netherlands • New Zealand • Norway • Peru • Philippines • Poland • Portugal • Puerto Rico • Romania • Russia • Saudi Arabia • Singapore Slovakia • Slovenia • South Africa • Spain • Sweden • Switzerland • Taiwan • Thailand • Turkey • Ukraine • United Kingdom • United States • Venezuela

About the Author

Ivan Pepelnjak, CCIE #1354, has over 10 years of experience in designing, installing, troubleshooting, and operating large corporate and service provider WAN and LAN networks. He is currently the technical director of NIL Data Communications, a high-tech data communications company in Slovenia (www.NIL.si). His previous activities include LAN and SNA product development.

Ivan is recognized as a Cisco routing authority in Europe and led the design or implementation of several large service provider and enterprise networks throughout Europe. He is the author of highly successful Advanced BGP, OSPF, and EIGRP Configuration and Troubleshooting courses offered by Cisco Systems to its European partners and customers.

About the Technical Reviewers

Don Slice, CCIE #1929, is an Escalation Engineer in RTP, North Carolina, and was formerly a senior engineer on the routing protocols team in the RTP TAC. He is an acknowledged expert in EIGRP, OSPF, and general IP routing issues and is well known for his knowledge of DECnet, CLNS/ISIS, and DNS, among other things. Don provides escalation support to Cisco engineers worldwide.

Russ White, CCIE #2635, is an Escalation Engineer focusing on routing protocols and architecture that supports Cisco engineers worldwide. Russ is well known within Cisco for his knowledge of EIGRP, BGP, and other IP routing issues.

Dedications

This book is dedicated to my wife, Karmen.

Acknowledgments

Every major project is a result of teamwork and this book is no exception. First of all, I'd like to thank my development editor, Allison Johnson, who helped me with the intricacies of writing a book, and the rest of the editorial team from Cisco Press: acquisition editors Tracy Hughes and Kathy Trace and executive editor Alicia Buckley. My special thanks go to the technical reviewers, Russ White and Don Slice, who not only corrected my errors and omissions, but also included several useful suggestions based on their experience with EIGRP. Russ went even beyond that and sometimes helped me to explain myself better.

There are also a number of people who shared their good and bad EIGRP experiences with me during the development and delivery of the Advanced EIGRP Configuration and Troubleshooting course. They are too numerous to mention, but the contributions of several individuals stand out. I'd like to thank Holger Scherrer from Cisco Europe, Marc Calderan from Comtech, and Janez Gruden from NIL for their pointed questions and the sharing of their experiences.

Finally, this book would never have been written without the continuous support and patience of my family, especially my wife, Karmen, and my children, Maja and Monika.

Contents at a Glance

Contents

Introduction

Network architects who wanted to build multiprotocol networks in the early 1990s were faced with a tough dilemma. Most of the protocols running in enterprise network, namely IPX from Novell and AppleTalk from Apple, had no scalable routing protocols that enabled the network architect to build reliable large networks. The situation was only slightly better in the IP world—the older and proven routing protocols such as Routing Information Protocol (RIP) or Interior Gateway Routing Protocol (IGRP) were reliable, but slow, and the newer emerging routing protocols, such as Open Shortest Path First (OSPF), were complex and unproven in the field.

Cisco Systems decided to bridge the gap between the existing technology and customer requirements with a new routing protocol, named Enhanced Interior Gateway Routing Protocol (EIGRP), that combined the simplicity and reliability of the old routing protocols, such as IGRP, with the fast convergence of the new breed of the routing protocols like OSPF. EIGRP was extremely easy to configure, but still allowed the network architect all the fine-tuning and tight control over route exchange that was lost with OSPF. Even more, EIGRP was the first routing protocol to support all three major protocol families found in the enterprise networks: IP, IPX, and AppleTalk.

The benefits of EIGRP made it an immediate success in many environments, particularly in the networks where IPX or AppleTalk were a major component of the network. The situation was slightly different for the customers running pure IP networks; some of them were afraid of the proprietary nature of EIGRP and decided to implement OSPF instead.

NOTE   Whenever I run an OSPF or EIGRP workshop for network architects or support engineers, I ask the audience about the protocol mix in their customer environments. The results vary by vertical markets and countries and are extremely varied—from almost no OSPF to almost no EIGRP, with the median being OSPF and EIGRP being implemented in approximately half of the networks. I've even seen some large Internet service providers (ISP) implementing EIGRP in their new networks.

Being beta-tester of IOS 9.21, I was one of the early adopters of EIGRP and designed and implemented several large EIGRP networks in recent years. Initially, I shared the widespread belief that EIGRP is easy to configure and requires little network design. It was only when I started developing an Advanced EIGRP Configuration and Troubleshooting course as part of the family of routing protocol courses developed by my company for Cisco EMEA Training, that I became aware of the intricate internal details of EIGRP and the poorly understood distributed nature of the protocol.

Running the advanced EIGRP course and the follow-up consulting engagements exposed to a wide range of customer networks, allowed me to experience various EIGRP-related problems that could largely be traced to the lack of network design and lack of advanced EIGRP knowledge. Although the initial lack of advanced EIGRP knowledge was addressed by the EIGRP course, the customers were asking for more in-depth material with case studies and detailed troubleshooting information. A book on EIGRP within the Cisco Press series looked like a perfect solution to meet those requirements.

Objectives

This book is targeted to be a definitive, detailed reference on EIGRP. It covers all EIGRP technologies, protocols, and data structures to give you the background information you need when implementing or troubleshooting EIGRP networks. Even more important, it gives you design guidelines that help you design more robust and more scalable EIGRP networks.

The book builds the design guidelines on a number of case studies. Although these case studies come from live networks, I've tried to combine the experience I gained from working with several customers into a more generic prototype customer network that addresses a larger range of design requirements. The case studies will give you insight into the problems that occur in real-life networks when EIGRP is designed or implemented improperly. You're also invited to solve the exercises associated with the case studies as they either reinforce the particular EIGRP behavior explained in the case study or address additional EIGRP features that might be relevant to the network under discussion.

Intended Audience

The audience for this book is any network designer, administrator, or engineer who needs to design, implement, or troubleshoot EIGRP networks. Basic knowledge of TCP/IP and a basic understanding of routing are assumed throughout the book.

Organization

The book is split in three parts to help you focus on the EIGRP topics that are most relevant to you.

The first part of the book focuses on the technology of EIGRP. Chapter 1, "EIGRP Concepts and Technology," describes the high-level concepts of EIGRP and the algorithms used to compute optimum routing topology in a network. Chapter 2, "Advanced EIGRP Concepts, Data Structures, and Protocols," describes the details of EIGRP protocols and data structures. Chapter 3, "IPX EIGRP," and Chapter 4, "AppleTalk EIGRP," cover the IPX-specific and AppleTalk-specific aspects of EIGRP.

Even with the detailed information on EIGRP you receive in the first part of the book, it's sometimes hard to visualize how EIGRP will behave in a large, redundantly built network. Therefore, the second part of the book focuses on real-life scalability issues you'll face when building large EIGRP-based networks.

Chapter 5, "Scalability Issues in Large Enterprise Networks," describes step-by-step EIGRP operation in a large, unstructured enterprise network and gives you insight into the distributed nature of EIGRP and the complex interactions between various routers in the network. The chapter also illustrates the need for scalability tools deployment in large EIGRP networks. The next few chapters describe various scalability tools, from route summarization and route filters in Chapter 6, "EIGRP Route Summarization," and Chapter 7, "Route Filters," to default routes and integration with additional routing protocols in Chapter 8, "Default Routes," and Chapter 9, "Integrating EIGRP with Other Enterprise Routing Protocols." These chapters are all based on case studies of various network designs. All the case studies are based on customer networks I've seen. Most of the case studies combine shortcomings of several networks and might therefore seem slightly extreme, but each and every symptom or failure that is described in this book has been observed in a live production network.

Ideas from Chapter 5 to Chapter 9 are applicable to all three protocol families supported by EIGRP, but the configurations and solutions are given only for IP EIGRP, giving you a complete toolbox for scalable IP network design. Similar, although less powerful, toolboxes are given in Chapter 10, "Designing Scalable IPX EIGRP Networks," for IPX EIGRP and in Chapter 11, "Designing Scalable AppleTalk EIGRP Networks," for AppleTalk EIGRP.

The third part of the book focuses on WAN issues and tries to give you WAN-specific sets of tools similar to the scalability tools described in the second part of the book. Chapter 12, "Switched WAN Networks and Their Impact on EIGRP," describes the specifics of switched WAN networks, ranging from X.25 or Frame Relay to SDMS or ATM. Chapter 13, "Running EIGRP over WAN Networks," focuses on successful EIGRP implementation over switched WAN networks and Chapter 14, "EIGRP and Dial-Up Networks," describes EIGRP usage over dial-up networks.

Security becomes ever more important in the computer networks and the secure exchange of routing information can help to increase the overall network security. Chapter 15, "Secure EIGRP Operation" focuses on EIGRP-related security issues and describes several possible intrusion or denial-of-service attacks on EIGRP-based networks and the tools that you can deploy with EIGRP to minimize your exposure to those attacks.

With the increasing time pressure being applied to all of us, it's not realistic to expect that you'll be able to read this book linearly in its entirety. Individual chapters are designed to be as self-sufficient as possible, but you will always benefit from understanding the underlying issues before reading a chapter focusing on a particular aspect of EIGRP. I would therefore recommend the following:

- Read the first part of the book to get acquainted with EIGRP technology before reading the more focused chapters later in the book. Chapter 1 is mandatory reading and you can probably skip Chapter 2 until you need to focus on issues described in it.
- You can skip IPX- or AppleTalk-related chapters if you are interested in IP only. The reverse is not true; you have to read the chapters that describe common EIGRP features even if you're dealing only with IPX or AppleTalk.
- If you're interested only in a particular scalability topic, such as route summarization, you'll get most out of the corresponding chapter if you also read Chapter 1, which describes DUAL, and Chapter 5, which describes issues in large enterprise networks.
- If your focus is WAN implementation of EIGRP, you should read Chapter 1 and Chapter 2 to get a detailed understanding of EIGRP, including the transport protocol, flow-control, and pacing. Chapter 12 and Chapter 13 are mandatory reading if you want to design reliable EIGRP-based WAN networks. You might want to continue with Chapter 5 to Chapter 9 after solving initial WAN issues to make your network more scalable.
- For those of you interested primarily in dial-up issues, Chapters 1, 2, and 14 will get you started, and I strongly recommend that you continue with the second part of the book to understand the scalability issues of your network.
- If you are interested in network security, Chapter 15 will give you the information you need to make EIGRP information exchange more secure. The secure information exchange shall always be combined with route filters described in Chapter 7.

Additional Background and Reference Information

With the Internet changing the way we work and learn, it's only appropriate that the background and reference information for a technology-oriented book be available in an interactive form on a Web site. A Web site for this book, reachable at www.ciscopress.com/eigrp, gives you the following:

- Links to other material related to EIGRP, including material on Cisco Connection Online
- Solutions to selected exercises
- Router configurations that were used to generate the printouts in the book so that you can reproduce the scenarios described in the book in your lab

The Web site is also designed to be interactive to enable you to share the information made available with other readers—from submitting your own solutions to exercises in the book to providing feedback or additional information.

Applicability of EIGRP

I'd like to conclude this introduction with the applicability of EIGRP in today's major networking segments: enterprise and service provider networks. Although the titles of some of the chapters might give you the impression that EIGRP is mostly an enterprise-oriented routing protocol that cannot be used in service provider environments, that is a completely wrong impression. Several large service providers use EIGRP very successfully. EIGRP has also proved to be very useful in several service provider networks I've designed because it has fewer topology limitations than OSPF. Based on that experience, I've included several case studies in Chapter 9 that address the service-provider issues, such as integration with Border Gateway Protocol (BGP). On the other hand, most new service-provider oriented technologies such as MPLS/VPN (Virtual Private Networks based on Multi-Protocol Label Swapping) or RRR (Routing for Resource Reservation) are first implemented within the framework of OSPF, giving OSPF a slight edge in the service-provider market.

EIGRP Technology

CHAPTER 1

EIGRP Concepts and Technology

This chapter explains the Enhanced Interior Gateway Routing Protocol (EIGRP) concepts and technologies. These concepts are common to all three protocol families supported by EIGRP (IP, IPX, and AppleTalk) and are covered in several sections:

- "Introduction to EIGRP" compares EIGRP to other routing protocols.

- "Initial IP EIGRP Configuration" documents the basic commands needed to start IP EIGRP in the Cisco IOS.

- "EIGRP Concepts" explains EIGRP Metrics and Distances.

- "DUAL—The Heart of EIGRP" describes the core algorithm of EIGRP.

EIGRP data structures, protocols, and advanced concepts are covered in Chapter 2, "Advanced EIGRP Concepts, Data Structures, and Protocols." The IPX EIGRP and AppleTalk EIGRP configurations are covered in Chapter 3, "IPX EIGRP," and Chapter 4, "AppleTalk EIGRP."

EIGRP Concepts—Metrics and Distances

You can better understand the technology used in EIGRP by comparing it with other protocols well known to the internetworking industry. As you know, routing protocols have two major approaches:

- Routing by rumor (also called distance-vector) is used by protocols, such as Interior Gateway Routing Protocol (IGRP), Routing Information Protocol (RIP), and Border Gateway Protocol (BGP), where each router knows only what its neighbors tell it.

- Routing by propaganda (also called link-state) is used by protocols, such as Open Shortest Path First (OSPF) or Intermediate System-to-Intermediate System (IS-IS), where all the routers in a region of the network share a common understanding of the region's topology.

Technology used in EIGRP (DUAL—Diffused Update Algorithm) is similar to distance vector protocols:

- The router uses only the information it receives from its directly connected neighbors to make its routing decisions. Received information can be further filtered for security or traffic-engineering reasons.
- The router announces only the routes it's using to its directly connected neighbors. Information sent to neighbors can also be filtered before being sent.

However, a number of significant differences make EIGRP perform better than traditional distance-vector protocols:

- EIGRP stores all routes received from all neighbors in its topology table, not just the best route it has received so far. (Compare that with RIP, which stores only the best route and discards all others.) Knowledge of more than one route enables EIGRP to quickly switch to an alternate route should the current route disappear.
- EIGRP takes an active role and queries its neighbors when a destination becomes unreachable and it has no alternate route. Routers running traditional distance-vector protocols passively wait for their neighbors to find better routes and report them. Because the convergence process is active, rather than passive (just waiting for a route to time out), EIGRP's convergence is comparable to the best link-state protocols.

Definition **Topology table** is the data structure where EIGRP stores all routes it has received from its neighbors.

Troubleshooting/Monitoring Tip

It's widely believed that EIGRP stores only the loop-free routes it receives from its neighbors because these routes appear in the default printout of the topology table (similar to the printout in Example 1-1).

Example 1-1 *Default EIGRP Topology Table Printout*

```
C2522>show ip eigrp topology
IP-EIGRP Topology Table for process 1

Codes: P - Passive, A - Active, U - Update, Q - Query, R - Reply,
       r - Reply status

P 1.0.0.1/32, 1 successors, FD is 22900736
        via 1.0.0.1 (22900736/128256), Serial2
P 1.0.0.3/32, 1 successors, FD is 2297856
        via 1.0.0.3 (2297856/128256), Serial1
P 1.0.0.2/32, 1 successors, FD is 128256
        via Connected, Loopback0
P 1.0.0.4/32, 1 successors, FD is 2297856
        via 1.0.0.4 (2297856/128256), Serial0
```

In reality, the other routes are stored in a topology table but they are not printed. You have to use the **all-links** option to see them. Such a printout for the same topology table as in Example 1-1 is displayed in Example 1-2.

Example 1-2   *Printout of the Whole EIGRP Topology Table*

```
C2522>show ip eigrp topology all-links
IP-EIGRP Topology Table for process 1

Codes: P - Passive, A - Active, U - Update, Q - Query, R - Reply,
       r - Reply status

P 1.0.0.1/32, 1 successors, FD is 22900736, serno 2
        via 1.0.0.1 (22900736/128256), Serial2
        via 1.0.0.4 (24436736/23924736), Serial0
P 1.0.0.3/32, 1 successors, FD is 2297856, serno 5
        via 1.0.0.3 (2297856/128256), Serial1
        via 1.0.0.4 (2809856/2297856), Serial0
P 1.0.0.2/32, 1 successors, FD is 128256, serno 1
        via Connected, Loopback0
        via 1.0.0.4 (3321856/2809856), Serial0
P 1.0.0.4/32, 1 successors, FD is 2297856, serno 3
        via 1.0.0.4 (2297856/128256), Serial0
        via 1.0.0.3 (2809856/2297856), Serial1
```

If you compare the entries for all the routes in Example 1-2 with the corresponding entries in Example 1-1, you'll notice that each route contains an extra entry that's hidden by the default printout.

- EIGRP uses the hello protocol between the neighbors to enable early detection of neighbor failure and faster convergence. Normal distance-vector protocols rely on routing update timeouts to detect this condition.

- EIGRP uses the reliable transport protocol to send and receive routing updates, which eliminates the need for periodic full updates.

These features make EIGRP a modern routing protocol with convergence and link-usage performance comparable to other modern protocols, such as OSPF or IS-IS.

Initial IP EIGRP Configuration

Initial IP EIGRP configuration is extremely simple:

- Start the EIGRP process with the **router eigrp <as-number>** configuration command.

- Assign interfaces to the EIGRP process using the **network <major-network>** router configuration command. All subnets belonging to the specified major network are assigned to the EIGRP process.

NOTE	The **as-number** used in the EIGRP process does not have to be the globally unique Autonomous System number assigned to service providers and multihomed end-customers in the Internet by numbering authorities such as InterNIC or RIPE. You can use any number as long as you use the same number on all the routers running EIGRP. If you own a legal Autonomous System number, it's recommended that you use that number for consistency.

When a major network is specified in the EIGRP process with the **network** command, all the directly connected subnets of that major network are entered in the EIGRP topology table, EIGRP neighbors are discovered on all the interfaces belonging to the specified major network, and the routing information is exchanged with those neighbors. If you use several major networks in your internetwork (for example, if you're using private class-C address space 192.168.1.0—192.168.255.0), only those networks that directly connect to the router must be specified with the **network** command.

NOTE	You can use the **passive-interface** router configuration command, described in more detail in Chapter 2, to stop EIGRP from running on an interface that belongs to a major network specified with the **network** command. However, you can't stop EIGRP from inserting the directly connected subnets belonging to the major network specified in the **network** command into the topology table and propagating them to other EIGRP-speaking routers prior to IOS 12.0(4)T. The **mask** option of the **network** command was introduced in IOS 12.0(4)T to give EIGRP true classless behavior.

These two commands are usually the only two commands that you need to configure IP EIGRP in a small enterprise network. Additional EIGRP configuration is necessary in larger networks for fine-tuning or to deploy the scalability features.

EIGRP Concepts—Metrics and Distances

Like any other protocol, EIGRP uses metrics to select the best route toward the destination. This section explains the two types of metrics that EIGRP uses: the vector metric and the composite metric. The rules for adjusting vector metric and the conversion process between vector and composite metric are defined.

Unlike other routing protocols, such as RIP or OSPF, EIGRP performs a two-step process in computing the metric of a route. Several different properties are associated with a route (vector metric):

- Total delay from the router to the destination subnet
- Minimum bandwidth on the path to the destination subnet

- Maximum load and minimum reliability of any link on the path toward the destination subnet
- Minimum MTU of any link toward the destination subnet
- Hop count

The vector metric is used in combination with K-values to compute a single number called *composite metric* and sometimes *distance*. This number is used in all comparisons when the router is trying to decide which route is the best.

Definition   **Vector metric** is a six-element vector containing parameters (bandwidth, delay, load, reliability, hop count, and MTU) that describe the distance between a router and the destination subnet. The vector metric is used in all EIGRP routing updates.

Composite metric or **Distance** is an integer number used to compare different routes toward the same destination subnet. It's only used internally in the router and is never sent to EIGRP neighbors. EIGRP distance is completely unrelated to IOS administrative distance.

K-values are numbers (K1 through K5) used in transformation of vector metrics to a composite metric.

Troubleshooting/Monitoring Tip

You can print the detailed vector and composite metric of a single EIGRP route from the topology table. The command to do it is **show ip eigrp topology <address> <mask>** (see Example 1-3).

Example 1-3   *EIGRP Vector and Composite Metrics as Displayed by the **show ip eigrp topology** Command*

```
C2522>show ip eigrp topology 1.0.0.4 255.255.255.255
IP-EIGRP topology entry for 1.0.0.4/32
  State is Passive, Query origin flag is 1, 1 Successor(s), FD is 40640000
  Routing Descriptor Blocks:
  1.0.0.4 (Serial0), from 1.0.0.4, Send flag is 0x0
      Composite metric is (40640000/128256), Route is Internal
      Vector metric:
        Minimum bandwidth is 64 Kbit
        Total delay is 25000 microseconds
        Reliability is 255/255
        Load is 197/255
        Minimum MTU is 576
        Hop count is 1
```

Computing a Composite Metric

The formula to transform vector metric into the composite metric is a two-step process:

Step 1   Composite metric = K1*BW + K2*BW/(256-load) + K3*DLY where

BW   10 Gbps/bandwidth

DLY   delay in tens of microseconds

Step 2   (Necessary only when K5 is not equal to 0)

Composite metric = Composite metric * K5 / (reliability + K4)

The default values of K1 and K3 are 1, and all the other factors have a default value of 0. The default composite metric is therefore a sum of the total delay and the inverse bandwidth.

K2, K4, and K5 are leftovers from IGRP times; they don't work correctly with EIGRP. IGRP used periodic routing updates that reflected current load and reliability conditions, whereas EIGRP uses event-triggered routing updates that reflect interface load and reliability at the time of the event (route loss or reappearance). Therefore, *Load* and *Reliability* in EIGRP vector metric are quite useless, and it makes no sense to use them in composite metric calculations.

You can change the default values of the K-values for IP EIGRP with a command in the EIGRP routing process configuration, as shown in Table 1-1.

Table 1-1   *Setting K-Values in the EIGRP Routing Process*

Task	Command
Change EIGRP K-values	**metric weights** *TOS K1 K2 K3 K4 K5*
Reset K-values to default values	**no metric weights**

For EIGRP to work correctly, it's crucial that the K-values match between EIGRP neighbors. The K-values are therefore checked in hello packets before the EIGRP routers establish adjacencies.

Design/Configuration Tip

You can use nondefault K-values to achieve EIGRP behavior that mimics other routing protocols in the following ways:

- To emulate RIP, set delays on all interfaces to equal value and set all Ks, except K3, to 0.

- To emulate OSPF, set interface delay to OSPF cost and set all Ks, except K3, to 0.

- To select a route with maximum end-to-end bandwidth, set all Ks, except K1, to 0.

NOTE	The composite metric is always 1 if you set all K-values to 0. This turns EIGRP into a routing protocol that selects all alternate paths toward a destination, regardless of whether they form a loop or not. Setting all K-values to 0 leads to traffic loops in many meshed networks. Loops also are guaranteed to occur if you turn off EIGRP split horizon.

Computing Vector Metric

Determining the vector metric is a straightforward process for a connected subnet; the proper parameters are copied from the interface definition and inserted in the route description in the topology table. The interface parameters influencing EIGRP vector metric for connected routes are highlighted in the printout in Example 1-4.

Example 1-4 *Interface Parameters Influencing EIGRP Vector Metric for Connected Subnets*

```
C2522>show interface serial 0
Serial0 is up, line protocol is up
  Hardware is HD64570
  Interface is unnumbered. Using address of Loopback0 (1.0.0.2)
  MTU 576 bytes, BW 64 Kbit, DLY 20000 usec, rely 255/255, load 1/255
  Encapsulation HDLC, loopback not set, keepalive set (10 sec)
  Last input 00:00:02, output 00:00:03, output hang never
  Last clearing of "show interface" counters never
  Queuing strategy: fifo
  Output queue 0/40, 0 drops; input queue 0/75, 0 drops
  30 second input rate 0 bits/sec, 0 packets/sec
  30 second output rate 0 bits/sec, 0 packets/sec
    ... more interface statistics ...
```

Default interface values for bandwidth and delay are set based on actual hardware in the router, as shown in Table 1-2.

Table 1-2 *Default Bandwidth and Delay for Various Interfaces*

Interface Type	Bandwidth (kbps)	Delay (microseconds)
Ethernet	10000	1000
Token ring	16000	630
Fddi	100000	100
Serial interface	1544	20000
Low-speed serial interface[1]	115	20000
ISDN BRI	64[2]	20000
ISDN PRI	64	20000
Dialer interface	56	20000
Channelized T1 or E1	n * 64	20000
Async interface	tty line speed	100000
Loopback	8000000	5000

1. Low-speed serial interfaces include WIC on 1600/2600/3600 series, sync/async interfaces on 252x routers, sync/async serial modules on 2600/3600, etc.

2. Also true in U.S.

Although the default values of bandwidth and delay are usually correct for LAN interfaces, at least the bandwidth tends to be incorrect for the WAN interfaces. Bandwidth—and sometimes delay—must be specified for each WAN interface or subinterface using the following commands in (sub)interface configuration mode, as shown in Table 1-3.

Table 1-3 *Setting Interface Bandwidth and Delay*

Task	Command
Set (sub)interface bandwidth	**bandwidth <bw-in-kbps>**
Set (sub)interface delay	**delay <delay-in-tens-of-microseconds>**

The bandwidth specified on a (sub)interface affects only load calculation, EIGRP routing calculations, and EIGRP pacing. The delay specified on (sub)interface affects only EIGRP routing calculations. These parameters have no other impact on router operation, performance, or traffic shaping on the outgoing interface.

NOTE   The units used in configuring interface delay (tens-of-microseconds) are different from the units used to display the delay with **show interface** command (microseconds). EIGRP uses the delay in tens of microseconds (as entered with the **delay** command) to calculate the composite metric.

Design/Configuration Tip

Setting proper bandwidth is particularly tricky on VLAN interfaces, more so in cases where different routers attach to the same virtual LAN through different technologies (for example, ATM LAN on one end, and Ethernet or Fast Ethernet on the other end). It's recommended that you set the bandwidth to a sensible value that's the same on all routers attached to the same virtual LAN.

The vector metric of a route received from a neighbor is computed from the received vector metric and the parameters of the interface through which the route was received using the formulas in Equation 1-1.

Equation 1-1

$$Delay_{New} = Delay_{Received} + Delay_{Interface}$$

$$Bandwidth_{New} = \min(Bandwidth_{Received}, Bandwidth_{Interface})$$

$$MTU_{New} = \min(MTU_{Received}, MTU_{Interface})$$

$$HopCount_{New} = HopCount_{Received} + 1$$

After the vector metric is adjusted to compensate for the inbound interface vectors, it is stored in the topology table.

The vector metric is never adjusted in the outgoing updates; the router always reports the values it has in its topology table to its neighbors and relies on them to adjust the values themselves.

A simple example of vector metric propagation is shown in Figure 1-1 where the bandwidth on the Frame Relay links is configured as indicated in the figure and the delay on all interfaces has default values from Table 1-2.

Figure 1-1   *Vector Metric Propagation Example*

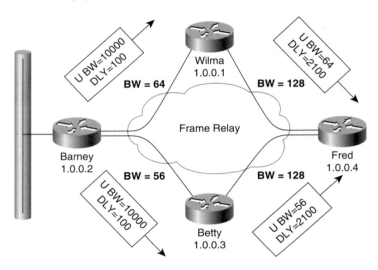

When the Ethernet interface on router Barney becomes active, Barney announces the subnet configured on the Ethernet interface with 10 Mbps bandwidth and a delay of 100 microseconds. Wilma and Betty receive this update, add the delay of the incoming interface to the announced delay and minimize the bandwidth according to formulas in Equation 1-1. The new vector metric is announced further to router Fred that performs the same operation.

DUAL—The Heart of EIGRP

The central algorithm of EIGRP is the *Diffusing Update Algorithm (DUAL)* that relies on protocols (such as the *hello protocol* and the *reliable transport protocol*) and data structures (such as the *neighbor table* and the *topology table*) to provide all the routers in a network with consistent information leading to optimum route selection. Figure 1-2 relates DUAL to all these other components.

Figure 1-2   *Map of EIGRP Components*

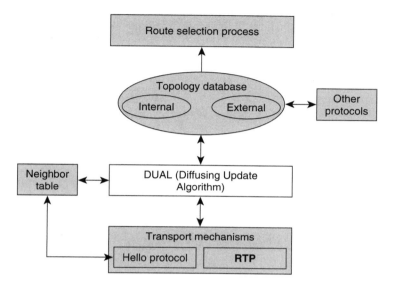

We start our exploration of DUAL with some terminology definitions, followed by a detailed look at the behavior of the DUAL algorithm in various scenarios, from adding a new route to losing a route or adjacency with a neighboring router.

NOTE	Throughout our discovery of EIGRP operation, we use extensive debugging capabilities built in Cisco IOS. I strongly urge readers who want to achieve an in-depth understanding of EIGRP operation to do the same in a lab environment. I also strongly discourage extensive use of EIGRP debugging (or any other debugging facility) in a production network.

DUAL Terminology

Before discussing details of DUAL, it's beneficial to define a few terms that are used throughout the rest of this chapter. The best place to start is with the definition of *upstream* and *downstream* routers.

Upstream and Downstream Routers

Imagine a network where the routed data toward a particular destination subnet flows from A toward F through X and C, as presented in Figure 1-3.

Figure 1-3   *Sample Routed Data Flow*

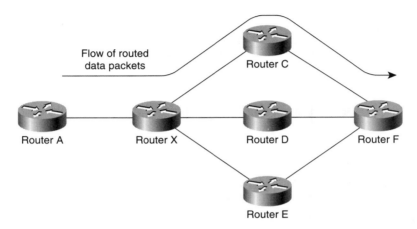

From the standpoint of router X, router C acts as a downstream router and router A acts as an upstream router. (Imagine the data flow as a river to get a better understanding of upstream/downstream concepts.) Figure 1-4 demonstrates the concept of upstream and downstream routers in the network displayed in Figure 1-3 from the perspective of router X.

Definition   The **downstream router** (for a subnet) is the router that is closer to the destination subnet and that the current router uses to forward data packets toward the destination subnet.

The **upstream router** (for a subnet) is a router that is further away from the destination subnet than the current router and that uses the current router to forward data packets toward the destination subnet.

Figure 1-4   *Upstream and Downstream Routers*

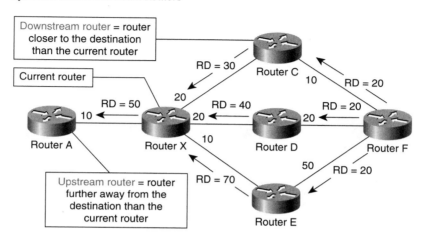

Reported Distance and Feasibility Distance

Each EIGRP router uses its topology table to select the best route toward each destination in the table. The vector metric of the best route is reported to the router's neighbors. The composite metric (or distance) of this route is called *reported distance*.

Definition	**Reported distance** is the distance reported to the current router from a neighbor.

Each router adds its interface metrics to the distance reported by its neighbor to get its own distance to the reported destination. The reported distance propagation in the network from Figure 1-4 is illustrated in Figure 1-5.

NOTE	Although the composite distances cannot be simply added together because the operation performed on the vector metric is not linear, we'll assume that we can add them to simplify the examples in this section.

Figure 1-5 *Distance Propagation*

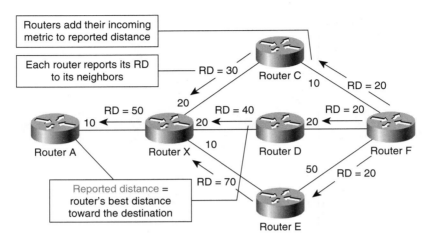

The router on the lowest-cost path toward the destination becomes the *successor* for a particular subnet as shown in Figure 1-6. The successor for a subnet is also the downstream router for the same subnet.

Figure 1-6 *EIGRP Successor*

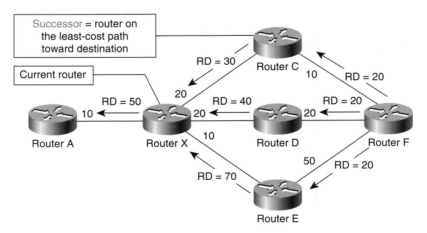

Definition	The **successor** is the next-hop router for traffic from the current router toward the destination.

Sometimes an EIGRP neighbor does not become a successor, but it unambiguously does not use the current router as its successor. In these scenarios, the neighbor is a *feasible successor*, meaning it can become a successor if the route through the current successor is gone.

For example, router D in Figure 1-6 is not the successor of router X because the combined reported distance (40) and interface distance (20) is higher than the minimum distance of router X (50). It's also evidently not using router X as its successor because the reported distance of router D (40) is lower than the distance of router X (50).

Many possible ways of finding out whether a specific router is not an upstream router exist. EIGRP designers decided to use one of the most reliable (and most restrictive) ones:

> A router is definitely not an upstream router if its reported distance is lower than the current best metric to a given destination. For a router to be an upstream router with a reported distance that is less than the current best metric, it must have a negative interface distance, which is impossible by design.

Definition	With this rule in mind, we can define several new terms:

The **feasible successor** is a router that is closer to the destination than the current router. A feasible successor is guaranteed not to be an upstream router of the current router.

A neighbor is a feasible successor if it meets *feasibility condition*.

Feasibility distance is the minimum distance from the current router toward the destination since the last time a DUAL computation completed. A neighbor meets the **feasibility condition** if its reported distance is strictly lower than the feasibility distance.

A neighbor is a *feasible successor* if it meets the *feasibility condition*.

A *feasible successor* on the least-cost path is a *successor*. All these concepts are illustrated in Figure 1-7.

Figure 1-7 *Feasible Successor*

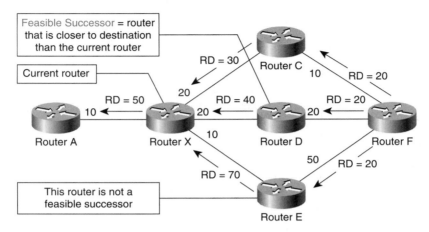

Router D is not a successor for router X because the distance of the path through router D is 60 (the reported distance of 40 plus the interface distance of 20). It is a feasible successor because its reported distance (40) is lower than the feasibility distance of router X (50) (or the best path router X has available, through router C). Router E is not a feasible successor because its reported distance (70) is greater than the feasibility distance of router X.

Simple DUAL Operation—Adding New Routes

With all the EIGRP terms defined, you can start exploring the workings of DUAL. We'll start with the easiest operations (route addition and metric decrease) and work our way through more and more complex scenarios, finally arriving at a full diffusing computation. A test network of four routers is used for all examples. The routers are connected with Permanent Virtual Circuits (PVC) through a Frame Relay network. The PVCs (also called Data Link Connection Identifier or DLCI) have the Committed Information Rates (CIR) depicted in Figure 1-8.

All DLCIs from Barney are configured on unnumbered point-to-point interfaces and the DLCIs between Betty, Fred, and Wilma are on a common partially meshed subnet, as shown in Figure 1-9.

When a new subnet becomes reachable through Barney, for example, with the commands in Example 1-5, Router Barney immediately informs all its neighbors about the new route, as shown in Example 1-6.

Figure 1-8   *EIGRP Test Network*

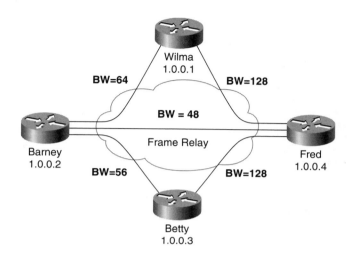

Figure 1-9   *EIGRP Test Network—Logical View*

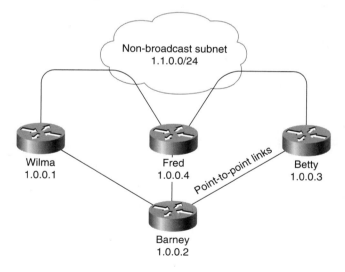

Example 1-5 *Insert a New Subnet in the Network by Configuring an IP Address on a Loopback Interface*

```
Barney(config)#interface loopback 1
Barney(config-if)#ip address 1.0.0.5 255.255.255.255
```

Example 1-6 *New Connected Subnet—Router Informs Its Neighbors*

```
Barney#debug eigrp packet update query reply
EIGRP Packets debugging is on
    (UPDATE, QUERY, REPLY)
Barney#debug eigrp fsm
EIGRP FSM Events/Actions debugging is on
Barney#
DUAL: dual_rcvupdate(): 1.0.0.5/32 via Connected metric 128256/0
DUAL: Find FS for dest 1.0.0.5/32. FD is 4294967295, RD is 4294967295 found
DUAL: RT installed 1.0.0.5/32 via 0.0.0.0
... Barney found out about the new route, it's time to inform its neighbors ...
DUAL: Send update about 1.0.0.5/32. Reason: metric chg
DUAL: Send update about 1.0.0.5/32. Reason: new if
EIGRP: Enqueuing UPDATE on Serial0.1 iidbQ un/rely 0/1 serno 128-128
EIGRP: Enqueuing UPDATE on Serial1.1 iidbQ un/rely 0/1 serno 128-128
EIGRP: Enqueuing UPDATE on Serial2.1 iidbQ un/rely 0/1 serno 128-128
```

More Debugging Output Explanations

Sending updates on an interface is not an easy process for EIGRP. (You will find out the reasons for this in the "Reliable Transport Protocol" section in Chapter 2.) The process of sending updates is composed of three steps:

Step 1 Individual route updates are enqueued for an interface.

Step 2 Route updates enqueued for an interface are bundled into a packet when the interface is ready to send more EIGRP traffic.

Step 3 The update packet is sent toward individual neighbors reachable over that interface.

This three-step process creates three debugging lines for each neighbor on Barney, as shown in Example 1-7.

Example 1-7 *Debugging Printout Associated with Sending a Single EIGRP Update Packet to an EIGRP Neighbor*

```
EIGRP: Enqueuing UPDATE on Serial2.1 iidbQ un/rely 0/1 serno 128-128
EIGRP: Enqueuing UPDATE on Serial2.1 nbr 1.0.0.1 iidbQ un/rely 0/0
  peerQ un/rely 0/0 serno 128-128
EIGRP: Sending UPDATE on Serial2.1 nbr 1.0.0.1
  AS 1, Flags 0x0, Seq 264/84 idbQ 0/0 iidbQ un/rely 0/0 peerQ
  un/rely 0/1 serno 128-128
```

To keep these examples simple and easy to understand, we'll omit the first two messages in the debugging outputs. In our simple examples, we don't lose anything by doing this because we always process only one route (so the batching process changes nothing) and the interfaces are always ready to send more EIGRP traffic.

Each of Barney's neighbors (Wilma, Betty, and Fred) process the incoming updates from Barney and find that Barney has announced the best route toward the new subnet. Barney becomes their successor, as shown in Example 1-8.

Example 1-8   *Router Receives a New Route from Its Neighbor*

```
Fred#
EIGRP: Received UPDATE on Serial0.1 nbr 1.0.0.2
  AS 1, Flags 0x0, Seq 255/134 idbQ 0/0 iidbQ un/rely 0/0
DUAL: dest(1.0.0.5/32) not active
DUAL: dual_rcvupdate(): 1.0.0.5/32 via 1.0.0.2 metric 53973248/128256
Barney's reported distance toward the destination subnet is 128256 when converted
into EIGRP composite metric. Fred's own composite metric of the direct path to Barney
through interface Serial 0.1 is 53973248, as seen from the last debugging line above.
DUAL: Find FS for dest 1.0.0.5/32. FD is 4294967295, RD is 4294967295
found
Fred's current feasibility distance for subnet 1.0.0.5 is infinity (4294967295),
which is also its reported distance. Obviously Barney offers a better route which
is immediately selected and installed.
DUAL: RT installed 1.0.0.5/32 via 1.0.0.2
```

After selecting the route offered by Barney, Fred has to inform its neighbors about the new route. Its updates to Wilma and Betty are obvious; it reports the metric through the best path it has to this new destination as its new reported distance, as shown in Example 1-9.

Example 1-9   *Fred Sends the Information about the New Best Route to Its Other Neighbors*

```
Fred#
DUAL: Send update about 1.0.0.5/32. Reason: metric chg
DUAL: Send update about 1.0.0.5/32. Reason: new if
01:46:46: EIGRP: Enqueuing UPDATE on Serial0.1 nbr 1.0.0.2 iidbQ un/rely 0/0 peerQ
un/rely 0/0 serno 90-90
01:46:46: EIGRP: Enqueuing UPDATE on Serial0 nbr 1.1.0.1 iidbQ un/rely 0/0 peerQ un/
rely 0/0 serno 90-90
01:46:46: EIGRP: Enqueuing UPDATE on Serial0 nbr 1.1.0.3 iidbQ un/rely 0/0 peerQ un/
rely 0/0 serno 90-90
```

The real question is, what is Fred sending to Barney and why? The debugging outputs on Fred don't tell us what's going on and Barney is also silent about this update, so the only help is a packet analyzer, such as Sniffer, which tells us that Fred is sending Barney a poison update (a regular update with the delay set to infinity) to prevent any potential loops.

Our current knowledge of EIGRP can be formulated in a set of rules.

Basic DUAL Rules

DUAL Rule 1:   Whenever a router chooses a new successor, it informs all its other neighbors about the new reported distance.

DUAL Rule 2:   Every time a router selects a successor, it sends a poison update to its successor (a poison reverse).

DUAL Rule 3:   A poison update is sent to all neighbors on the interface through which the successor is reachable unless split-horizon is turned off, in which case, it's sent to only the successor.

The first few steps in propagation of the new subnet as observed in the debugging printouts are also illustrated in Figure 1-10.

Figure 1-10 *First Step in New Route Propagation*

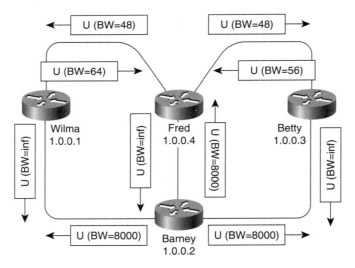

To understand the various bandwidth values in Figure 1-10, note the following:

- The bandwidths on links from Barney to Wilma, Fred, and Betty are 64 kbps, 48 kbps, and 56 kbps, respectively.

- EIGRP takes the minimum of the reported and interface bandwidths to compute the new bandwidth.

After processing Barney's update, Fred receives two more updates: one from Wilma and one from Betty. They both offer Fred a better route than the route going directly through the Frame Relay link to Barney. Fred follows the same steps as before (see Example 1-10).

Example 1-10 *Router Fred Receives an Update from Router Betty*

```
Fred#
EIGRP: Received UPDATE on Serial0 nbr 1.1.0.3
  AS 1, Flags 0x0, Seq 131/145 idbQ 0/0 iidbQ un/rely 0/0
DUAL: dest(1.0.0.5/32) not active
DUAL: dual_rcvupdate(): 1.0.0.5/32 via 1.1.0.3 metric 46866176/46354176
```

Fred received an update from Betty. Betty's reported distance is 46354176. Fred's distance composite metric for this path is 46354176 (see Example 1-11).

Example 1-11 *Router Fred Receives an Update from Betty—Continued*

```
DUAL: Find FS for dest 1.0.0.5/32. FD is 53973248, RD is 53973248
DUAL:        1.0.0.2 metric 53973248/128256
DUAL:        1.1.0.3 metric 46866176/46354176 found Dmin is 46866176
```

The new route from Betty is compared with the route from Barney already in Fred's topology table. The new route has a lower distance (from Fred's perspective) and the successor for network 1.0.0.5 is changed. Fred has to inform its neighbors about the better route (see Example 1-12).

Example 1-12 *The Router Fred Selects the Better Route Offered by Router Betty*

```
DUAL: RT installed 1.0.0.5/32 via 1.0.0.2
DUAL: RT installed 1.0.0.5/32 via 1.1.0.3
DUAL: Send update about 1.0.0.5/32. Reason: metric chg
DUAL: Send update about 1.0.0.5/32. Reason: new if
```

However, before the updates from Fred can be sent out, another update is received from Wilma, and it's even better (see Example 1-13).

Example 1-13 *Router Fred Receives an Update from Router Wilma*

```
EIGRP: Received UPDATE on Serial0 nbr 1.1.0.1
  AS 1, Flags 0x0, Seq 86/146 idbQ 2/0 iidbQ un/rely 0/0
DUAL: dest(1.0.0.5/32) not active
DUAL: dual_rcvupdate(): 1.0.0.5/32 via 1.1.0.1 metric 41152000/40640000
DUAL: Find FS for dest 1.0.0.5/32. FD is 46866176, RD is 46866176
```

continues

Example 1-13 *Router Fred Receives an Update from Router Wilma (Continued)*

```
DUAL:         1.1.0.3 metric 46866176/46354176
DUAL:         1.1.0.1 metric 41152000/40640000
DUAL:         1.0.0.2 metric 53973248/128256 found Dmin is 41152000
```

Because the newly received route is selected as the best route, the distance of the route Fred is using decreases, so Fred has to propagate this lower reported distance to its neighbors (see Example 1-14).

Example 1-14 *New Best Route Selected and Propagated to Fred's Neighbors*

```
DUAL: RT installed 1.0.0.5/32 via 1.1.0.3
DUAL: RT installed 1.0.0.5/32 via 1.1.0.1
DUAL: Send update about 1.0.0.5/32. Reason: metric chg
EIGRP: Enqueuing UPDATE on Serial0.1 nbr 1.0.0.2
EIGRP: Enqueuing UPDATE on Serial0 nbr 1.1.0.1
EIGRP: Enqueuing UPDATE on Serial0 nbr 1.1.0.3
```

Fred sends a poison update to Wilma (*DUAL Rule 2*) and Betty (*DUAL Rule 3*, Betty is reachable through the same interface as Wilma), and a regular update to Barney (*DUAL Rule 1*). These updates are displayed in Figure 1-11.

Figure 1-11 *Fred Received a Better Route for 1.0.0.5/32 Through Wilma*

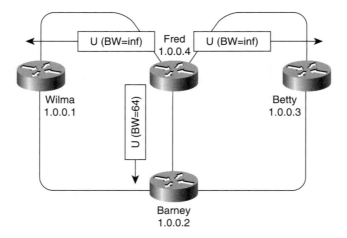

Barney receives Fred's update, stores it in the topology table, and otherwise completely ignores it. The corresponding debugging printouts can be found in Example 1-15.

Example 1-15 *A Route Received That Is Not Better Than the One the Router Already Has*

```
Barney#
EIGRP: Received UPDATE on Serial0.1 nbr 1.0.0.4
  AS 1, Flags 0x0, Seq 158/269 idbQ 0/0 iidbQ un/rely 0/0 DUAL: dest(1.0.0.5/32) not
  active
DUAL: dual_rcvupdate(): 1.0.0.5/32 via 1.0.0.4 metric 54997248/41152000
DUAL: Find FS for dest 1.0.0.5/32. FD is 128256, RD is 128256
DUAL: 0.0.0.0 metric 128256/0
DUAL: 1.0.0.4 metric 54997248/41152000 found Dmin is 128256
```

At the end of this data exchange, Fred has three routes toward 1.0.0.5 in its topology table. They are displayed in Example 1-16.

Example 1-16 *Final Topology Table Entries on Router Fred for Network 1.0.0.5/32*

```
Fred#show ip eigrp topology 1.0.0.5 255.255.255.255
IP-EIGRP topology entry for 1.0.0.5/32
  State is Passive, Query origin flag is 1, 1 Successor(s), FD is 41152000
  Routing Descriptor Blocks:
  1.1.0.1 (Serial0), from 1.1.0.1, Send flag is 0x0
      Composite metric is (41152000/40640000), Route is Internal
      Vector metric:
        Minimum bandwidth is 64 Kbit
        Total delay is 45000 microseconds
        Reliability is 255/255
        Load is 1/255
        Minimum MTU is 1500
        Hop count is 2
  1.1.0.3 (Serial0), from 1.1.0.3, Send flag is 0x0
      Composite metric is (46866176/46354176), Route is Internal
      Vector metric:
        Minimum bandwidth is 56 Kbit
        Total delay is 45000 microseconds
        Reliability is 255/255
        Load is 1/255
        Minimum MTU is 1500
        Hop count is 2
  1.0.0.2 (Serial0.1), from 1.0.0.2, Send flag is 0x0
      Composite metric is (53973248/128256), Route is Internal
      Vector metric:
        Minimum bandwidth is 48 Kbit
        Total delay is 25000 microseconds
        Reliability is 255/255
        Load is 1/255
        Minimum MTU is 1500
        Hop count is 1
```

Exercise 1-1

Find out which route in Fred's routing table comes from Wilma, Betty, and Barney. Which router is the successor? Which router is the feasible successor? How many feasible successors does Fred have and why?

NOTE   You have seen how EIGRP reacts to a new route and to a decrease in the route metric (receiving a better route). The operation of EIGRP in these scenarios is indistinguishable from the operation of a well-implemented distance-vector protocol (for example, RIP v2).

DUAL Behavior on Route Loss

The DUAL algorithm covered so far can be summarized in the pseudocode shown in Example 1-17.

Example 1-17 *DUAL Behavior on Receiving Routes with Better Metrics*

```
Receiving update packet:
  Install information in topology table
  If ReceivedUpdate is better or equal than the current best route then
    Select the new best route
    Send update packets to all neighbors
  Else
      ????
  End If
```

The previous section covered DUAL behavior only under favorable conditions; a new or a better route was received. The real power of DUAL lies, however, in handling unfavorable conditions—route loss or metric increase.

It turns out that the DUAL algorithm handles these conditions in a pretty straightforward way that can be summarized in the following extensions to the previous algorithm (see Example 1-18).

Example 1-18 *High-Level Overview of a DUAL Algorithm*

```
Receiving update packet:
  Install information in the topology table
  If ReceivedUpdate is better or equal than the current best route then
    Select the new best route
    Send update packets to all neighbors
  Else
    If ReceivedUpdate was not received from current successor then
    Store the information in topology table, ignore the update
    Else
      Try to find a better route
    End If
  End If
```

Before going into details, we have to answer the following questions:

1 Why should EIGRP try to find a better route every time the successor reports an increase in the route metric?

2 How does EIGRP indicate a route loss?

3 How does EIGRP handle other events such as a link failure or neighbor loss?

To answer the first question, consider the example in Figure 1-12, where a four-router network is implemented with leased lines of various speeds.

Figure 1-12 *Example Network 1*

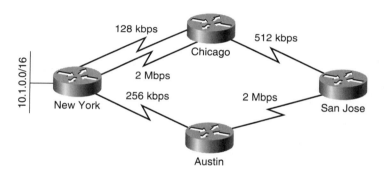

When the 2-Mbps line fails between Chicago and New York, the Chicago router could switch over to the 128-kbps line immediately and report the increased metric to the San Jose router. If the San Jose router accepts the increased metric without trying to find an alternate route, the result is suboptimal routing because the new best route toward New York really goes through Austin. It's therefore mandatory to look for an alternate route every time the successor reports an increased route metric.

Exercise 1-2

Assuming that the delay on all serial links is set to the same value and that the bandwidth is set as indicated in the previous figure, answer the following questions:

1. Where does the traffic from Austin to network 10.1.0.0/16 flow?

2. How many routers have a successor *and* a feasible successor for network 10.1.0.0/16?

The two previous questions listed at the top of this section, namely "How does EIGRP indicate a route loss?" and "How does EIGRP handle other events such as a link failure or neighbor loss?" are easier to answer:

- EIGRP reports a route loss with a normal update packet by setting the *delay* portion of vector metric to infinity (−1).

- EIGRP handles the loss of a directly connected subnet as an update packet with the *delay* set to infinity received from an external source in the router (loss of an external route that has been redistributed into EIGRP is handled in a similar fashion).

- EIGRP handles link loss as the loss of a directly connected subnet plus a loss of one or more neighbors if there are EIGRP neighbors reachable through the lost interface.

- EIGRP handles a neighbor loss as if it had received an update packet from that neighbor with *delay* set to infinity for every route received from that neighbor.

To illustrate these points, see what happens when router Fred in our test network (refer to Figure 1-12) loses its Frame Relay link (subnet 1.1.0.0/24).

NOTE   Only the relevant portions of debugging outputs are shown; detailed DUAL computation printouts are deleted for clarity reasons.

The following debugging options were used to generate the printouts (see Example 1-19).

Example 1-19 *EIGRP Debugging Is Enabled on Router Fred*

```
Fred#show debug
EIGRP:
  EIGRP FSM Events/Actions debugging is on
  EIGRP Packets debugging is on
    (UPDATE, QUERY, REPLY)
```

Link loss is first handled as the loss of a directly connected subnet (see Example 1-20).

Example 1-20 *Interface Is Lost on Router Fred*

```
DUAL: dual_rcvupdate(): 1.1.0.0/24 via Connected metric 4294967295/4294967295
DUAL: Find FS for dest 1.1.0.0/24. FD is 20512000, RD is 20512000
DUAL:    0.0.0.0 metric 4294967295/4294967295
DUAL:    1.0.0.2 metric 54869248/41024000 not found Dmin is 54869248
DUAL: Dest 1.1.0.0/24 entering active state.
```

Neighbor loss is forced for every neighbor reachable over that subnet. Every advertisement received from those neighbors is examined and deleted from the topology table. Additional processing is done if the neighbor was the successor for a particular route (see Example 1-21).

Example 1-21 *All the Neighbors Reachable Through the Lost Interface Are Lost*

```
DUAL: linkdown(): start - 1.1.0.3 via Serial0.2
DUAL: Destination 1.0.0.1/32
DUAL: Removing dest 1.0.0.1/32, nexthop 1.1.0.3
DUAL: Best path rejected - forcing active
DUAL: Destination 1.1.0.0/24
DUAL: Clearing handle 2, count is now 2
DUAL: Destination 1.0.0.3/32
DUAL: Find FS for dest 1.0.0.3/32. FD is 20640000, RD is 20640000
DUAL:    1.1.0.3 metric 4294967295/4294967295
DUAL:    1.1.0.1 metric 47378176/46866176
DUAL:    1.0.0.2 metric 54485248/46354176 not found Dmin is 47378176
DUAL: Dest 1.0.0.3/32 entering active state.
DUAL: Set reply-status table. Count is 2.
DUAL: Not doing split horizon
DUAL: Destination 1.0.0.2/32
DUAL: Removing dest 1.0.0.2/32, nexthop 1.1.0.3
DUAL: Best path rejected - forcing active
DUAL: Destination 1.0.0.5/32
DUAL: Removing dest 1.0.0.5/32, nexthop 1.1.0.3
DUAL: Best path rejected - forcing active
DUAL: Destination 1.0.0.4/32
DUAL: linkdown(): finish
```

The same algorithm is repeated for every neighbor reachable over the lost subnet (see Example 1-22).

Example 1-22 *The Second Neighbor Reachable Through Serial 0.2 Is Also Lost*

```
DUAL: linkdown(): start - 1.1.0.1 via Serial0.2
DUAL: Destination 1.0.0.1/32
DUAL: Removing dest 1.0.0.1/32, nexthop 1.1.0.1
DUAL: RT installed 1.0.0.1/32 via 1.0.0.2
DUAL: Destination 1.1.0.0/24
DUAL: Clearing handle 1, count is now 1
DUAL: Destination 1.0.0.3/32
DUAL: Clearing handle 1, count is now 1
DUAL: Destination 1.0.0.2/32
```

continues

Example 1-22 *The Second Neighbor Reachable Through Serial 0.2 Is Also Lost (Continued)*

```
DUAL: Removing dest 1.0.0.2/32, nexthop 1.1.0.1
DUAL: RT installed 1.0.0.2/32 via 1.0.0.2
DUAL: Destination 1.0.0.5/32
DUAL: Removing dest 1.0.0.5/32, nexthop 1.1.0.1
DUAL: RT installed 1.0.0.5/32 via 1.0.0.2
DUAL: Destination 1.0.0.4/32
DUAL: linkdown(): finish
```

Exercise 1-3

To understand all the details of the previous debugging printout, you have to know the exact contents of the EIGRP topology table of router Fred. You can compute the topology table by hand or set up the four-router lab and print out the topology table on Fred. You can find the necessary lab instructions on the accompanying Web site at www.ciscopress.com/eigrp.

Local Computation

An EIGRP router faced with an increased metric from its successor can find a better route immediately if the new best route goes through a feasible successor. The action in this case is immediate; the new route is selected and updates are sent to all the neighbors to inform them of the change in the network topology. This is exactly what happens in our test network when Fred loses subnet 1.1.0.0/24; Barney is the feasible successor for network 1.0.0.2 and the best (well, the only remaining) route toward that network also goes through Barney. The corresponding debugging outputs are shown in Example 1-23.

Example 1-23 *Route Loss with a Feasible Successor Available in the Topology Table*

```
Fred#debug ip eigrp 1 1.0.0.2 255.255.255.255
IP Target enabled on AS 1 for 1.0.0.2/32
IP-EIGRP AS Target Events debugging is on
Fred#show debug
IP routing:
  IP-EIGRP AS Target Events debugging is on
EIGRP:
  EIGRP FSM Events/Actions debugging is on
  EIGRP Packets debugging is on
    (UPDATE, QUERY, REPLY)
Fred#
DUAL: linkdown(): start - 1.1.0.3 via Serial0.2
DUAL: Destination 1.0.0.2/32
DUAL: Removing dest 1.0.0.2/32, nexthop 1.1.0.3
DUAL: Best path rejected - forcing active
DUAL: linkdown(): finish
DUAL: linkdown(): start - 1.1.0.1 via Serial0.2
DUAL: Destination 1.0.0.2/32
```

Example 1-23 *Route Loss with a Feasible Successor Available in the Topology Table (Continued)*

```
DUAL: Removing dest 1.0.0.2/32, nexthop 1.1.0.1
DUAL: RT installed 1.0.0.2/32 via 1.0.0.2
DUAL: linkdown(): finish
```

NOTE   The debugging printout changed between IOS versions 11.2 and 11.3T. IOS 11.2 prints the whole topology table indicating the best route selected, whereas IOS 11.3T informs you only that a new best route is installed. A sample IOS 11.2 printout is shown in Example 1-24.

Example 1-24 *Printout from Example 1-23 as Displayed under IOS 11.2*

```
DUAL: linkdown(): start - 1.1.0.1 via Serial0.2
DUAL: Destination 1.0.0.2/32
DUAL: Find FS for dest 1.0.0.2/32. FD is 41152000, RD is 41152000
DUAL:    1.1.0.1 metric 4294967295/4294967295
DUAL:    1.0.0.2 metric 53973248/128256 found Dmin is 53973248
DUAL: Removing dest 1.0.0.2/32, nexthop 1.1.0.1
DUAL: RT installed 1.0.0.2/32 via 1.0.0.2
```

The switch over to the feasible successor is immediate and local to the router. The route stays *passive* (no diffusing computation exists for the route) and no other routers are involved. With this knowledge, we can write the first approximation of our algorithm to select alternate routes (see Example 1-25).

Example 1-25 *DUAL Selection of Alternate Routes*

```
Try to find a better route:
  Find the new best route in topology table
  If NewBestRoute goes through a feasible successor then
    Select the NewBestRoute
    Send update packets to all neighbors
  Else
    Ask other neighbors about an alternate route
  End If
```

It's worth noting that EIGRP behavior might be random in some border cases. Assume that the internal order of neighbors in router Fred is different, and the linkdown events are processed in a different sequence. (The linkdown event for neighbor 1.1.0.1 is processed before the linkdown event for neighbor 1.1.0.3.) The route with the minimum reported distance for network 1.0.0.2/32 after the neighbor 1.1.0.1 is lost does not go through a feasible successor and router Fred starts a diffusing computation, as seen in Example 1-26.

Example 1-26 *Alternate Route Loss Sequence—Best Route Is Not a Feasible Successor*

```
Fred#
DUAL: linkdown(): start - 1.1.0.1 via Serial0.2
DUAL: Destination 1.0.0.2/32
DUAL: Find FS for dest 1.0.0.2/32. FD is 41152000, RD is 41152000
DUAL:    1.1.0.1 metric 4294967295/4294967295
DUAL:    1.0.0.2 metric 53973248/128256
DUAL:    1.1.0.3 metric 46866176/46354176 not found Dmin is 46866176
DUAL: Dest 1.0.0.2/32 entering active state.
DUAL: Set reply-status table. Count is 2.
DUAL: Not doing split horizon
DUAL: linkdown(): finish
```

NOTE   Although a router with a feasible successor can select an alternate route immediately, its upstream neighbors might not be so lucky—a fact often overlooked by EIGRP network designers. Consider the network in Figure 1-12. When the Chicago router loses its 2-Mbps link to New York, it already has a feasible successor and can switch over to a 128-kbps link immediately. However, when the Chicago router reports an increased route metric to the San Jose router, the San Jose router has no feasible successor and has to start a diffusing computation.

Diffusing Computation

When an EIGRP router cannot find an alternate route (no alternate route exists, *or* the new best route still goes through the successor reporting increases in the route metric, *or* the new best route does not go through a feasible successor), it starts a diffusing computation by asking all its neighbors about an alternate route. A diffusing computation is performed in a series of steps:

Step 1   The route in question is marked *active* in the topology table.

Step 2   A reply-status table is created to track replies expected from the neighbors.

Step 3   A query is sent to the neighbors.

Step 4   Responses are collected from all the neighbors and stored in the topology table. The response status of individual neighbors is tracked in the reply-status table.

Step 5   The best response is selected in the topology table and the new best route is installed in the routing table.

Step 6   If necessary, an update is sent to the neighbors to inform them of the changed network topology.

Starting a Diffusing Computation

The router starting the diffusing computation has already gone through several steps:

- Its topology table reflects the changed state of the network. (It contains information about increased or infinite metric from a successor.)

- The new (temporary) best route toward the destination is already selected in the topology table but it either goes through a successor reporting the change or through a neighbor that is not a feasible successor, so it cannot be used immediately.

The first few steps in the diffusing computation are performed in the router:

Step 1   The route in the topology table is marked active. This flag serves to prevent query loops.

Step 2   A timer is started to guarantee network convergence in a reasonable time.

Step 3   The router creates a data structure to track responses from all neighbors involved in the diffused computation.

When all these preparatory steps are finished, the router sends a query packet to its neighbors. The query packet includes the new temporary best vector metric (or infinity if all the paths to a subnet were lost) to inform the neighbors about the topology change that triggered the diffusing computation.

In the test network, the bandwidth of a loopback interface on router Barney was changed from its default value to 16 kbps, forcing an EIGRP reconvergence for that particular route, as seen in the debugging printout in Example 1-27.

Example 1-27 *Router Initiates a Diffusing Computation*

```
Barney#show debug
EIGRP:
  EIGRP FSM Events/Actions debugging is on
  EIGRP Packets debugging is on
    (UPDATE, QUERY, REPLY)
Barney#conf t
Enter configuration commands, one per line. End with CNTL/Z.
Barney(config)#interface loopback 1
Barney(config-if)#bandwidth 16
Barney(config-if)#
DUAL: dual_rcvupdate(): 1.0.0.5/32 via Connected metric 160128000/0
DUAL: Find FS for dest 1.0.0.5/32. FD is 5127936, RD is 5127936
DUAL:    0.0.0.0 metric 160128000/0
DUAL:    1.0.0.4 metric 54997248/41152000 not found Dmin is 54997248
DUAL: Dest 1.0.0.5/32 entering active state.
DUAL: Set reply-status table. Count is 3.
DUAL: Not doing split horizon
EIGRP: Enqueuing QUERY on Serial0.1 nbr 1.0.0.4 serno 91-91
EIGRP: Enqueuing QUERY on Serial1.1 nbr 1.0.0.3 serno 91-91
EIGRP: Enqueuing QUERY on Serial2.1 nbr 1.0.0.1 serno 91-91
```

NOTE	The debugging outputs in the section titled, "Simple DUAL Operation—Adding New Routes," in this chapter, are similar to the debugging output in Example 1-28. In both situations, we reduce three lines of debugging output into a single line that's most significant for DUAL discussions—the line that tells us which packet type was enqueued for which neighbor, as shown in Example 1-29.

Example 1-28 *The Actual EIGRP Debugging Printout upon Sending a Packet to an EIGRP Neighbor*

```
EIGRP: Enqueuing QUERY on Serial1.1 iidbQ un/rely 0/1 serno 91-91
EIGRP: Enqueuing QUERY on Serial0.1 nbr 1.0.0.4 iidbQ un/rely 0/0 peerQ un/rely 0/
0 serno 91-91
EIGRP: Sending QUERY on Serial0.1 nbr 1.0.0.4
  AS 1, Flags 0x0, Seq 129/106 idbQ 0/0 iidbQ un/rely 0/0 peerQ un/rely 0/1 serno
  91-91
```

Example 1-29 *The Shortened EIGRP Debugging Printout*

```
EIGRP: Enqueuing QUERY on Serial0.1 nbr 1.0.0.4 serno 91-91
```

Receiving a Query Packet and Responding to It

The router receiving a query packet uses the following rules to process the query:

- If the router sending the query previously supplied topology information about the route being queried, the information in the query overwrites the information previously received from the neighbor sending the query.

- If the router receives a query about a route that is not in its topology table, it immediately replies with an infinite metric and stops query processing. (If the router never received any information about the route from any neighbor, it makes no sense to further propagate the search for that route.)

- If the route is already active (for example, the diffusing computation has encountered a query loop), the router replies with its current best path and stops query processing.

- If the query is not received from a successor, the router replies with its current best route. The route stays passive, and the router completes its part of diffused computation.

- If the query is received from the only successor and there is no other EIGRP neighbor, the router replies with infinite metric (stub router case).

- The router selects the new best route toward the destination. If that route goes through a feasible successor, the router selects the alternate route (local computation) and reports the new best route to the query originator.

- If no alternate route exists *or* the new best route still points to the router from which the query was received *or* the new best route does not go through a feasible successor *then* the router recursively propagates the query to its neighbors.

These rules are summarized in Table 1-4.

Table 1-4   *Action Taken upon Receiving an EIGRP Query*

Condition	Action
Route not in topology table	Reply with infinity.
Route already active	Reply with current best metric (could be infinity).
Query received from nonsuccessor	Reply with current best route.
Query received only from successor, no other EIGRP neighbors	Reply with infinity.
Query received from successor	Select new best route. If it goes through a feasible successor, reply with new best route, otherwise extend diffused computation.

Debugging outputs illustrating various scenarios are included in Example 1-30 through Example 1-33.

Example 1-30 *Query Received for a Route Not in the Topology Table*

```
EIGRP: Received QUERY on Serial0.2 nbr 1.1.0.3
  AS 1, Flags 0x0, Seq 83/130 idbQ 0/0 iidbQ un/rely 0/0 peerQ un/rely 0/0
DUAL: dest(1.0.0.5/32) not active
DUAL: dual_rcvquery():1.0.0.5/32 via 1.1.0.3 metric 161152000/160640000,
RD is 4294967295
DUAL: Find FS for dest 1.0.0.5/32. FD is 4294967295, RD is 4294967295 found
DUAL: Send reply about 1.0.0.5/32 to 1.1.0.3
```

Example 1-31 *Query Received While the Route Is Active*

```
EIGRP: Received QUERY on Serial0.1 nbr 1.0.0.4
  AS 1, Flags 0x0, Seq 110/129 idbQ 0/0 iidbQ un/rely 0/0
DUAL: dual_rcvquery():1.0.0.5/32 via 1.0.0.4 metric 161664000/161152000,
RD is 160128000
DUAL: Send reply about 1.0.0.5/32 to 1.0.0.4
EIGRP: Enqueuing REPLY on Serial0.1 nbr 1.0.0.4 iidbQ un/rely 0/1 peerQ un/rely
0/0 serno 92-92
```

Example 1-32 *Query Received from a Neighbor That Is Not the Current Successor*

```
EIGRP: Received QUERY on Serial0.1 nbr 1.0.0.2
  AS 1, Flags 0x0, Seq 242/178 idbQ 0/0 iidbQ un/rely 0/0 peerQ un/rely 0/0
DUAL: dual_rcvquery():1.0.0.5/32 via 1.0.0.2 metric 160640000/160128000,
RD is 41152000
DUAL: Find FS for dest 1.0.0.5/32. FD is 41152000, RD is 41152000
DUAL:    1.1.0.1 metric 41152000/40640000
DUAL:    1.1.0.3 metric 46866176/46354176
DUAL:    1.0.0.2 metric 160640000/160128000 found Dmin is 41152000
DUAL: Send reply about 1.0.0.5/32 to 1.0.0.2
DUAL: RT installed 1.0.0.5/32 via 1.1.0.1
EIGRP: Enqueuing REPLY on Serial0.1 nbr 1.0.0.2 iidbQ un/rely 0/1 peerQ un/rely
0/0 serno 202-202
```

Example 1-33 *Query Received from the Successor, but There Is No Feasible Successor*

```
DUAL: dual_rcvquery():1.0.0.5/32 via 1.1.0.1 metric 161152000/160640000,
RD is 41152000
DUAL: Find FS for dest 1.0.0.5/32. FD is 41152000, RD is 41152000
DUAL:    1.1.0.1 metric 161152000/160640000
DUAL:    1.1.0.3 metric 161152000/160640000
DUAL:    1.0.0.2 metric 160640000/160128000 not found Dmin is 160640000
DUAL: Dest 1.0.0.5/32 entering active state.
DUAL: Set reply-status table. Count is 3.
DUAL: Not doing split horizon
DUAL: Going from state 1 to state 3
EIGRP: Enqueuing QUERY on Serial0.2 nbr 1.1.0.1 serno 204-204
EIGRP: Enqueuing QUERY on Serial0.2 nbr 1.1.0.3 serno 204-204
EIGRP: Enqueuing QUERY on Serial0.1 nbr 1.0.0.2 serno 204-204
```

Finishing a Diffusing Computation

Whenever a router that initiated a query receives a reply from its neighbor, it stores the received data in its topology table and marks the appropriate entry in the reply table. When all the replies are received, one step in the diffusing EIGRP computation is finished, and the router has all the information it needs to select the new best route. If the router initiated the diffusing computation, the overall diffusing computation is complete; otherwise, the router reports its results to the neighbor it received the query from in a reply packet.

After the diffusing computation is complete, the router that initiated the computation has the best overall route known in its topology table, and it also uses the proper downstream router. The other routers involved in the diffusing computation might not know the optimum route yet, so the diffusing computation results must be distributed to those routers as well. This step takes place only if the new best route was supplied by one of the replying neighbors; otherwise, the neighbors already know the new best route because it was supplied in the original query, and the extra update step is unnecessary.

These last steps generate the debugging outputs in Example 1-34 and Example 1-35.

Example 1-34 *Reply Received from One of the Neighbors*

```
Fred#debug eigrp packet update query reply
Fred#debug eigrp fsm

EIGRP: Received REPLY on Serial0.1 nbr 1.0.0.4
  AS 1, Flags 0x0, Seq 108/129 idbQ 0/0 iidbQ un/rely 0/0
DUAL: dual_rcvreply(): 1.0.0.5/32 via 1.0.0.4 metric 54997248/41152000
DUAL: Count is 3
DUAL: Clearing handle 2, count is now 2
```

Example 1-35 *The Diffused Computation Is Finished, and Reply and Update Packets Are Sent*

```
Fred#debug eigrp packet update query reply
Fred#debug eigrp fsm

EIGRP: Received REPLY on Serial0.1 nbr 1.0.0.2
  AS 1, Flags 0x0, Seq 376/300 idbQ 0/0 iidbQ un/rely 0/0
DUAL: dual_rcvreply(): 1.0.0.5/32 via 1.0.0.2 metric 160640000/160128000
DUAL: Count is 1
DUAL: Clearing handle 0, count is now 0
DUAL: Freeing reply status table
DUAL: Find FS for dest 1.0.0.5/32. FD is 4294967295, RD is 161152000 found
DUAL: Send reply about 1.0.0.5/32 to 1.1.0.3
DUAL: RT installed 1.0.0.5/32 via 1.1.0.3
DUAL: RT installed 1.0.0.5/32 via 1.0.0.2
DUAL: RT installed 1.0.0.5/32 via 1.0.0.2
DUAL: Send update about 1.0.0.5/32. Reason: new if
DUAL: Going from state 3 to state 1
EIGRP: Enqueuing REPLY on Serial0.2 nbr 1.1.0.3 serno 299-299
EIGRP: Enqueuing UPDATE on Serial0.1 nbr 1.0.0.2 serno 300-300
EIGRP: Enqueuing UPDATE on Serial0.2 nbr 1.1.0.3 serno 300-300
EIGRP: Enqueuing UPDATE on Serial0.2 nbr 1.1.0.1 serno 300-300
```

A Diffused Computation Example

To further illustrate the details of a diffusing computation, the example network illustrated in Figure 1-13 is used. The network includes elements of the local diffusing computations as well as a diffusing computation triggered by an update packet.

Throughout these examples, assume that the delays on the links are equal (20 msec) and that the route selection is done purely on the basis of minimum end-to-end bandwidth.

Figure 1-13 *Network Used to Illustrate Diffusing Computations*

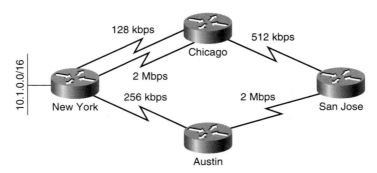

Exercise 1-4

Before reading the rest of the example, figure out the topology table contents for route 10.1.0.0/16 on all four routers. Which routers have more than one entry in the topology table? Which routers have a successor and a feasible successor? Where does the traffic from Austin to New York flow?

The Chicago router has two entries for network 10.1.0.0/16 in its topology table—the best entry points to the 2-Mbps link into New York, and alternate entry points to the 128-kbps link. Both entries have a greater EIGRP distance than the entry in the New York router, which has a bandwidth of 10 Mbps. The New York router is thus both the successor and the feasible successor for the Chicago router.

When the 2-Mbps link between Chicago and New York fails and the successor for network 10.1.0.0/16 is lost, the Chicago router immediately selects the alternate route over a 128-kbps link because the new best route goes through a feasible successor. The Chicago router also informs the San Jose router about the reduced minimum bandwidth of the route. This first step is shown in Figure 1-14.

Figure 1-14 *An Alternate Link between Chicago and New York Is Selected after a 2 Mbps Link Failure*

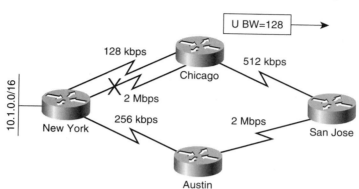

The San Jose router has only one entry for network 10.1.0.0/16 in its topology table, which is pointing toward the Chicago router. The reported bandwidth of that entry was 2 Mbps and San Jose's own bandwidth was 512 kbps. When the update is received from the Chicago router, San Jose's own cost is increased and the San Jose router tries to find an alternate route. It has no feasible successor, so it must start a diffusing computation and send the queries to all other neighbors (for example, Austin) as seen in Figure 1-15.

Figure 1-15 *A Diffusing Computation Is Started in the San Jose Router*

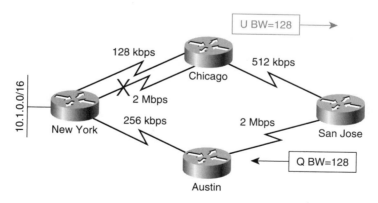

NOTE   Note that although the network design includes redundancy and feasible successors, a diffusing computation nonetheless begins. The presence of a feasible successor does not always guarantee that the convergence is immediate.

Another important fact is that the route from San Jose toward network 10.1.0.0/16 remains stable throughout the duration of the diffusing computation, pointing to the old downstream neighbor (Chicago). This guarantees that the traffic always reaches the destination network even during network convergence periods, although it might not always take the optimal path.

The topology table in the Austin router contained two entries for network 10.1.0.0/16: an entry pointing toward San Jose with a bandwidth of 512 kbps, and an alternate entry pointing toward New York with a bandwidth of 256 kbps. The New York router is also a feasible successor because its own EIGRP distance is less than the reported distance of the Austin router.

When the Austin router receives a query packet from the San Jose router, it stores the information from the query packet in its topology table. The old entry from the San Jose router is overwritten with the new information including the reduced minimum bandwidth. Because the query was received from the current successor, the Austin router needs to rerun DUAL to make certain it is using the optimum path. Luckily, Austin has a feasible successor for this destination (through the New York router) and therefore immediately selects this alternate path. The San Jose router is informed about the new best route via a reply packet and the New York router is informed about the change in network topology via a poison update packet. These packets are highlighted in Figure 1-16.

Figure 1-16 *The Austin Router Selects an Alternate Route Toward New York*

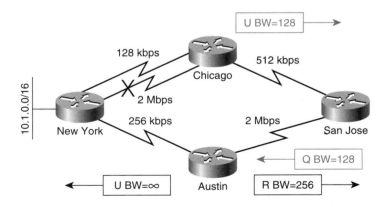

Exercise 1-5

Answer the following questions:

- What were the contents of the topology table of the New York router before the Chicago–New York link failure?

- Is the poison update packet from Austin to New York necessary?

- What does the New York router do after receiving the poison update packet from Austin?

The San Jose router receives the reply packet from Austin and stores the received information in its topology table. It can also complete the diffusing computation because the Austin router was the only one queried. The topology table contains two entries: one from Chicago with a minimum bandwidth of 128 kbps, and another one from Austin with a minimum bandwidth of 256 kbps. The route through Austin is selected and installed in the routing table of the San Jose router.

As one of the last steps in the network convergence process, the San Jose router has to inform all other routers that it has changed the path it is using to this destination. An update is sent to the Chicago router listing the better bandwidth. The last step in network convergence is displayed in Figure 1-17.

Figure 1-17 *The San Jose Router Completes the Diffusing Computation and Informs the Other Neighbors about a Better Route*

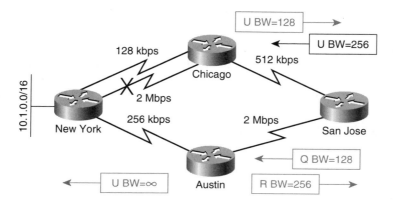

Exercise 1-6

Answer the following questions:

- What does the Chicago router do after it receives the update packet from the San Jose router?

- How many packets does the Chicago router send after it receives the update packet from the San Jose router?

Monitoring Diffusing Computation

A diffusing computation should be a transparent operation that runs behind the scenes, but we could make a similar statement about networks in general and we all know it's not always true. In reality, a large percentage of EIGRP problems and the majority of all EIGRP network meltdowns arise from failed diffusing computations— from too many computations being performed and too many routers being involved in the computation. Therefore, monitoring diffusing computations is crucial for successful EIGRP troubleshooting. You can monitor diffusing computations in your network in several ways:

- Use EIGRP debugging commands. This approach is useful only in small networks (where you wouldn't expect any problems anyway) or when you are trying to troubleshoot events related to a particular route. Generic EIGRP debugging in large networks doesn't lead to good results.

- Use the EIGRP event log in the router. The information in the event log is similar to information gathered with the debugging commands (although more cryptic) and requires extensive EIGRP knowledge to be properly understood. Therefore, using the EIGRP event log to try to understand the extent of diffused computation in your network is discouraged.

- Use **show ip eigrp topology** and **show ip eigrp neighbor** commands. These commands give network operators or the troubleshooting engineers useful insight into the extent of a diffusing computation and the potential bottlenecks that could cause convergence problems.

Table 1-5 lists the commands that give you rapid insight into overall EIGRP performance while you are troubleshooting.

Table 1-5   *Commands Used in Diffused Computation Monitoring*

To Display . . .	. . . Use the Following Command
Routes currently under diffused computation	**show ip eigrp topology active**
Routes currently being converged	**show ip eigrp topology pending**
Whether this router is a potential bottleneck	**show ip eigrp neighbor detail**

The **show ip eigrp topology active** command displays all the routes for which a diffusing computation is being performed. This command identifies both the extent of diffusing computation (how many routes are currently active and how many routers are involved) as well as potential bottlenecks (routers that don't reply to queries) and convergence problems (long diffusing computation times). An example of a diffusing computation being identified with this command is shown in Example 1-36.

Example 1-36 *Monitoring Diffusing Computations with the **show ip eigrp topology active** Command*

```
Fred#show ip eigrp topology active
IP-EIGRP Topology Table for process 1

Codes: P - Passive, A - Active, U - Update, Q - Query, R - Reply,
       r - Reply status

A 1.0.0.5/32, 1 successors, FD is 161152000, Q
    2 replies, active 00:00:02, query-origin: Successor Origin
        via 1.1.0.3 (161152000/160640000), r, Serial0.2, serno 323
        via 1.0.0.2 (160640000/160128000), Serial0.1, serno 327
    Remaining replies:
        via 1.1.0.1, r, Serial0.2
```

Potential EIGRP performance problems can be identified by the following symptoms:

- Consistently high numbers of active routes indicate a constant source(s) of route flaps and network instabilities.

- Long active times indicate slow overall network convergence and potential bottlenecks.

- Long active times experienced while waiting for replies from a small number of neighbors indicate a communication bottleneck with those neighbors (on this router or on the neighbor router) or a communication problem beyond those neighbors.

- Long active times experienced while waiting for replies from several neighbors indicate an interface bottleneck or a highly redundant topology.

Another useful command to help you identify whether the current router is a potential convergence bottleneck is **show ip eigrp topology pending**, which lists all active routes as well as those routes for which there are pending outgoing updates (see Example 1-37 for a sample printout).

Example 1-37 *Monitoring Network Convergence with the **show ip eigrp topology pending** Command*

```
Fred#show ip eigrp topology pending
IP-EIGRP Topology Table for process 1

Codes: P - Passive, A - Active, U - Update, Q - Query, R - Reply,
       r - Reply status

P 1.0.0.5/32, 1 successors, FD is 46866176, U
        via 1.1.0.3 (46866176/46354176), Serial0.2, serno 329
        via 1.0.0.2 (53973248/10127872), Serial0.1, serno 327
```

If a particular router constantly displays several passive pending routes, that router definitely represents a bottleneck. To further verify whether the router under inspection represents the convergence bottleneck, you can use the **show ip eigrp neighbor detail** command to display all packets waiting to be sent from this router to its neighbors. This command can help you identify the link and the neighbor that's slowing down the convergence of the route in Example 1-37. As seen in Example 1-38, the only neighbor with an outstanding update packet is the neighbor 1.1.0.1, where the potential bottleneck lies.

Example 1-38 *Monitoring Potential Bottlenecks with the* **show ip eigrp neighbor detail** *Command*

```
Fred#show ip eigrp neighbor detail
IP-EIGRP neighbors for process 1
H    Address                 Interface    Hold Uptime     SRTT     RTO      Q     Seq
                                          (sec)           (ms)             Cnt   Num
2    1.1.0.3                 Se0.2         172 02:13:17   16       5000     0     233
     Version 11.3/1.0, Retrans: 9, Retries: 0
1    1.1.0.1                 Se0.2         121 02:13:35   49       5000     1     190
     Version 11.3/1.0, Retrans: 13, Retries: 0
     UPDATE seq 355 ser 334-334 Sent Sequenced
0    1.0.0.2                 Se0.1          13 20:08:05   19       5000     0     418
     Version 11.3/1.0, Retrans: 1, Retries: 0
```

When the **show ip eigrp neighbor detail** command displays several packets in the *Sequenced* state, the bottleneck is the router under inspection. When the packets displayed by this command are in the *Sent Sequenced* state, the bottleneck is either the transmission media (which might be lossy) or the remote router (which is not acknowledging the packets in a timely manner). Interface-related bottlenecks are also easy to spot with the **show ip eigrp interface** command, where several pending routes indicate a transmission media bottleneck.

When you are designing a network, you have several options when faced with a high number of diffusing computations in an EIGRP network:

- Reduce the number of route flaps in the network.
- Reduce the diameter of diffusing computations.
- Reduce the number of neighbors or the number of routers running EIGRP.
- Increase the available EIGRP bandwidth between the neighbors.

All these measures are covered in detail in Part II and Part III of this book.

Stuck-in-Active Routes

Diffusing computation rules, as discussed in the section entitled, "Diffusing Computation," in this chapter, require that a router receive replies from all the neighbors it queried before it can select the new best route. Under the following extreme circumstances, a neighbor might fail to respond to a query:

- In the event of a neighbor failure, for example, a neighbor router reload that hasn't yet been noticed through the hello mechanism

- In the event of a transmission media congestion or overload

- In the event of software or hardware errors

In all these circumstances, the router originating the diffusing computation is blocked from completing the computation. To prevent these types of deadlock situations, EIGRP contains a built-in safety measure—a maximum time a diffusing computation can take. Whenever a diffusing computation takes longer than the timeout value, the diffusing computation is prematurely aborted; the adjacency with any nonresponding neighbors is cleared, and the computation proceeds as though these neighbors replied with an infinite metric. The route for which the computation is aborted is said to be *stuck in active*.

Stuck-in-Active (SIA) routes are a major source of EIGRP-related problems, especially because of their distributed nature. Consider the network in Figure 1-18.

Figure 1-18 *Sample Network Prone to SIA Events*

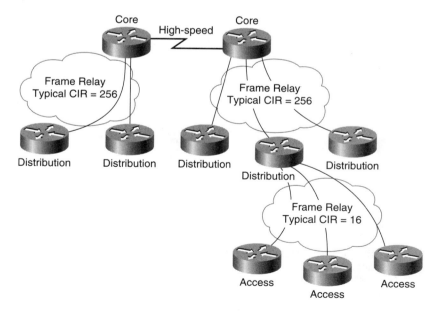

Whenever there is a DLCI failure between the distribution and core layers, a core router starts a diffusing computation for all the routes previously reachable over the failed DLCI. Because the network does not contain any redundancy, there are no feasible successors and the diffusing computation spreads to all the remaining routers in the whole network including all the access routers. The link speed between distribution and access routers is very low; hence, there is a high probability that these links will be overloaded and become convergence bottlenecks. Unfortunately, the SIA event does not occur between the distribution and access routers; the first router to experience SIA timeout is most likely to be the core router initiating the diffusing computation. This router tries to recover from SIAs by clearing the adjacency with the router that timed out (in its perspective), namely the other core router. The net result of this action is network partitioning, the loss of several routes resulting in even more diffused computations, and probably more SIA events between other routers in this network. The end result of this chain of events can be a network meltdown resulting in several minutes of complete network outage.

It is clear from the previous example that the SIA event should be avoided if at all possible by the use of several available design and configuration techniques. Most techniques try to avoid or prevent the original reasons for an SIA event, but one technique tries to prevent the resulting catastrophe without removing the original causes—the extension of the stuck-in-active timer.

The default Stuck-in-Active timeout is three minutes, which should be enough for all properly designed networks. You can extend the timeout during a troubleshooting session if necessary, but you should consider this to be only a temporary measure that prevents network meltdowns. If when troubleshooting, you use this stopgap measure, you must adjust the timeout on all EIGRP speaking routers in the network (see Table 1-6).

Table 1-6   *Changing the SIA Timeout*

Task	Command
Change the Stuck-in-Active timeout	**router eigrp <AS>** **timers active-time <timeout-in-minutes>**
Disable the Stuck-in-Active check	**router eigrp <AS>** **timers active-time disabled**

SIA events are usually caused by several route flaps (or the loss of many routes) combined with slow-speed or lossy links in large networks. The usual causes can be categorized along these lines:

- **Flapping interface**—A single constantly flapping interface can introduce a constant stream of diffusing computations in the network; every time the interface goes down, all the routers in the network have to agree that there is no alternate route to the lost subnet. Over a period of time the number of outstanding queries can grow to the extent that one of the diffusing computations exceeds the SIA timeout.

- **Configuration change**—EIGRP-related configuration changes normally clear the adjacency between the router on which the changes were made and its neighbors (see the section titled, "Adjacency Resets—Causes and Consequences," in Chapter 2, "Advanced EIGRP Concepts, Data Structures, and Protocols" for more details), potentially resulting in several lost routes and diffusing computations. These can lead to SIA events in combination with slow-speed links as illustrated in the example network.

- **Lossy links**—EIGRP packets might get lost on lossy links resulting in retransmissions that might in turn lead to an extended convergence period when combined with several diffusing computations (caused by, for example, flapping interfaces or configuration changes).

- **Heavily loaded links**—Heavily loaded links usually experience packet drops that can cause EIGRP retransmissions finally resulting in SIA routes (see also lossy links).

- **Misconfiguration of the bandwidth parameter**—Recent EIGRP implementations try to prevent WAN link overload by pacing EIGRP data packets based on configured interface bandwidth. Misconfiguring the bandwidth on an interface can lead to packet loss or extremely low throughout; both of which can slow down the transmission of query and reply packets, thus increasing the overall time required to complete a diffusing computation.

- **Old EIGRP code**—Old EIGRP implementation (up to IOS versions 10.3(11) and 11.0(8)) as well as early maintenance releases of some IOS versions (for example, early IOS 11.2) contain several EIGRP-related software defects that can result in delayed retransmissions, lost packets, and finally, SIA events. The obvious remedy in this scenario is an IOS upgrade.

- **Routing loops with multiple (E)IGRP processes**—Blind two-way redistribution between multiple IGRP and/or EIGRP processes can lead to redistribution loops that trigger repetitive diffusing computations in all involved EIGRP processes (see also lossy links and flapping interface for more details).

- **Redistributed IGRP routes**—Automatic IGRP to EIGRP redistribution performed whenever IGRP and EIGRP are using the same AS number can lead to complex two-way multipoint redistribution scenarios that could cause routing loops (see also routing loops). More details can be found in Chapter 9, "Integrating EIGRP with Other Enterprise Routing Protocols."

- **Frame-Relay**—Several SIA-related configuration problems are usually encountered in Frame-Relay environments: flapping interfaces, lossy or heavily loaded links, and misconfigured bandwidth parameters. See Chapter 12, "Switched WAN Networks and Their Impact on EIGRP" and Chapter 13, "Running EIGRP over WAN Networks" for more details.

Summary

EIGRP is a modern routing protocol that combines simplicity and filtering capabilities of the distance-vector routing protocols such as Routing Information Protocol (RIP) or Interior Gateway Routing Protocol (IGRP) with fast convergence of link-state routing protocols such as Open Shortest Path First (OSPF) protocol. EIGRP is also the only routing protocol that supports all three layer-3 protocols most commonly found in enterprise networks: IP, IPX, and AppleTalk.

Configuring EIGRP in a small network is easy and does not require any network design. Therefore, EIGRP is the routing protocol of choice in most networks that do not require multivendor interoperability. An EIGRP network where no real network design was done can grow to a fairly large size without problems, but might also unexpectedly collapse when the number of routers or the number of changes per time unit exceeds a certain hard-to-specify limit. On the other hand, everyone designing and implementing a network based on a link-state routing protocol, such as OSPF, becomes aware of the need to implement network segregation with areas early on in the network growth cycle. The net result is that fewer large OSPF or IS-IS networks experience unexpected outages, but this result is not strictly technology-related. Remember, although EIGRP has the ability to cope with more abuse than link-state protocols, it can also break without warning when it cannot take any more.

NOTE   I've seen several large EIGRP networks that experienced fairly frequent outages and meltdowns, most of which were the result of missing design elements and improper implementation. I, therefore, strongly urge the reader to do a proper network design even though EIGRP does not require it in early stages when the network is still small. I also recommend using as many scalability features discussed in Part II of this book as possible to make your network as scalable and as stable as possible.

CHAPTER 2

Advanced EIGRP Concepts, Data Structures, and Protocols

This chapter builds on EIGRP concepts and algorithms described in Chapter 1, "EIGRP Concepts and Technology." The following sections focus on protocols and data structures used by EIGRP:

- "EIGRP Transport Mechanisms and Protocols" describes the reliable transport between EIGRP neighbors.

- "EIGRP Neighbors" provide the details about the concept of EIGRP neighbors and adjacencies.

- "EIGRP Topology Table" describes the details of how EIGRP stores routing information.

- "Building Routing Tables from EIGRP Topology Tables" explains the process of building the main routing table from an EIGRP topology table.

Throughout this chapter, we'll use an approximate structure map of EIGRP detailing how the processes, protocols, and data structures of EIGRP are joined together (see Figure 2-1).

Figure 2-1 *Overall Map of EIGRP Processes, Protocols, and Data Structures*

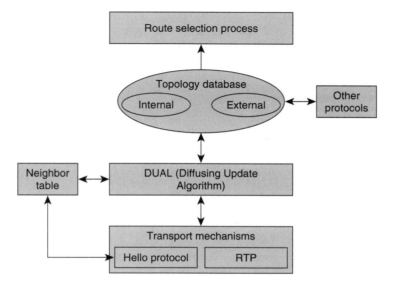

EIGRP Transport Mechanisms and Protocols

Throughout the discussion of the DUAL algorithm and its operation in Chapter 1, we made hidden assumptions that the data delivery between routers is reliable and that the routers have some means of finding their neighboring routers. These two assumptions are crucial to proper operation of the DUAL algorithm. Therefore, it's not surprising that one of the major parts of EIGRP addresses reliable neighbor discovery and data delivery. These parts of EIGRP are highlighted in Figure 2-2.

EIGRP's designers were faced with two choices when designing the EIGRP transport protocol. They could use an already existing protocol (for example, TCP) or they could design their own. They probably felt that TCP was too complex for transporting routing data and that it lacked one of the major features they wanted to implement in EIGRP: multicast data delivery. Other transport protocols under development at that time (for example, the protocol OSPF uses to transport LSAs between routers) lacked the robustness and adaptability that are the crucial benefits of TCP. Design of a proprietary transport protocol was, therefore, the only remaining option.

Figure 2-2 *The EIGRP Transport Protocol and Its Position in the Overall EIGRP Structure*

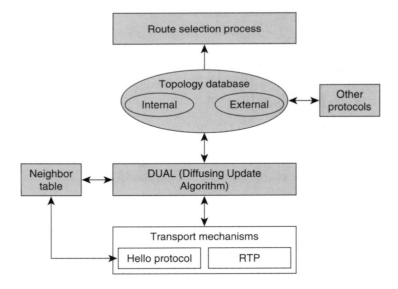

As currently implemented, the EIGRP transport protocol fulfills all the major requirements:

- EIGRP neighbors are dynamically discovered using the EIGRP hello protocol.
- The hello protocol also discovers neighbor loss.
- All data transfer is reliable.
- The transport protocol allows unicast or multicast data transfer.
- The transport protocol adapts itself to changing network conditions and variations in neighbor responsiveness.
- With proper configuration, EIGRP behaves as a good neighbor and limits its bandwidth usage to give other applications fair access to transmission media (see Part III of this book for more details).

EIGRP Encapsulation Methods and Packet Format

Multicast or broadcast addresses used to deliver EIGRP hello packets depend on an underlying protocol family. IP uses multicast, whereas IPX and AppleTalk use broadcast addresses as shown in Table 2-1.

Table 2-1   *Multicast Addresses Used by EIGRP over Different Protocols*

Underlying Protocol Family	Multicast/Broadcast Address Used for EIGRP
IP	224.0.0.10
IPX	<network-number>.ffff.ffff.ffff
AppleTalk	Cable range broadcast

Every EIGRP packet begins with a common header shown in Figure 2-3. The common header contains the EIGRP version number, packet type (Opcode) as specified in Table 2-2, sequence number and acknowledge number fields (described in detail in the section, "Sequence Numbers and Acknowledgments," in this chapter) as well as the packet checksum, and EIGRP Autonomous System number.

Figure 2-3 *The EIGRP Packet Header*

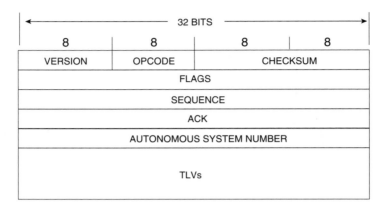

Table 2-2 *EIGRP Packet Types*

OPcode	Type
1	Update
3	Query
4	Reply
5	Hello
6	IPX SAP

Additional information in the EIGRP packets is encoded using Type/Length/Value (TLV) encoding which allows for easy future extensions to the protocol. The various TLVs defined in the current EIGRP implementation are listed in Table 2-3.

Table 2-3   *Type/Length/Value (TLV) Types Used in Current EIGRP Implementation*

Number	TLV Type
General TLV Types	
0x0001	EIGRP Parameters
0x0003	Sequence
0x0004	Software Version 12
0x0005	Next Multicast Sequence
IP-Specific TLV Types	
0x0102	IP Internal Routes
0x0103	IP External Routes
AppleTalk-Specific TLV Types	
0x0202	AppleTalk Internal Routes
0x0203	AppleTalk External Routes
0x0204	AppleTalk Cable Configuration
IPX Specific TLV Types	
0x0302	IPX Internal Routes
0x0303	IPX External Routes

Each TLV entry contains the entry type (2 bytes), entry length (2 bytes), and the entry-specific information. To illustrate the concept of TLVs, refer to Figures 2-4 and 2-5, which display the TLV format for IP internal and external routes. More details on the individual fields in these two TLVs can be found in sections, "Internal EIGRP Routes," and "External Routes and Additional Route Attributes," later in this chapter.

Figure 2-4   *The IP Internal Routes TLV*

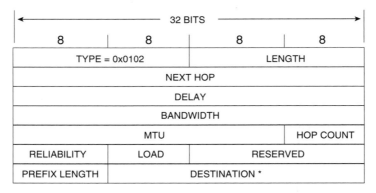

* This field is variable. If it is less than or more than 3 octets, the TLV will be padded with
zeros to the next 4-octet boundary. For example, if the destination address is 10.1, the
Destination field will be 2 octets and will be followed with a pad of 0x00. If the address is
192.168.16.64, the Destination field will be 4 octets and will be followed with a pad of 0x000000.

Figure 2-5   *The IP External Routes TLV*

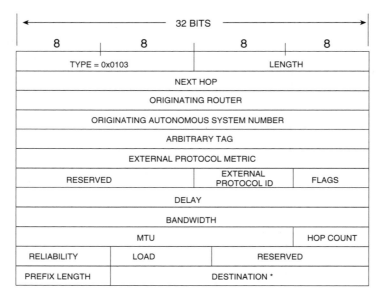

* This field is variable. If it is less than or more than 3 octets, the TLV will be padded with
zeros to the next 4-octet boundary. For example, if the destination address is 10.1, the
Destination field will be 2 octets and will be followed with a pad of 0x00. If the address is
192.168.16.64, the Destination field will be 4 octets and will be followed with a pad of 0x000000.

Hello Protocol

The EIGRP hello protocol achieves three goals that are necessary for proper EIGRP operation:

- It discovers new neighbors as they become reachable. Neighbor discovery is automatic and does not require extra manual configuration.

- It verifies neighbor configuration and allows neighbors to communicate only if they are configured in a compatible way.

- It constantly monitors neighbor availability and detects neighbor loss.

The hello protocol is implemented as a unidirectional protocol where each router sends multicast packets over all interfaces on which it runs EIGRP. Every EIGRP-speaking router receives these multicast packets and is thus able to discover all its neighbors.

Hello packets also carry the basic information about the router sending the packets:

- Its IOS version and EIGRP code version

- The K-values the router is using

- The holdtime that should be used to detect neighbor loss

These values are encoded using a special syntax that allows for easy future extension. A sample EIGRP hello packet, as decoded by Network General's Sniffer, is displayed in Example 2-1.

Example 2-1 *EIGRP Hello Packet as Decoded by Sniffer*

```
EIGRP:   Version          = 2
EIGRP:   Opcode           = 5 (Hello)
EIGRP:   EIGRP Checksum   = EFCF (correct)
EIGRP:   Subnets in Local Net          = 0 Unused
EIGRP:   Networks in Autonomous System = 0 Unused
EIGRP:   Sequence number               = 0 Unused
EIGRP:   Autonomous System number      = 1
EIGRP:
EIGRP:   Type             = 0
EIGRP:   Subtype          = 1
EIGRP:   Length           = 12 Bytes
EIGRP:   Holdtime             = 15 Seconds
EIGRP:   Type             = 0
EIGRP:   Subtype          = 4
EIGRP:   Length           = 8 Bytes
EIGRP:   Routing level        = 2
```

NOTE   The printout in the example was taken with an older version of Network General's software, which did not decode all the EIGRP fields correctly. You should be aware of this fact if you are not using the latest version of Sniffer software.

Each router verifies the K-values in incoming hello packets—which must be equal to the values the router is using itself—as well as the source address of the hello packet. The hello packet source address has to lie in one of the subnets configured on the interface through which the hello packet was received and must be different from any address configured on the router itself; otherwise, the packet is considered to be a spoofing attempt and is ignored.

NOTE   EIGRP hello packets are always sent from the primary IP address configured on the interface, but the receiving router checks the packet's source IP address against all IP subnets configured on the interface. If you reverse the primary and secondary subnets on two adjacent routers, EIGRP still works. If, on the other hand, the primary IP address of one router is not in the address space of the other router, EIGRP does not start.

The hello protocol uses two timers to detect neighbor loss: The *hello interval* specifies how often a router sends the EIGRP hello packets over an interface, and the *hold timer* specifies how long a router waits while receiving no traffic from a given neighbor before declaring that neighbor dead. The default hello and hold timers depend on interface and encapsulation type as specified in Table 2-4.

NOTE   In older IOS versions, a hello packet had to be received to reset the hold timer. Newer IOS versions, starting with IOS 11.2, reset the hold timer every time an EIGRP packet is received from the adjacent router.

Table 2-4   *Default EIGRP Hello and Hold Timers*

Interface Type	Encapsulation	Hello Timer (sec)	Hold Timer (sec)
LAN interface	Any	5	15
WAN interface	HDLC or PPP	5	15
	NBMA interface (X.25, Frame Relay, SMDS or Dialer) with bandwidth <= T1	60	180
	NBMA interface with bandwidth > T1	5	15
	Point-to-point subinterface over NBMA interface	5	15

The default values of hello timers can lead to a situation where EIGRP neighbors connected to the same IP subnet use different hello and hold timers, for example, in the network in Figure 2-6.

Figure 2-6   *Frame Relay Network Where Neighbors Use Different Hello and Hold Timers*

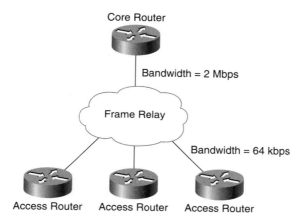

To resolve this problem, each router specifies its own hold timer in its hello packets, and every EIGRP router uses the hold timer specified by the neighbor's hello packet to time out that particular neighbor; this effectively allows the hello protocol to dynamically adjust to neighbor requirements. This property of EIGRP hello protocol is one of the major advantages of EIGRP as it enables different neighbor failure detection timers in different sites of the same WAN cloud.

To illustrate the proper use of asymmetrical EIGRP hello/hold timers, consider two dial-backup examples: a company that has remote sites dialing into the central site in case of Frame Relay failure (see Figure 2-7), and another company where the central site dials out to the remote sites (see Figure 2-8). In both cases, the applications require very fast recovery from Frame Relay failure (around 10 seconds).

Figure 2-7   *Dial-In Dial-Backup Design*

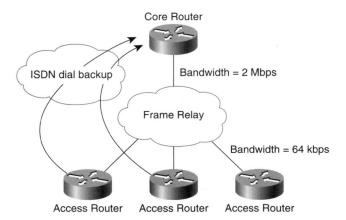

In this dial-in scenario, the access routers have to detect DLCI failure (and corresponding neighbor loss) very quickly to be able to start dial-backup procedures. The timeout on hello packets coming from the core router should be very small, resulting in small hello and hold timers on the core router. The hello and hold times on the access routers are not as important because the core router does not have to detect neighbor failures as quickly.

In the dial-out scenario, the core router has to detect neighbor loss in a short timeframe, resulting in strict requirements for hello and hold timers on access routers. The hello and hold timers on the core router are not as important because the access routers don't rely on neighbor failure detection for proper routing.

Figure 2-8   *Dial-Out Backup Design*

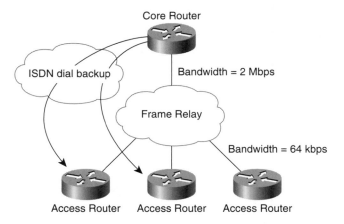

Exercise 2-1

It's not absolutely correct that the access routers don't need to detect neighbor failure to reroute traffic. Consider the return traffic from access to core site. This drawback can be avoided using proper EIGRP metrics. Design the proper EIGRP metrics, static routes, and dial-up parameters in both dial backup scenarios to guarantee the following:

- The return traffic also flows over the ISDN line when the ISDN call is established.

- The ISDN call is dropped when the Frame-Relay DLCI is reestablished.

You can change the hello and hold timers on a per-interface basis in interface configuration mode with the commands from Table 2-5.

Table 2-5   *Changing the Hello and Hold Timers*

To Change . . .	. . . Use the Following Command
EIGRP/IP hello timer	**ip hello-interval eigrp <as> <seconds>**
EIGRP/IP hold timer used by other routers to detect this router's failure	**ip hold-time eigrp <as> <seconds>**
EIGRP/IPX hello timer	**ipx hello-interval eigrp <as> <seconds>**
EIGRP/IPX hold timer used by other routers to detect this router's failure	**ipx hold-time eigrp <as> <seconds>**
Change EIGRP/AT timers	**appletalk eigrp-timers <hello> <hold>**

You can also turn off the hello protocol on a per-interface basis using the commands in Table 2-6 in router configuration mode.

Table 2-6   *Disabling and Enabling EIGRP Hello Protocol on a Per-Interface Basis*

Task	Command
Disable EIGRP hello protocol on a single interface	**router eigrp <as>** **passive-interface <interface>**
Re-enable EIGRP hello protocol	**router eigrp <as>** **no passive-interface <interface>**

The **passive-interface** command can only be used for interfaces with IP addresses falling within the networks specified by the EIGRP routing process **network** command. You cannot use the **no passive-interface** command to enable EIGRP protocol on an interface that does not belong to the EIGRP process.

The **passive-interface** command has a number of side effects:

- No adjacencies are ever established over the passive interface.

- No routing updates are accepted over the passive interface.

- The subnet of the passive interface remains in the EIGRP process and appears in the EIGRP topology table as an internal route.

Monitoring EIGRP Hello Protocol

No easy way to monitor the EIGRP hello protocol or the hello and hold timers that various neighbors are using exists. To find the values the router itself is using, you have to look through the interface part of the router's configuration; to find the values used by the neighbors, you can resort to a couple of tricks.

To find the hello timer used by a neighbor, use EIGRP packet debugging together with EIGRP targeted debugging and debug timestamps. See Example 2-2 for a sample measurement.

Example 2-2   *Commands Used to Measure Neighbor's Hello Timer*

```
Fred#debug eigrp packet hello
EIGRP Packets debugging is on
   (HELLO)
Fred#debug ip eigrp neighbor 1 1.0.0.2
IP Neighbor target enabled on AS 1 for 1.0.0.2
IP-EIGRP Neighbor Target Events debugging is on
Fred#conf term
Enter configuration commands, one per line. End with CNTL/Z.
Fred(config)#service timestamps debug datetime msec
Fred(config)#^Z
Fred#term mon
Fred#
*Mar 3 00:01:18.924: EIGRP: Received HELLO on Serial0.1 nbr 1.0.0.2
*Mar 3 00:01:18.928: AS 1, Flags 0x0, Seq 0/0 idbQ 0/0 iidbQ ...
*Mar 3 00:01:23.528: EIGRP: Received HELLO on Serial0.1 nbr 1.0.0.2
*Mar 3 00:01:23.532: AS 1, Flags 0x0, Seq 0/0 idbQ 0/0 iidbQ ...
*Mar 3 00:01:28.332: EIGRP: Received HELLO on Serial0.1 nbr 1.0.0.2
*Mar 3 00:01:28.336: AS 1, Flags 0x0, Seq 0/0 idbQ 0/0 iidbQ ...
*Mar 3 00:01:32.936: EIGRP: Received HELLO on Serial0.1 nbr 1.0.0.2
*Mar 3 00:01:32.940: AS 1, Flags 0x0, Seq 0/0 idbQ 0/0 iidbQ ...
```

The difference in timestamps between debugging printouts is a good approximation of the hello interval used by the neighbor.

WARNING	This method works well only for unloaded links; for loaded links you should use repeated measurements and average the measured values.

To find the hold time the neighbor is specifying in its hello packets, use the **show ip eigrp neighbor** command repeatedly. When the *hold time* value for a certain neighbor increases, the router has just received a hello packet from that neighbor and the *hold time* value represents an approximate value of the hold timer specified by that neighbor. For example, the value in the *Hold* column for neighbor 1.1.0.3 in Example 2-3 would jump to 180 (the default *hold timer* on low-speed Frame Relay link) when a hello packet is received from that neighbor.

Example 2-3   *Show Command Used to Determine Hold Time Specified by an EIGRP Neighbor*

```
Fred#show ip eigrp neighbor
IP-EIGRP neighbors for process 1
H    Address        Interface    Hold Uptime      SRTT     RTO      Q    Seq
                                 (sec)            (ms)              Cnt  Num
2    1.1.0.3        Se0.2        126  18:02:06    20       5000     0    240
1    1.1.0.1        Se0.2        137  18:02:14    32       5000     0    197
0    1.0.0.2        Se0.1         12  18:02:27    25       5000     0    431
```

Reliable Transport Protocol

EIGRP reliable transport protocol (RTP) guarantees timely, reliable, and efficient exchange of routing data between EIGRP neighbors using mechanisms encountered in all transport protocols such as sequencing, acknowledgments and retransmission for reliable delivery and flow control, and pacing for efficient and fair bandwidth usage. A major difference between RTP and most of the other reliable transport protocols is its support for concurrent unicast and multicast transmission.

RTP uses two types of packets: unreliable packets that are used internally by RTP (ack packet) or that don't have to be acknowledged (hello packet), and reliable packets carrying routing data that always have to be acknowledged. Both types of packets can be either unicast or multicast; the rules are outlined in Table 2-7.

Table 2-7   *Unicast and Multicast EIGRP Packets*

Packet Type/Reliability	Unreliable	Reliable
Unicast	ACK	Reply IPXSAP Response
Multicast	Hello	Update Query IPXSAP Flash Update IPXSAP General Query

All reliable multicast packets can also be sent as unicast packets. Multicast packets are used whenever possible and EIGRP reverts to a unicast version of multicast packets in the following circumstances:

- When sending packets over transmission media types that do not support hardware multicasting (for example, X.25, or Frame Relay)
- When retransmitting a packet to a neighbor that did not acknowledge the packet in multicast timeout interval

You can discover which packet type is used over a particular media by using either debugging or show commands. In the debugging printouts, you can see whether the EIGRP data packet was sent to the interface as a whole or to a particular neighbor. For example, on router Fred, the Ethernet interface is capable of hardware multicasting, whereas the serial Frame Relay interface uses unicast packets. The difference between these interfaces can be seen in the debugging outputs in Example 2-4.

Example 2-4   *Unicast Versus Multicast Debugging Outputs*

```
Fred#debug eigrp packet update query reply
EIGRP: Enqueuing QUERY on Serial0.2 iidbQ un/rely 0/1 serno 38-38
EIGRP: Enqueuing QUERY on Ethernet0 iidbQ un/rely 0/1 serno 38-38
EIGRP: Enqueuing QUERY on Serial0.2 nbr 1.1.0.1 iidbQ un/rely 0/0 peerQ un/rely 0/
0 serno 38-38
EIGRP: Enqueuing QUERY on Serial0.2 nbr 1.1.0.3 iidbQ un/rely 0/0 peerQ un/rely 0/
0 serno 38-38
EIGRP: Sending QUERY on Ethernet0
  AS 1, Flags 0x0, Seq 53/0 idbQ 0/0 iidbQ un/rely 0/0 serno 38-38
EIGRP: Sending QUERY on Serial0.2 nbr 1.1.0.1
  AS 1, Flags 0x0, Seq 52/241 idbQ 0/0 iidbQ un/rely 0/0 peerQ un/rely 0/1 serno 38-38
EIGRP: Sending QUERY on Serial0.2 nbr 1.1.0.3
  AS 1, Flags 0x0, Seq 52/271 idbQ 0/0 iidbQ un/rely 0/0 peerQ un/rely 0/1 serno 38-38
```

In the multicast mode of operation, the packet is enqueued and sent to an interface (Ethernet 0 in our example). In the unicast mode, the packet is enqueued to an interface, further enqueued for each individual neighbor reachable over that interface, and finally sent to each individual neighbor as a unicast packet.

You can also use the **show ip eigrp interface** command to find out whether multicast EIGRP packets are used over an interface. The values to look for are the *Un/reliable mcasts* values. If these values are all zero, the interface does not support hardware multicasting, and EIGRP RTP uses strictly unicast packets; if the values are nonzero, the multicast mode is used whenever possible. For example, the router that generated the printout in Example 2-5 used multicast only on the Ethernet interface and used exclusively unicast packets over the serial interfaces.

Example 2-5 *show ip eigrp interfaces detail Printout*

```
Fred#show ip eigrp interfaces detail
IP-EIGRP interfaces for process 1
                        Xmit Queue     Mean        Pacing Time      Multicast
Interface     Peers     Un/Reliable    SRTT        Un/Reliable      Flow Timer
Se0.1           0          0/0          0           666/25333         36037
   Next xmit serial <none>
   Un/reliable mcasts: 0/0 Un/reliable ucasts: 20/24
   Mcast exceptions: 0 CR packets: 0 ACKs suppressed: 1
   Retransmissions sent: 1 Out-of-sequence rcvd: 0
Se0.2           2          0/0          124         250/9500          19604
   Next xmit serial <none>
   Un/reliable mcasts: 0/0 Un/reliable ucasts: 13/41
   Mcast exceptions: 0 CR packets: 0 ACKs suppressed: 4
   Retransmissions sent: 16 Out-of-sequence rcvd: 6
Et0             1          0/0          21          0/10              88
   Next xmit serial <none>
   Un/reliable mcasts: 0/14 Un/reliable ucasts: 10/3
   Mcast exceptions: 1 CR packets: 1 ACKs suppressed: 1
   Retransmissions sent: 1 Out-of-sequence rcvd: 0
```

Sequence Numbers and Acknowledgments

Each reliable transport protocol must employ some variant of sequencing and sequence numbers to detect lost packets, retransmissions, and reordered packets. Several widely known sequencing techniques exist:

- Sequencing every application session (for example, TCP)
- Sequencing node-to-node traffic (for example, LLC2 or X.25)
- Using byte count as a sequence number (TCP) or packet count as a sequence number (LLC2 and X.25)

None of these methods can be used for EIGRP because they don't work in mixed unicast/multicast operation. To implement mixed unicast/multicast transport protocol, you can use one of two approaches:

- Use different sequence numbers for unicast peer-to-peer flows and multicast peer-to-interface flows.

- Use the same sequence numbers for all packets, but accept that the sequence numbers received by the peer are nonsequential.

EIGRP's designers decided to use the second approach. EIGRP sequence numbers could have been generated on a per-interface or per-routing process basis, but the second option was chosen. Every time an EIGRP routing process generates a new data packet, the packet carries the next higher sequence number. These data packets are, in generic conditions, destined for different neighbors. Each neighbor therefore sees a nonsequential stream of packets arriving from any of the source routers, making traditional windowing and retransmission algorithms useless. The only possible solution to this dilemma is to use a window size of 1; each packet received by a router has to be individually acknowledged. The EIGRP transport protocol uses a stop-and-wait (or ping-pong) mode of operation, which might delay network convergence in some scenarios, but ensures conservative bandwidth usage due to round-trip delays.

Each individual data packet is normally acknowledged by an ACK packet carrying the same sequence number, but it could also be acknowledged by another unicast data packet traveling in the opposite direction (piggybacked ACK). The return data packet is most often a reply packet sent as a response to a query packet, but the piggyback acknowledgment can happen at any time there is a unicast data packet enqueued to travel in the opposite direction. To enable both acknowledgment modes, each EIGRP packet carries two fields (sequence number and acknowledgment number) that have the values specified in Table 2-8.

Table 2-8   *Values in Sequence Number and ACK Number Fields in Various EIGRP Packets*

Condition	Sequence Number	ACK Number
Data packets before the first packet is received from remote neighbor	Current sequence number	0
Data packets after the first packet is received from remote neighbor	Current sequence number	Last sequence number received from the neighbor
ACK packet	0	Last sequence number received from the neighbor
hello packet	0	0

The normal RTP operation (no packet loss) in both explicit-ACK and piggyback-ACK scenarios is shown in Figure 2-9.

Figure 2-9   *Simple RTP Sequencing and Acknowledging*

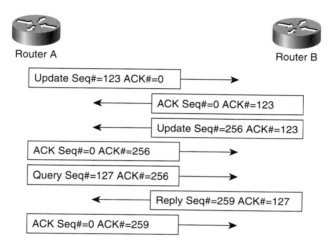

In Figure 2-9, router A sent the first update packet without receiving a previous packet from router B; the ACK number field was therefore 0. The update packet was acknowledged because router B had nothing to send to router A at that time. Some time later, router B sent another update packet with its own sequence number. The ACK field in this packet carries the last sequence number received from router A. Router A acknowledges the update package. As seen from the first part of the diagram, every data packet re-acknowledges the last data packet received from the remote router. These continuous acknowledgments can help RTP recover from lost ACK packets on lossy links with constant EIGRP traffic.

Later on, router A sends a query packet, which is immediately replied to with a reply packet. The reply packet can also serve as a piggyback acknowledgment; no ACK packet from router B is needed. Router A must send a separate ACK packet because no more traffic is going from Router A to Router B.

The detailed sequencing operation of EIGRP RTP can also be seen in the debugging outputs in Example 2-6.

Example 2-6 *EIGRP RTP Debugging*

```
Fred#debug eigrp packet update query reply ack
Fred#debug ip eigrp neighbor 1 1.0.0.2
Fred#
EIGRP: Received QUERY on Serial0.1 nbr 1.0.0.2
  AS 1, Flags 0x0, Seq 544/132 idbQ 0/0 iidbQ un/rely 0/0 ...
EIGRP: Enqueuing ACK on Serial0.1 nbr 1.0.0.2
  Ack seq 544 iidbQ un/rely 0/0 peerQ un/rely 1/0
EIGRP: Sending ACK on Serial0.1 nbr 1.0.0.2
  AS 1, Flags 0x0, Seq 0/544 idbQ 1/0 iidbQ un/rely 0/0 ...
EIGRP: Enqueuing REPLY on Serial0.1 nbr 1.0.0.2 iidbQ un/rely 0/1 ...
EIGRP: Sending REPLY on Serial0.1 nbr 1.0.0.2
  AS 1, Flags 0x0, Seq 134/544 idbQ 0/0 iidbQ un/rely 0/0 ...
EIGRP: Received ACK on Serial0.1 nbr 1.0.0.2
  AS 1, Flags 0x0, Seq 0/134 idbQ 0/0 iidbQ un/rely 0/0 ...
EIGRP: Enqueuing QUERY on Serial0.1 nbr 1.0.0.2 iidbQ un/rely 0/...
EIGRP: Sending QUERY on Serial0.1 nbr 1.0.0.2
  AS 1, Flags 0x0, Seq 136/544 idbQ 0/0 iidbQ un/rely 0/0 ...
```

You can see the SEQ number and ACK number fields in the EIGRP data packet in the "Seq . . ." part of the packet printout. The first number is the packet sequence number; the second number is the acknowledgment number. As seen from the debugging output, EIGRP packets only get a sequence number when they are sent; the lines displaying packets being enqueued into a particular interface or neighbor queue carry no sequence or acknowledgment number. The only exception being the ACK packet which has no sequence number and the acknowledgment number is put into the packet at the moment it's enqueued.

Retransmissions and Retransmission Timers

The sequence number and acknowledgment number fields carried in EIGRP packets enable RTP to recover from various packet loss conditions. The easiest case where the original packet is lost is handled by retransmitting the packet as long as it's not acknowledged (see Figure 2-10).

Figure 2-10 *RTP Recovery after Packet Loss*

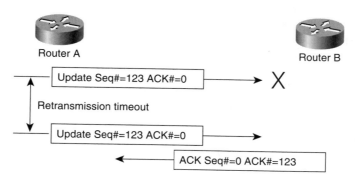

If the acknowledgment is lost, the sending router can't detect this condition and handles the exception as though the original packet is lost—by retransmitting the original packet. The receiving router can detect duplicate packets because it always stores the last sequence number received from each neighbor. It discards the duplicate and acknowledges the data packet (see Figure 2-11).

Figure 2-11 *RTP Recovery after Acknowledgment Loss*

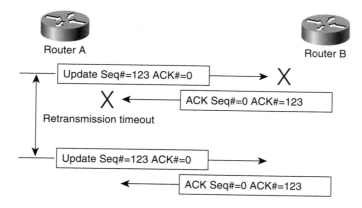

Crucial to the efficient and optimal operation of every transport protocol is the choice of the retransmission timeout. If the retransmission timeout is too short, the transport protocol does not use bandwidth effectively because it generates too many unnecessary retransmissions. If the timeout is too long, the throughput drops rapidly as soon as any errors or drops are encountered. To ensure continuous, efficient operation, every transport protocol constantly adjusts the retransmission timeouts to match changing network conditions and variations in peer responsiveness.

EIGRP RTP measures *Round Trip Time (RTT)* on every packet exchange. RTT is defined as the interval between the packet being sent over an interface and the acknowledgment for that packet being received from a neighbor. After each RTT measurement, RTP computes a *Smoothed Round Trip Time (SRTT)* for every neighbor using the formula in Equation 2-1, the SRTT of each interface is computed as well; it's the average SRTT of all neighbors reachable over that interface.

Equation 2-1

$$SRTT_{New} = SRTT_{Old} \times 0.8 + RTT \times 0.2$$

In Equation 2-2, the initial retransmission timeout (RTO) is defined as below.

Equation 2-2

$$RTO_{Initial} = 6 \times \max (SRTT, PacingInterval)$$

The *Pacing Interval* of an interface (defined in more detail in Part III of this book) is also used in the RTO calculation in Equation 2-2 to prevent retransmission timeout from expiring while the packet is still being stuck in the EIGRP output queue.

RTO is increased by 50 percent after each retransmission, as shown in Equation 2-3.

Equation 2-3

$$RTO_{New} = RTO_{Old} \times \frac{3}{2}$$

The retransmission timeout cannot be smaller than 200 msec or larger than 5 seconds (see Equation 2-4).

Equation 2-4

$$RTO_{Final} = \min(5000, \max (200, RTO_{Computed}))$$

RTP does not retry indefinitely; if the packet is not acknowledged after 16 retries *and* the time spent retrying this packet is longer than the neighbor hold timer, the neighbor is declared dead.

You can display the SRTT time, the interface SRTT timer, and current RTO values with the various show commands, for example, with the **show ip eigrp neighbors** command as seen in Example 2-7.

Example 2-7 *Per-Neighbor SRTT and RTO Values*

```
Fred#show ip eigrp neighbors
IP-EIGRP neighbors for process 1
H       Address         Interface    Hold Uptime      SRTT      RTO       Q     Seq
                                     (sec)                      (ms)      Cnt   Num
0       1.0.0.2         Se0.1         10  00:00:13      20       756       0     547
2       1.1.0.3         Se0.2        170  05:25:26      24      1140       0     318
1       1.1.0.1         Se0.2        170  05:25:32      50      1140       0     272
```

NOTE   The previous example also illustrates the interaction between SRTT and the interface pacing timer. The RTO value for all neighbors is larger than six times SRTT due to the large interface pacing timers displayed in Example 2-9.

The **show ip eigrp neighbors** command displays current SRTT and RTO values. The RTO value is the initial RTO value if there is no packet currently being sent to that neighbor or the actual RTO value if RTP is currently retransmitting a packet toward that neighbor.

The number of retransmissions done for each neighbor can be inspected using **show ip eigrp neighbor detail** command. (A sample printout appears in Example 2-8.)

Example 2-8 *Detailed Printout of Per-Neighbor Retries and Retransmissions*

```
Fred#show ip eigrp neighbors detail
IP-EIGRP neighbors for process 1
H       Address         Interface    Hold Uptime      SRTT      RTO       Q     Seq
                                     (sec)                      (ms)      Cnt   Num
2       1.1.0.3         Se0.2        173  00:00:06       0      4500       1     0
        Last startup serial 142
        Version 11.3/1.0, Retrans: 2, Retries: 2, Waiting for Init,
          Waiting for Init Ack
        UPDATE seq 186 ser 15-142 Sent 6968 Init Sequenced
1       1.1.0.1         Se0.2        166  00:08:38      42      1140       0     303
        Version 11.3/1.0, Retrans: 7, Retries: 0
0       1.0.0.2         Se0.1         14  00:09:48      49      3036       0     576
        Version 11.3/1.0, Retrans: 2, Retries: 0
```

This show command displays the total number of retransmissions done for each neighbor (the *Retrans:* value) as well as the current retry count (the *Retries:* value) for the packet currently being sent. The packet being retransmitted is also displayed and is indicated by the keyword *Sent*.

The **show ip eigrp interface** command displays the average SRTT for each interface (the *Mean SRTT* value). See Example 2-9 for a sample printout.

Example 2-9 *Interface Average SRTT Values*

```
Fred#show ip eigrp interface
IP-EIGRP interfaces for process 1
                      Xmit Queue   Mean    Pacing Time    Multicast     Pending
Interface    Peers   Un/Reliable   SRTT    Un/Reliable    Flow Timer    Routes
Se0.1        1         0/0         20        3/126           126           0
Se0.2        2         0/0         37        5/190           528           0
Se1          0         0/0          0       10/10              0           0
Et0          0         0/0          0        0/10            164           0
```

Current RTO value is also displayed in all debugging outputs when the router is retransmitting packets. Example 2-10 illustrates such a retransmission sequence.

Example 2-10 *Retry Counters and RTO Values in Debugging Printouts*

```
Fred#debug eigrp packet update query reply ack
...
EIGRP: Sending UPDATE on Serial0.2 nbr 1.1.0.1
  AS 1, Flags 0x1, Seq 178/0 idbQ 1/0 iidbQ un/rely 0/0 ...
EIGRP: Sending UPDATE on Serial0.2 nbr 1.1.0.1, retry 1, RTO 3000
  AS 1, Flags 0x1, Seq 178/0 idbQ 0/0 iidbQ un/rely 0/0 ...
EIGRP: Sending UPDATE on Serial0.2 nbr 1.1.0.1, retry 2, RTO 4500
  AS 1, Flags 0x1, Seq 178/0 idbQ 0/0 iidbQ un/rely 0/0 ...
EIGRP: Sending UPDATE on Serial0.2 nbr 1.1.0.1, retry 3, RTO 5000
  AS 1, Flags 0x1, Seq 178/0 idbQ 0/0 iidbQ un/rely 0/0 ...
```

Mixed Multicast/Unicast Operation

Multicast RTP sequencing and acknowledging is performed in a very similar way to unicast operation; the major significant difference is that the router sending the multicast packet must track which neighbors should acknowledge the packet and then retransmit the packets that were not acknowledged by individual neighbors as unicast packets. Another difference between unicast and multicast transmission is that the multicast packets can never carry piggybacked acknowledgment; the ACK number field is always zero (see Figure 2-12).

In Figure 2-12, router A is transmitting a multicast update. The update packet is queued internally to the transmission lists of all three neighbors reachable over the interface (router B to router D) and taken off each individual transmission list when it's acknowledged by an individual router.

Figure 2-12 *Sample Multicast Transmission with Proper Acknowledgments*

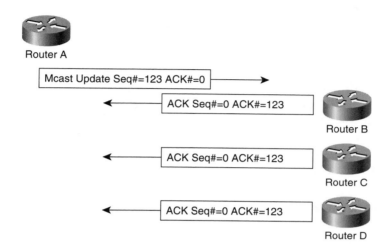

In the event that one of the routers misses the multicast packet (or the ACK packet is lost), the packet is re-sent as a unicast packet to the nonresponding router. These retransmissions follow the usual unicast rules, as explained in the previous section (see Figure 2-13).

Figure 2-13 *Multicast Transmission with Unicast Retransmission*

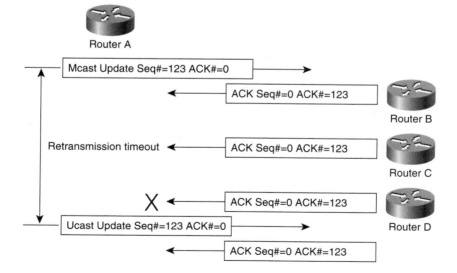

In Figure 2-13, the ACK packet from router D was lost. Router A received the ACK packets from router B and router C and removed the update packet from their transmission lists, but the update packet remains in the transmission list of router D. After the RTO timeout, the unicast retransmission procedure is started.

The multicast/unicast transmission model has one potential drawback: A single unresponsive router could stall the traffic between all neighbors on a broadcast-capable subnet. To prevent this situation, EIGRP uses special mechanisms (multicast flow control and conditional receive) to allow the responsive neighbors to continue receiving multicast packets while the unicast versions of the same packets are independently delivered to the unresponsive neighbors. When the unresponsive neighbors eventually catch up with the rest of the routers (for example, when they have acknowledged all outstanding packets), they can resume receiving multicast traffic.

You can discover the number of times EIGRP handles unresponsive neighbors in a special manner by using the **show ip eigrp interface detail** command. For example, look at the Ethernet 0 values in Example 2-11.

Example 2-11 *Using **show ip eigrp interface detail** Command to Multicast Exceptions*

```
Fred#show ip eigrp interface detail
IP-EIGRP interfaces for process 1
                        Xmit Queue   Mean      Pacing Time    Multicast      Pending
Interface    Peers    Un/Reliable   SRTT      Un/Reliable    Flow Timer     Routes
Se0.1          1         0/0          0         13/506          1370            0
  Next xmit serial <none>
  Un/reliable mcasts: 0/0 Un/reliable ucasts: 90/126
  Mcast exceptions: 0 CR packets: 0 ACKs suppressed: 2
  Retransmissions sent: 14 Out-of-sequence rcvd: 48
Se0.2          2         0/0         115         5/190           676             0
  Next xmit serial <none>
  Un/reliable mcasts: 0/0 Un/reliable ucasts: 135/250
  Mcast exceptions: 0 CR packets: 0 ACKs suppressed: 8
  Retransmissions sent: 59 Out-of-sequence rcvd: 11
Et0            2         0/0         440         0/10           1952             0
  Next xmit serial <none>
  Un/reliable mcasts: 0/46 Un/reliable ucasts: 44/28
  Mcast exceptions: 6 CR packets: 6 ACKs suppressed: 5
  Retransmissions sent: 13 Out-of-sequence rcvd: 5
```

The Mcast exceptions value is the number of times EIGRP processed some of the neighbors in an exceptional way. The CR packets value is the number of Conditional Receive packets the EIGRP process had to send over the interface to prepare the neighbors for split multicast/unicast reception mode.

EIGRP Neighbors

The section "Hello Protocol" in this chapter discussed the EIGRP hello protocol and the way it's used to find new neighbors and detect existing neighbor failures. This section focuses more on the neighbor table itself, the concept of adjacency, and the actions taken when the adjacency is established or torn down. The role of the neighbor table in overall EIGRP operation is highlighted in Figure 2-14.

Figure 2-14 *Position of EIGRP Neighbor Table in Overall EIGRP Structure*

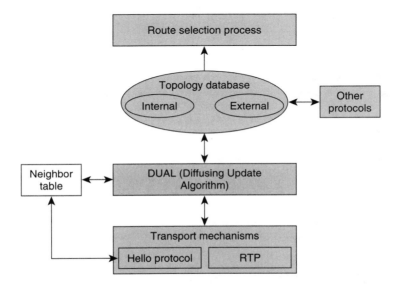

We use two tools to illustrate the actions taken by EIGRP: adjacency debugging and neighbor logging, which you enable by using the commands in Table 2-9.

Table 2-9 *Enabling EIGRP Neighbor Debugging and Logging*

Task	Command
Debug EIGRP neighbor events	**debug eigrp neighbor**
Log adjacency establishments and losses	**router eigrp <as>** **eigrp log-neighbor-changes**
Log adjacency establishments and losses for EIGRP/IPX	**ipx router eigrp <as>** **log-neighbor-changes**
Log adjacency establishments and losses for EIGRP/AppleTalk	**appletalk eigrp log-neighbor-changes**

Use of EIGRP neighbor logging is strongly recommended because it provides an extremely usable EIGRP troubleshooting tool as well as a historical view of the EIGRP problems (assuming that the syslog messages get logged somewhere, of course).

NOTE   Logging to an internal buffer is also enabled in the router with the **logging buffered** command. In EIGRP's case, the buffered logging enables the neighbor changes to get logged in the internal buffer in the router in addition to being logged to the syslog server. If the neighbor that bounced and was reported in the message is used to reach the syslog server, the message that was sent to the syslog server gets lost. Use the **service timestamps** command to enable the logging timestamps to track the timing of the neighbor changes.

Discovering New Neighbors

You can discover new neighbors by means of hello protocol. Every router sends its own multicast hello messages over all interfaces that belong to the EIGRP process and listens to multicast messages from other routers coming through the same set of interfaces. As soon as a hello message from a previously unknown neighbor is received, EIGRP tries to establish full adjacency with that neighbor and starts an initial topology table exchange.

The hello protocol in EIGRP is extremely optimistic when compared to other similar hello protocols. It does not verify a two-way adjacency like OSPF does, which can lead to interesting problems in some WAN networks (for example, X.25).

Example 2-12 displays a sample sequence observed when a new neighbor is discovered.

Example 2-12 *New Neighbor Discovery*

```
Fred#debug eigrp packet hello
EIGRP Packets debugging is on
    (HELLO)
Fred#debug eigrp neighbors
EIGRP Neighbors debugging is on
Fred#debug ip eigrp neighbor 1 1.0.0.2
IP Neighbor target enabled on AS 1 for 1.0.0.2
IP-EIGRP Neighbor Target Events debugging is on
Fred#

EIGRP: Received HELLO on Serial0.1 nbr 1.0.0.2
   AS 1, Flags 0x0, Seq 0/0 idbQ 0/0
EIGRP: New peer 1.0.0.2
%DUAL-5-NBRCHANGE: IP-EIGRP 1: Neighbor 1.0.0.2 (Serial0.1) is up: new adjacency
```

Initial Topology Table Exchange

An EIGRP router tries to exchange its topology table with the new neighbor as soon as it's discovered. The initial topology table exchange is signaled by the INIT flag in the first update packet sent to the new neighbor. However, the neighbor might not be ready for the topology table exchange yet (for example, maybe it hasn't received the hello message from this router yet), which might lead to interesting scenarios like the one in Figure 2-15.

In the scenario of Figure 2-15, the link between router A and router B has just been established (for example, a Frame Relay DLCI became active). Router A received a hello packet from a previously unknown neighbor (router B) and immediately tried to exchange a topology table by sending an update packet with INIT flag set to 1. Router B, however, hasn't heard from router A yet; from its perspective, the packet is coming from an unknown neighbor and is therefore immediately dropped without further processing. Router A retransmitted the initial update packet, but router B continued to drop the retransmitted packets as long as it hasn't seen the hello packet from router A. At that moment router B tried to exchange the topology table with router A, so it also sent an update packet with INIT flag set to 1. Router A recognized router B as a valid neighbor; the initial update packet was processed and acknowledged in the yet again retransmitted initial update packet from router A. The rest of the update packets are exchanged with piggybacked acknowledgments because they were already enqueued in the neighbor's transmission list (see the section, "Sequence Numbers and Acknowledgments," in this chapter for details). The last update packet in the database exchange is finally acknowledged with an ACK packet because there are no more enqueued data packets that could carry the piggyback acknowledgment.

Figure 2-15 *Initial Database Exchange—Typical Scenario*

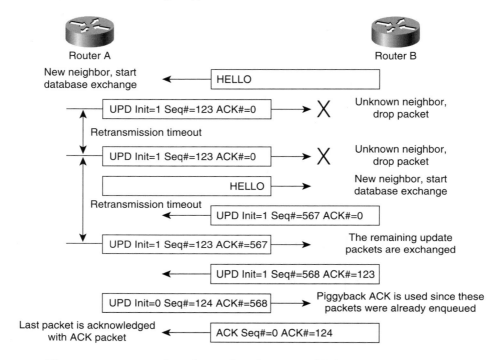

The same sequence, when observed on the router with the debugging turned on, would look similar to the printout in Example 2-13.

Example 2-13 *Initial Database Exchange as Observed on a Router*

```
Fred#debug eigrp packet hello update query reply
EIGRP Packets debugging is on
    (UPDATE, QUERY, REPLY, ACK)
Fred#
EIGRP: New peer 1.0.0.2
%DUAL-5-NBRCHANGE: IP-EIGRP 1: Neighbor 1.0.0.2 (Serial0.1) is up: new adjacency
EIGRP: Enqueuing UPDATE on Serial0.1 nbr 1.0.0.2 iidbQ un/rely 0/1 peerQ un/rely 0/
0 serno 2-30
EIGRP: Sending UPDATE on Serial0.1 nbr 1.0.0.2
  AS 1, Flags 0x1, Seq 39/0 idbQ 0/0 iidbQ un/rely 0/0 peerQ ...
EIGRP: Sending UPDATE on Serial0.1 nbr 1.0.0.2, retry 1, RTO 3000
  AS 1, Flags 0x1, Seq 39/0 idbQ 0/0 iidbQ un/rely 0/0 peerQ ...
EIGRP: Received UPDATE on Serial0.1 nbr 1.0.0.2
  AS 1, Flags 0x1, Seq 54/0 idbQ 0/0 iidbQ un/rely 0/0 peerQ ...
EIGRP: Sending UPDATE on Serial0.1 nbr 1.0.0.2, retry 2, RTO 4500
  AS 1, Flags 0x1, Seq 39/54 idbQ 0/0 iidbQ un/rely 0/0 peerQ ...
EIGRP: Received ACK on Serial0.1 nbr 1.0.0.2
  AS 1, Flags 0x0, Seq 0/39 idbQ 0/0 iidbQ un/rely 0/0 peerQ un/rely 0/1
```

Adjacency Resets—Causes and Consequences

In the section, "Hello Protocol," in this chapter, you saw one of the most frequently encountered reasons for adjacency resets: The neighbor is declared dead when the hold timer expires without receiving any hello packets from the neighbor. In this section, the other reasons for adjacency resets are described along with the way EIGRP recovers from software- or operator-induced resets. Whatever the reason for the adjacency reset, whether it is a reset triggered by an external event, an operator requested reset, or an IOS-generated reset, the results are always the same:

- The neighbor (or several neighbors) is removed from the neighbor table and EIGRP loses all information about that neighbor.

- A *linkdown()* event is generated for the neighbor (see the section, "Dual Behavior on Route Loss," in Chapter 1 for details). All the routes received from the neighbor are removed from the topology table and either local or diffused computation is started for all those routes where the now-dead neighbor was the successor.

The most obvious reasons an adjacency would be reset are the following ones listed in Table 2-10.

Table 2-10 *Various Reasons to Reset EIGRP Adjacency*

Action	Effects on EIGRP Adjacencies
No packets are received from the neighbor within *hold timer.*	Neighbor is declared dead (see the section "Hello Protocol").
A single reliable packet is retransmitted at least 16 times and for a period larger than the *hold timer.*	Neighbor is declared dead (see the section "Retransmissions and Retransmission Timers" for additional details).
The interface goes down (line down or line protocol down).	All neighbors reachable over that interface are declared dead.
The interface is shut down by an operation action.	Same as the previous entry.
A network is removed from EIGRP process.	All neighbors belonging to that network are declared dead.

The network operator can clear the EIGRP adjacency in a number of different ways. See Table 2-11 for corresponding privileged-mode commands.

Table 2-11 *Commands Used to Clear EIGRP Neighbors*

To Clear Adjacency with . . .	. . . Use the Following Exec Command
A single IP neighbor	**clear ip eigrp neighbor** <ip-address>
A single IPX neighbor	**clear ipx eigrp neighbor** <ipx-address>
A single AppleTalk neighbor	**clear appletalk eigrp neighbor** <at-address>
All IP neighbors reachable over one interface	**clear ip eigrp neighbor** <interface>
All IPX neighbors reachable over one interface	**clear ipx eigrp neighbor** <interface>
All AppleTalk neighbors reachable over one interface	**clear apple eigrp neighbor** <interface>
All IP neighbors of all EIGRP processes	**clear ip eigrp neighbor**
All IPX neighbors of all EIGRP processes	**clear ipx eigrp neighbor**
All AppleTalk neighbors	**clear apple eigrp neighbor**

These commands would normally be used to recover from software errors (for example, inconsistencies in topology tables) and should not be used during normal network operation.

The last set of actions that can cause EIGRP adjacency resets are IOS-generated resets that follow changes in router configuration. Every time a network operator changes router configuration in a way that might influence the EIGRP topology table on the router itself or on its neighbors, the adjacency with these neighbors is reset to force a topology table purge and a full topology table exchange under new configuration parameters. An EIGRP adjacency reset following each configuration change that affects EIGRP process might be considered overkill (or a brute-force approach) but unfortunately that's the way EIGRP handles configuration changes.

TIP Because adjacency resets following a configuration change are a fact of life, network operators should follow a few rules to make their network more stable:

- Make EIGRP-related changes only during maintenance periods of your network. Any router configuration change that is linked to EIGRP operation might bring your network down for 5–60 seconds (depending on the hello timer values) because the EIGRP neighbors only reestablish adjacency after the hello packets are received by both routers.

- Any EIGRP-related changes cause a massive flurry of local and diffusing computations following the route loss caused by adjacency resets throughout your network, more so if the changes are done on the core routers with many neighbors. It's therefore strongly advisable to plan enough time for the network to recover from a potential meltdown situation within the maintenance period.

- All EIGRP-related changes on the core routers should be done in a batch to prevent repetitive adjacency resets. The best way to apply these changes is to store them in a file and download them to the router using any of the mechanisms available for configuration download (for example, TFTP, RSH, and so on).

The various configuration changes that can trigger EIGRP adjacency resets are documented in Table 2-12.

NOTE   MTU change no longer causes neighbor reset. The behavior was fixed by CSCdj90106 in IOS 11.3(6) and 12.0(1).

Table 2-12   *Configuration Changes That Can Cause EIGRP Adjacency Resets*

Configuration Change	Effect on EIGRP Adjacency
Change in interface bandwidth, delay, or MTU size	All neighbors reachable over that interface are reset
EIGRP split horizon is configured on the interface	
EIGRP summarization is configured on the interface	
IP, IPX, or AppleTalk address of the interface is changed	
Interface is configured as **passive-interface**	
Per-interface **distribute-list in** or **distribute-list out** is configured or removed	
ACL referenced in per-interface **distribute-list** is changed	
Autosummary is configured or removed	All adjacencies of the EIGRP process are reset
metric maximum-hop is configured	
Per-process **distribute-list in** or **distribute-list out** is configured	
ACL referenced in per-process **distribute-list** is changed	

Whenever the EIGRP adjacency is reset, the neighbor is not informed that it has been deleted from the EIGRP neighbor table. The neighbor only discovers that something unexpected has happened when it receives the initial topology table exchange packet (update packet with INIT flag set to 1). The reaction to the fact that the adjacency has been reset is rather unexpected; the neighbor that tries to reestablish the adjacency is declared dead by the other side. A typical scenario is shown in Figure 2-16.

Either the network operator or IOS itself triggered the adjacency reset on router A resulting in router B silently being removed from the neighbor table. Router B was not informed that it has been removed from router A's neighbor table, so it continues receiving hello packets from router A believing that everything is normal. Router A might continue receiving data packets from router B, but it ignores them because they are coming from an unknown neighbor. The situation at this point is a stalemate. Router A ignores router B, and router B does not know that anything exceptional happened.

Figure 2-16 *Recovery from Operator-Initiated or IOS-Triggered Adjacency Reset*

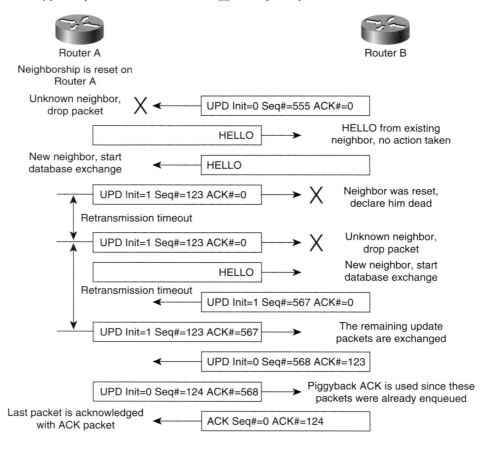

When router A receives the first hello packet from router B, it discovers a new neighbor and tries exchanging the topology table with it by sending an update packet with the INIT flag set to 1. Router B, upon receiving this packet, finally discovers that the adjacency was reset on router A and declares router A dead. Your first impression might be that this is not a very smart action because it prolongs the recovery process, but router B does not know whether router A reset the adjacency or experienced a reload. From router B's perspective, it's safer to declare router A dead and wait for the first hello packet to verify Router A's EIGRP configuration. The stalemate situation has now turned around; router B ignores router A.

Finally, the hello timer on router A triggers another hello packet that's received by router B. Router B discovers a new neighbor, starts initial database exchange, and the update packets start flowing between the neighbors (refer to the section, "Initial Topology Table Exchange," earlier in this chapter for additional details).

The unfortunate side effect of the way EIGRP handles recovery from adjacency resets is the long recovery time, which could be in the worst case twice the hello interval (or up to 2 minutes on a low-speed Frame Relay connection). This is yet another reason to approach router configuration changes that might result in EIGRP adjacency resets with extreme care.

Monitoring EIGRP Neighbors

IOS gives you a rich set of **show** commands that provide good insight into the EIGRP neighbor table, as well as a real-time logging mechanism that can alert you via a syslog mechanism or provide a historical view of EIGRP-related events in the network. Such a history can prove extremely beneficial when you are trying to reconstruct the potential reasons for EIGRP-related problems during a troubleshooting session.

The two **show** commands display the summary of the neighbor data or more detailed information and the information can be requested by the EIGRP AS number, by the interface over which the neighbor is reachable, or both. Table 2-13 documents all the various command options:

Table 2-13   *IOS Show Commands Used to Display the EIGRP Neighbor Table*

To Display . . .	. . . Use the Following Command
Summary information on all neighbors	**show ip eigrp neighbor**
Detailed information on all neighbors	**show ip eigrp neighbor detail**
Summary information on neighbors belonging to one EIGRP process and/or reachable over one interface	**show ip eigrp neighbor [<as>] [<interface>]**
Detailed information on neighbors belonging to one EIGRP process and/or reachable over one interface	**show ip eigrp neighbor detail [<as>] [<interface>]**

To get information on IPX or AppleTalk EIGRP neighbors, replace the *ip* keyword in Table 2-13 with *ipx* or *appletalk*.

The information displayed by the **show ip eigrp neighbor** command is explained in Figure 2-17, and the additional information displayed by the **show ip eigrp neighbor detail** command is explained in Figure 2-18.

Figure 2-17 *Information Displayed by the* **show ip eigrp neighbor** *Command*

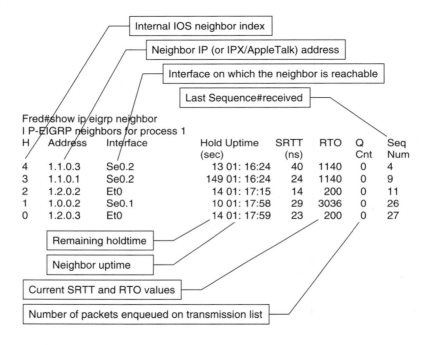

Figure 2-18 *Additional Information Displayed by the **show ip eigrp neighbor detail** Command*

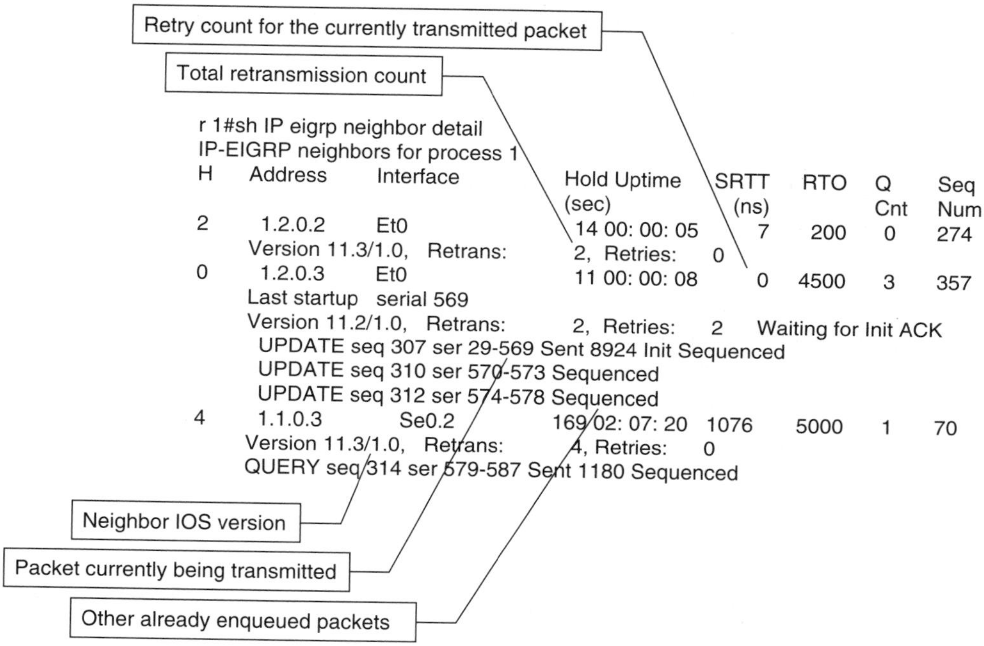

You configure the second troubleshooting tool, neighbor event logging, using the commands from Table 2-14.

Table 2-14 *Commands Used to Configure Neighbor Event Logging*

To Enable . . .	. . . Use the Following Command
IP neighbor event logging	**router eigrp <as>** **eigrp log-neighbor-changes**
IPX neighbor event logging	**ipx router eigrp <as>** **log-neighbor-changes**
AppleTalk neighbor event logging	**appletalk eigrp log-neighbor-changes**

The neighbor event logging facility logs all EIGRP neighbor-related changes using standard IOS logging mechanisms with the severity level *warning*. Sample event logging printouts as related to various events in the EIGRP network are shown in Examples 2-14 to 2-18. The operator-requested adjacency reset is shown in Example 2-14.

Example 2-14 *Adjacency with Wilma Is Cleared and Reestablished on Fred*

```
Fred#clear ip ei nei 1.2.0.2
Fred#
%DUAL-5-NBRCHANGE: IP-EIGRP 1: Neighbor 1.2.0.2 (Ethernet0) is down: manually
    cleared
%DUAL-5-NBRCHANGE: IP-EIGRP 1: Neighbor 1.2.0.2 (Ethernet0) is up: new adjacency
```

When the EIGRP-related configuration parameters are changed, all neighbors reachable over the affected interface are declared down (refer also to the section titled "Adjacency Resets—Causes and Consequences" earlier in this chapter for details) as seen in Example 2-15.

Example 2-15 *EIGRP-Related Interface Configuration Parameters Are Changed*

```
Fred#conf t
Enter configuration commands, one per line. End with CNTL/Z.
Fred(config)#interface ethernet 0
Fred(config-if)#delay 20
Fred(config-if)#
%DUAL-5-NBRCHANGE: IP-EIGRP 1: Neighbor 1.2.0.2 (Ethernet0) is down: interface delay
    changed
%DUAL-5-NBRCHANGE: IP-EIGRP 1: Neighbor 1.2.0.3 (Ethernet0) is down: interface delay
    changed
%DUAL-5-NBRCHANGE: IP-EIGRP 1: Neighbor 1.2.0.3 (Ethernet0) is up: new adjacency
%DUAL-5-NBRCHANGE: IP-EIGRP 1: Neighbor 1.2.0.2 (Ethernet0) is up: new adjacency
Fred(config-if)#ip summary-address eigrp 1 10.0.0.0 255.255.0.0
Fred(config-if)#
%DUAL-5-NBRCHANGE: IP-EIGRP 1: Neighbor 1.2.0.2 (Ethernet0) is down: summary
    configured
%DUAL-5-NBRCHANGE: IP-EIGRP 1: Neighbor 1.2.0.3 (Ethernet0) is down: summary
    configured
%DUAL-5-NBRCHANGE: IP-EIGRP 1: Neighbor 1.2.0.3 (Ethernet0) is up: new adjacency
%DUAL-5-NBRCHANGE: IP-EIGRP 1: Neighbor 1.2.0.2 (Ethernet0) is up: new adjacency
Fred(config-if)#^Z
```

When the adjacency is reset on the adjacent router, the EIGRP router discovers that the adjacency was restarted when it receives an update packet with INIT flag set to 1 (see the section titled "Adjacency Resets—Causes and Consequences" for details). The corresponding log messages are displayed in Example 2-16.

Example 2-16 *EIGRP Log Messages on Neighbor Restart*

```
Fred#wilma
Trying Wilma (1.0.0.1)...
Wilma#clear ip eigrp neighbor 1.2.0.1
```

Example 2-16 *EIGRP Log Messages on Neighbor Restart (Continued)*

```
Wilma#
%DUAL-5-NBRCHANGE: IP-EIGRP 1: Neighbor 1.2.0.2 (Ethernet0) is down: peer restarted
%DUAL-5-NBRCHANGE: IP-EIGRP 1: Neighbor 1.2.0.2 (Ethernet0) is up: new adjacency
```

Finally, when the neighbor fails (for example, due to operator-requested reload), the hold timer expires as seen in Example 2-17.

Example 2-17 *EIGRP Message upon Neighbor Failure*

```
Wilma#reload
Proceed with reload? [confirm]y
[Connection to wilma closed by foreign host]
Fred#
%DUAL-5-NBRCHANGE: IP-EIGRP 1: Neighbor 1.2.0.2 (Ethernet0) is down: holding time
    expired
Fred#term no mon
```

Unfortunately, the only time when EIGRP neighbor logging doesn't give you all the relevant information is when you would need it most, namely when you are trying to troubleshoot the Stuck-in-Active (SIA) events. The adjacency with a nonresponding neighbor is cleared when the EIGRP router experiences an SIA event, but this fact is not logged using the EIGRP neighbor logging mechanism; the only message logged is the fact that a route was found to be stuck in active. The only method left to you as you try to troubleshoot the SIA event is to correlate the SIA message with follow-on *new adjacency* messages that might be caused by adjacency being torn down following the SIA event. For example, if you are faced with the sequence shown in Example 2-18, it's very probable that the nonresponding neighbors have IP addresses 1.2.0.2, 1.1.0.3, and 1.1.0.1.

NOTE   EIGRP neighbor loss due to interface going down or due to an SIA event is logged after IOS 12.0(2).

Example 2-18 *EIGRP Log Messages Following an SIA Event*

```
Fred#show ip eigrp topology active
IP-EIGRP Topology Table for process 1

Codes: P - Passive, A - Active, U - Update, Q - Query, R - Reply,
       r - Reply status

A 1.3.0.3/32, 1 successors, FD is Inaccessible, QR
    3 replies, active 00:01:18, query-origin: Local origin
        via Connected (Infinity/Infinity), Loopback3
        via 1.2.0.3 (Infinity/Infinity), Ethernet0, serno 129
        via 1.2.0.2 (Infinity/Infinity), r, Ethernet0, serno 126
        via 1.1.0.1 (Infinity/Infinity), r, R, Serial0.2, serno 128
        via 1.0.0.2 (Infinity/Infinity), Serial0.1, serno 130
```

Example 2-18 *EIGRP Log Messages Following an SIA Event (Continued)*

```
      Remaining replies:
           via 1.1.0.3, r, Serial0.2
Fred#
%DUAL-3-SIA: Route 1.3.0.3/32 stuck-in-active state in IP-EIGRP 1. Cleaning up
%DUAL-5-NBRCHANGE: IP-EIGRP 1: Neighbor 1.2.0.2 (Ethernet0) is up: new adjacency
%DUAL-5-NBRCHANGE: IP-EIGRP 1: Neighbor 1.1.0.3 (Serial0.2) is up: new adjacency
%DUAL-5-NBRCHANGE: IP-EIGRP 1: Neighbor 1.1.0.1 (Serial0.2) is up: new adjacency
```

EIGRP Topology Table

The EIGRP topology table was mentioned throughout this chapter because it's one of the central elements of EIGRP. As seen in Figure 2-19, the topology table is used by DUAL process to store information received by the EIGRP neighbors as well as information received from other routing protocols. The route selection process that selects optimum routes and inserts them in the main IP routing table also uses it.

Figure 2-19 *EIGRP Topology Table and Its Relation to Various EIGRP Processes*

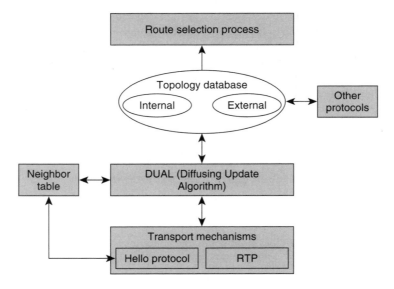

This section focuses more on how you can explore the contents of the topology table and how you can use the information stored in it to monitor or troubleshoot EIGRP. But before going into the description of various **show** commands, review the different ways information can be inserted or removed from the topology table:

Information can be inserted or updated in the topology table when any of the following occur:

- An update packet with a noninfinity delay is received.
- A reply packet with a noninfinity delay is received.
- A route is redistributed from another routing protocol.
- A directly connected subnet that falls within one of the networks configured in the EIGRP process becomes active.

Information in the topology table can be updated (but not inserted) when a query with a noninfinity delay is received from a neighbor. Finally, entries from a topology table are deleted when any of the following occur:

- A directly connected subnet becomes unreachable (layer 1 or layer 2 failure or the interface is shut down by the operator).
- An update, query, or reply packet is received with infinite delay.
- A redistributed route disappears from the source routing process.
- A neighbor is found dead.

EIGRP Topology Table Contents

You can display the basic information about the EIGRP topology table with the commands in Table 2-15.

Table 2-15 *Show Commands to Display Summary Information on the EIGRP Topology Table*

To Display . . .	. . . Use This Command
Summary information on all EIGRP topology tables	**show ip eigrp topology summary**
Summary information on the topology table of a single EIGRP process	**show ip eigrp topology <as> summary**
Routes that are used or could be potentially used in the topology table	**show ip eigrp topology [<as>]**
Summary information on all routes stored in the EIGRP topology table	**show ip eigrp topology [<as>] all-links**

To display IPX or AppleTalk topology tables, simply replace the **ip** keyword in the commands in Table 2-15 with **ipx** or **appletalk**. The optional **<as>** parameter cannot be used with AppleTalk because EIGRP/AT does not support multiple processes running in the router.

The **show ip eigrp topology summary** command produces a printout similar to the one in Example 2-19.

Example 2-19 *The show ip eigrp topology summary Command*

```
Fred#show ip eigrp topology summary
IP-EIGRP Topology Table for process 1
Head serial 1, next serial 156
9 routes, 0 pending replies, 0 dummies
IP-EIGRP enabled on 8 interfaces, neighbors present on 3 interfaces
Quiescent interfaces: Se0.2 Et0 Se0.1
Fred#
```

The most relevant information produced by this **show** command is the number of routes in the EIGRP topology table and the *next serial* field. The number of routes stored in the EIGRP topology table directly affects the memory usage and convergence speed. If the number of routes in an EIGRP topology table is much larger than the number of routes inserted from EIGRP into the IP routing table, it might indicate that your network is too highly meshed or that the EIGRP split horizon is turned off in the wrong place (see Chapter 13, "Running EIGRP over WAN Networks," for more details). Additional commands, such as **show ip eigrp topology all-links** must be used to verify any one of these assumptions.

The next serial field gives you information about the number of changes in the EIGRP topology table; every time a change is introduced into the topology table, the next serial number is increased by one. By monitoring this number over time, you can directly conclude how stable your network is.

The **show ip eigrp topology** command displays all the routes in the EIGRP topology table that are used or might be used in the future (for example, all routes received from a successor or a feasible successor). The printout you see on the router is similar to that in Figure 2-20.

Figure 2-20 *The show ip eigrp topology Command*

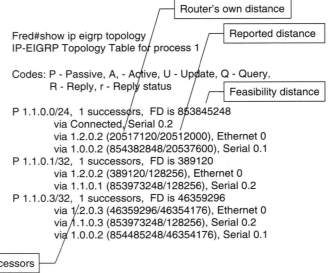

For each route in the EIGRP topology table, all entries received from successors or feasible successors are displayed. The entries are sorted in the order of increasing distance (the distance of the entry as seen from this router's perspective). The number of successors displays after the network prefix (all the remaining entries are feasible successors), together with the feasibility distance of the route. Each entry belonging to a route carries the neighbor IP address, the router's own distance, the neighbor's reported distance, and the interface through which the neighbor is reachable.

In contrast to the **show ip eigrp topology** command, the **show ip eigrp topology all-links** command displays all entries in the topology table, not just the entries received from successors or feasible successors. For example, compare the **show ip eigrp topology all-links** printout in Figure 2-21 with the **show ip eigrp topology** output from the same router in Figure 2-20.

Figure 2-21   *The show ip eigrp topology all-links Printout*

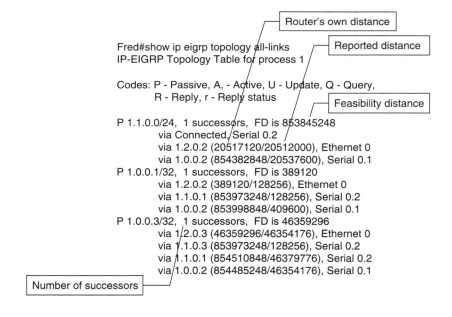

The difference between the printouts can be observed in entries for routes 1.0.0.1/32 and 1.0.0.3/32. The second printout shows that an entry for route 1.0.0.1/32 received from neighbor 1.0.0.2, which is clearly not a feasible successor because its reported distance (409600) is greater than router's own feasibility distance (389120). A similar entry for route 1.0.0.3/32 was received from neighbor 1.1.0.1.

Internal EIGRP Routes

All the printouts from the previous section give you only the summary information about the routes in the EIGRP topology table. To see details about a specific route (for example, the vector metric), you have to use the command **show ip eigrp topology [<as>] <ip-address> <subnet-mask>**. This command expands the information about the specified route as observed in the **show ip eigrp topology all-links** command to include all EIGRP attributes of the route.

The detailed information about the route 1.0.0.1/32 from the example in Figure 2-21 is displayed in Example 2-20.

Example 2-20 *The show ip eigrp topology <address> <mask> Printout for Internal Routes*

```
Fred#show ip eigrp topology 1.0.0.1 255.255.255.255
IP-EIGRP topology entry for 1.0.0.1/32
  State is Passive, Query origin flag is 1, 1 Successor(s), FD is 389120
  Routing Descriptor Blocks:
  1.2.0.2 (Ethernet0), from 1.2.0.2, Send flag is 0x0
      Composite metric is (389120/128256), Route is Internal
      Vector metric:
        Minimum bandwidth is 10000 Kbit
        Total delay is 5200 microseconds
        Reliability is 255/255
        Load is 1/255
        Minimum MTU is 1500
        Hop count is 1
  1.1.0.1 (Serial0.2), from 1.1.0.1, Send flag is 0x0
      Composite metric is (853973248/128256), Route is Internal
      Vector metric:
        Minimum bandwidth is 3 Kbit
        Total delay is 25000 microseconds
        Reliability is 255/255
        Load is 1/255
        Minimum MTU is 1500
        Hop count is 1
  1.0.0.2 (Serial0.1), from 1.0.0.2, Send flag is 0x0
      Composite metric is (853998848/409600), Route is Internal
      Vector metric:
        Minimum bandwidth is 3 Kbit
        Total delay is 26000 microseconds
        Reliability is 255/255
        Load is 1/255
        Minimum MTU is 1500
        Hop count is 2
Fred#
```

For every entry received from a neighbor, this command displays all the information from the **show ip eigrp topology all-links** command. The additional information displayed for every entry also includes the following:

- EIGRP route type (internal or external)

- Both composite metrics—reported distance from the neighbor and router's own distance

- Detailed vector metric with all six vector components

External Routes and Additional Route Attributes

The EIGRP topology table contains additional attributes for routes that were redistributed into EIGRP from other sources. You can display all these attributes by using the **show ip eigrp topology <address> <mask>** command. Two sample printouts of an external route are shown in Example 2-21 and Example 2-22. The first external route is a static route redistributed into EIGRP; the second external route comes from another EIGRP process.

Example 2-21 *Static Route Redistributed into EIGRP*

```
Fred#show ip eigrp topology 2.0.0.3 255.255.255.255
IP-EIGRP topology entry for 2.0.0.3/32
  State is Passive, Query origin flag is 1, 1 Successor(s), FD is 389120
  Routing Descriptor Blocks:
  1.2.0.3 (Ethernet0), from 1.2.0.3, Send flag is 0x0
      Composite metric is (389120/128256), Route is External
      Vector metric:
        Minimum bandwidth is 10000 Kbit
        Total delay is 5200 microseconds
        Reliability is 255/255
        Load is 1/255
        Minimum MTU is 1500
        Hop count is 1
      External data:
        Originating router is 1.0.0.5
        AS number of route is 0
        External protocol is Static, external metric is 0
        Administrator tag is 0 (0x00000000)
```

Example 2-22 *Route Redistributed into EIGRP from Another EIGRP Process*

```
Fred#show ip eigrp topology 2.0.0.1 255.255.255.255
IP-EIGRP topology entry for 2.0.0.1/32
  State is Passive, Query origin flag is 1, 1 Successor(s), FD is 414720
  Routing Descriptor Blocks:
  1.2.0.2 (Ethernet0), from 1.2.0.2, Send flag is 0x0
      Composite metric is (414720/409600), Route is External
      Vector metric:
        Minimum bandwidth is 10000 Kbit
        Total delay is 6200 microseconds
        Reliability is 255/255
        Load is 1/255
        Minimum MTU is 1500
        Hop count is 2
      External data:
        Originating router is 1.0.0.1
```

continues

Example 2-22 *Route Redistributed into EIGRP from Another EIGRP Process (Continued)*

```
AS number of route is 2
External protocol is EIGRP, external metric is 409600
Administrator tag is 0 (0x00000000)
```

The additional attributes of an external EIGRP route are listed in Table 2-16.

Table 2-16 *Attributes of External EIGRP Routes*

Attribute	Meaning
Originating router	Router ID of the router redistributing external route into this EIGRP process. The router ID is an IP address that follows the same rules as the router ID for OSPF or BGP.
AS number	AS number of originating BGP or EIGRP process.
External protocol	The originating protocol from which the route was redistributed into EIGRP.
External metric	The metric of the redistributed route in the originating protocol. For routes redistributed from OSPF this would be the OSPF cost, for RIP routes the hop count, and for the EIGRP routes the composite metric.
Administrator tag	32-bit quantity that can be set in the redistribution point with a route map. The administrator tag has no meaning for EIGRP itself. It can be used, however, to fine-tune redistribution.

Monitoring Network Convergence through the EIGRP Topology Table

All the commands discussed so far display all routes in the topology table. Sometimes, you might need to see only those routes that are in the convergence process, whether the routers are performing diffused computation on these routes or they haven't converged throughout the network yet because the update packets weren't propagated due to bandwidth constraints. Commands from Table 2-17 can help you focus on only the routes currently in the convergence phase.

Table 2-17   *Show Commands That Display Routes in the Convergence Phase*

Command	Printout
show ip eigrp topology active	Displays only the routes for which the diffused computation is performed
show ip eigrp topology pending	Displays the routes that haven't converged yet (for example, diffused computation is performed or outgoing updates are still pending)

Both commands display only the interesting entries in the EIGRP topology table together with the information that can help a network operator understand in which direction the potential convergence bottleneck lies. For example, consider the printout in Example 2-23.

Example 2-23 *The show ip eigrp topology active Command*

```
Fred#show ip eigrp topology active
IP-EIGRP Topology Table for process 1

Codes: P - Passive, A - Active, U - Update, Q - Query, R - Reply,
       r - Reply status

A 1.3.0.2/32, 1 successors, FD is Inaccessible, QR
    3 replies, active 00:00:12, query-origin: Local origin
        via Connected (Infinity/Infinity), Loopback2
        via 1.2.0.2 (20645120/20640000), Ethernet0
        via 1.1.0.3 (Infinity/Infinity), r, R, Serial0.2, serno 191
        via 1.0.0.2 (Infinity/Infinity), Serial0.1, serno 190
        via 1.1.0.1 (Infinity/Infinity), r, Serial0.2
    Remaining replies:
        via 1.2.0.3, r, Ethernet0
```

The printout shows that there is only one route in the EIGRP topology table for which the diffusing computation is currently being performed. The diffusing computation has been originated locally (see the *query-origin* field) and the route has been active for 12 seconds.

EIGRP is still in the process of sending at least one QUERY and one reply packet for this destination (the highlighted Q and R letters in the first line of the printout). The router is still waiting for three replies to complete the diffusing computation. All the neighbors that have not provided the reply yet are marked with a lowercase r (also highlighted in the printout). The replies thus far have to come from neighbors 1.1.0.3, 1.1.0.1 (both of which have previously sent information about this route to this router), and 1.2.0.3 (which has not sent any information about this route before, probably because the router under inspection was its downstream router).

As you have seen in this short example, **show ip eigrp topology active** is a powerful command that can identify the following:

- The amount of diffusing computation being currently performed in the EIGRP network (for example, the number of active routes).

- The approximate network convergence time—if the routes are active for a long time, the overall network convergence time is also long.

- The potential convergence bottlenecks—if the same router or a set of routers is not responding to queries for a number of destinations, those routers or their downstream neighbors obviously represent a potential convergence bottleneck.

Anomalies in EIGRP Topology Tables

Two scenarios where the information in the EIGRP topology table deviates from what you'd expect to see exist, and both of them are related to interactions between different routing protocols.

In the first scenario, an entry for a locally connected subnet with higher EIGRP distance might take precedence over a better entry learned from an EIGRP neighbor because the router uses the locally connected subnet due to its lower administrative distance (see Example 2-24).

Example 2-24 *Directly Connected Network Taking Precedence over a Better Route Learned from a Neighbor*

```
Fred#sh ip ei top all-links
IP-EIGRP Topology Table for process 1

Codes: P - Passive, A - Active, U - Update, Q - Query, R - Reply,
       r - Reply status

P 1.0.0.1/32, 1 successors, FD is 389120, serno 251
        via 1.2.0.2 (389120/128256), Ethernet0
        via 1.1.0.1 (20640000/128256), Serial0.2
        via 1.0.0.2 (53998848/409600), Serial0.1
Fred#conf t
Enter configuration commands, one per line. End with CNTL/Z.
Fred(config)#int loop 3
Fred(config-if)#ip addr 1.0.0.1 255.255.255.255
Fred(config-if)#band 10
Fred(config-if)#^Z
Fred#sh ip ei top all-links
IP-EIGRP Topology Table for process 1

Codes: P - Passive, A - Active, U - Update, Q - Query, R - Reply,
       r - Reply status

P 1.0.0.1/32, 1 successors, FD is 256128000, serno 254
        via Connected, Loopback3
        via 1.2.0.2 (389120/128256), Ethernet0
        via 1.1.0.3 (46891776/46379776), Serial0.2
        via 1.1.0.1 (20640000/128256), Serial0.2
        via 1.0.0.2 (53998848/409600), Serial0.1
```

Under specific circumstances (for example, when a locally connected subnet is configured on a loopback interface) it can block any equivalent route from an EIGRP neighbor even when it is not reachable. See Example 2-25 for an example.

Example 2-25 *Directly Connected Subnet Blocking a Better Route Learned from an EIGRP Neighbor*

```
Fred#conf t
Enter configuration commands, one per line. End with CNTL/Z.
Fred(config)#int loop 3
Fred(config-if)#ip address 1.0.0.1 255.255.255.255
Fred(config-if)#shutdown
Fred(config-if)#^Z
Fred#sh ip ei top all-links
IP-EIGRP Topology Table for process 1

Codes: P - Passive, A - Active, U - Update, Q - Query, R - Reply,
       r - Reply status

P 1.0.0.1/32, 0 successors, FD is Inaccessible, serno 255
          via 1.2.0.2 (389120/128256), Ethernet0
          via 1.1.0.3 (46891776/46379776), Serial0.2
          via 1.1.0.1 (20640000/128256), Serial0.2
          via 1.0.0.2 (53998848/409600), Serial0.1
```

An entry in a topology table might have infinite Feasibility Distance and zero successors although the topology table contains several legitimate entries when the router itself is using the route toward the same destination from some other source, such as a static route (see Example 2-26).

Example 2-26 *A Route from Another Source with a Better Administrative Distance Blocking an EIGRP Route*

```
Fred#show ip eigrp topology
IP-EIGRP Topology Table for process 1

Codes: P - Passive, A - Active, U - Update, Q - Query, R - Reply,
       r - Reply status

P 2.0.0.3/32, 1 successors, FD is 389120
          via 1.2.0.3 (389120/128256), Ethernet0
          via 1.0.0.2 (853973248/128256), Serial0.1

Fred#conf t
Enter configuration commands, one per line. End with CNTL/Z.
Fred(config)#ip route 2.0.0.3 255.255.255.255 null 0
Fred(config)#^Z
Fred#show ip route 2.0.0.3 255.255.255.255
Routing entry for 2.0.0.3/32
  Known via "static", distance 1, metric 0 (connected)
  Routing Descriptor Blocks:
  * directly connected, via Null0
```

continues

Example 2-26 *A Route from Another Source with a Better Administrative Distance Blocking an EIGRP Route (Continued)*

```
        Route metric is 0, traffic share count is 1

Fred#show ip eigrp topology all-links
IP-EIGRP Topology Table for process 1

Codes: P - Passive, A - Active, U - Update, Q - Query, R - Reply,
r - Reply status

P 2.0.0.3/32, 0 successors, FD is Inaccessible
        via 1.1.0.1 (853998848/409600), Serial0.2
        via 1.2.0.3 (389120/128256), Ethernet0
        via 1.1.0.3 (854485248/46354176), Serial0.2
        via 1.0.0.2 (853973248/128256), Serial0.1
        via 1.2.0.2 (414720/409600), Ethernet0
Fred#
```

You can display the anomalies where the EIGRP topology table has at least one good successor for a certain route that is ignored due to other sources of routing information with a special show command: **show ip eigrp topology zero-successor**. This command, when used on router Fred after the configuration changes in Example 2-25 and Example 2-26, yields the results in Example 2-27.

Example 2-27 *Displaying Entries in the EIGRP Topology Table with Zero Successors*

```
Fred#show ip eigrp topology zero
IP-EIGRP Topology Table for process 1

Codes: P - Passive, A - Active, U - Update, Q - Query, R - Reply,
       r - Reply status

P 1.0.0.1/32, 0 successors, FD is Inaccessible
        via 1.2.0.2 (389120/128256), Ethernet0
        via 1.1.0.3 (46891776/46379776), Serial0.2
        via 1.1.0.1 (20640000/128256), Serial0.2
        via 1.0.0.2 (53998848/409600), Serial0.1
P 2.0.0.3/32, 0 successors, FD is Inaccessible
        via 1.2.0.2 (414720/409600), Ethernet0
        via 1.2.0.3 (389120/128256), Ethernet0
        via 1.1.0.1 (20665600/409600), Serial0.2
        via 1.1.0.3 (46866176/46354176), Serial0.2
        via 1.0.0.2 (53973248/128256), Serial0.1
```

Building Routing Tables from EIGRP Topology Tables

The final step in EIGRP processing is the installation of the best routes from the EIGRP topology table (for example, the routes received from successors) into the main IP routing table. EIGRP best routes are not automatically copied into the main routing table. They have to compete with other routing sources. The *administrative distance* is used to compare routes from different routing sources and select the best ones.

EIGRP normally only installs routes to the successors in the main IP routing table. As many routes are installed as are permitted (up to the maximum of six) yielding equal-cost load balancing. EIGRP and IGRP are also the only routing protocols that support unequal-cost load balancing via a mechanism called *variance.*

NOTE   The administrative distance is usually the only means of comparing routes coming from different routing sources due to incompatible metrics used in different routing protocols. However, the administrative distance is used as the sole criteria even when comparing routes coming from two EIGRP processes even though the metrics could be compared in this scenario. If the two EIGRP processes have the same administrative distance, the route that was changed most recently (the latest flap) takes precedence and replaces the older (more stable) route. Therefore, it's mandatory to use different administrative distances for different EIGRP processes if they cover overlapping parts of your network. Some hints for proper administrative distance selection in these scenarios are given in Chapter 9, "Integrating EIGRP with Other Enterprise Routing Protocols."

Administrative Distance of EIGRP Routes

The EIGRP route selection process sets different administrative distances for internal and external routes, the defaults being 90 for internal routes and 170 for external routes. (For further explanation about using different distances for internal and external routes, see Chapter 9.) As shown in Table 2-18, you can change these distances in a variety of ways.

Table 2-18   *Different Ways of Setting Nondefault Administrative Distances of EIGRP Routes*

To Change . . .	. . . Use This Command
Default distances for internal and external routes in an EIGRP process	**router eigrp <as>** **distance eigrp <default-internal-distance>** **<default-external-distance>**
Distance of all internal routes received from a neighbor or a set of neighbors	**router eigrp <as>** **distance <distance> <neighbor-ip-address>** **<wildcard-bits>**
Distance of a select set of internal routes received from a neighbor or a set of neighbors	**router eigrp <as>** **distance <distance> <neighbor-ip-address>** **<wildcard-bits> <route-selection-ACL>**

The **distance eigrp** command sets the new defaults for both internal and external routes. Use this command to prefer one EIGRP process over another in the event that the address space of the two processes overlaps.

The **distance** command influences only the distance of internal EIGRP routes (nondefault value for external routes cannot be specified) and enables you to set different administrative distances for routes received from specific neighbors (matched by **neighbor-ip-address** and **wildcard-bits**) or matched by a route filter (standard or extended IP access list specified in **route-selection-ACL**). If you want to ignore internal EIGRP routes received from a neighbor or internal EIGRP routes matching a route filter, specify distance 255 (which means ignore this entry).

Use the **distance** command only in very special circumstances and with extreme care because side effects of this command are not easily evaluated.

EIGRP Variance and Its Influence on Traffic Load Sharing

EIGRP is the only protocol that can load-balance between unequal cost routes. To enable and fine-tune EIGRP load balancing, use the commands in Table 2-19.

Table 2-19   *Configure Unequal-Cost Load-Sharing with EIGRP*

Task	Configure With
Configure unequal-cost load balancing	**router eigrp <as>** **variance <factor>**
Configure proportional load balancing between unequal-cost routes	**router eigrp <as>** **traffic-share balanced**
Use only minimum-cost routes for load balancing	**router eigrp <as>** **traffic-share min across-interfaces**
Configure the maximum number of equal-cost or unequal-cost routes for a given destination	**route eigrp <as>** **maximum-paths <1 to 6>**
Configure per-packet load balancing over an interface on all platforms	**interface <int>** **no ip route-cache**
Configure Cisco Express Forwarding (CEF) per destination load balancing	**interface <int>** **ip route-cache cef** **ip load-sharing per-destination**
Configure CEF per-packet load balancing	**interface <int>** **ip route-cache cef** **ip load-sharing per-packet**

The **variance** command enables unequal-cost balancing under the following conditions:

- The router's own distance from the topology table entry is less than *feasibility distance × variance*.
- The alternate path toward the destination goes through a feasible successor.

The number of alternate paths that can be entered in the IP routing table is controlled by the maximum-paths command. (Only the best N entries that match feasibility condition are entered in the routing table.)

You configure the load-balancing mode on unequal-cost routes by using the **traffic-share** command. If you specify **traffic-share balanced**, the traffic is load-balanced inversely proportionally to the EIGRP composite metric. If, on the other hand, you specify **traffic-share min**, the routed traffic is balanced only across the minimum-cost paths, but all the other paths are already entered in the IP routing table to speed up the convergence process in case of a link or neighbor failure.

The load-balancing mechanism used by the router is dependent on the switching path taken for the interface in question as detailed in Table 2-20.

Table 2-20   *Load Sharing Mechanism Used Depending on the Switching Path*

Switching Path	Load Sharing Mechanism
Process switching	Per-packet load sharing
Fast switching, Optimum switching, Autonomous switching, Silicon switching, Netflow switching	Per-prefix load sharing (for example, all traffic for a certain prefix in the routing table flows over one interface)
Cisco Express Forwarding	Per source-destination-pair load sharing (for example, all traffic for a certain source-destination IP address pair flows over one interface)
Cisco Express Forwarding with per-packet load sharing configured	Per-packet load sharing

Designing EIGRP networks for unequal-cost load balancing is a nontrivial task as you'll see in the next section, but you'll be able to design successful networks using unequal-cost load-balancing by following these rules:

Variance Rule 1

Verify that the paths over which you want to load-balance the traffic lead to successors and feasible successors. In many intuitively correct designs, the neighbor you want to balance the load with is not a feasible successor in EIGRP terms.

Variance Rule 2

Always verify that the load-balancing mechanism works in both directions; if the load balancing works for traffic flowing in one direction it may not work for the return traffic.

Variance Rule 3

If there is more than one router connected to a LAN and you want to load-balance outgoing traffic from that LAN, you'll need additional mechanisms like Hot Standby Routing Protocol (HSRP) to select the proper exit point from the LAN.

Variance Rule 4

You can solve some load-balancing problems where load balancing intuitively works but does not work in reality due to feasible successor limitations by introducing another layer of routers to distribute the traffic.

Valid and Invalid Examples of Using Variance

In several commonly used designs, you might expect to get the desired load-sharing functionality, but the design does not work because it does not comply with EIGRP requirements for unequal-cost load sharing. Several examples are presented in this section, some with comments and solutions, the other as exercises.

One of the most common designs is load sharing between two unequal speed links between two adjacent routers. A simple network using this design appears in Figure 2-22.

The design requirement for this network is to provide proportional load balancing on parallel links between San Jose and Chicago in a 2:1 ratio for all traffic running over those two links. To evaluate whether this design yields the required load balancing functionality, you need to verify that all the variance rules are satisfied:

Variance Rule 1—Verification:

The San Jose router has two paths to the Chicago LAN. The Chicago router over the 2-Mbps link is the successor, and the same router over a 1-Mbps link is a feasible successor.

The Chicago router has two paths to the San Jose LAN. The San Jose router over the 2-Mbps link is the successor, and the same router over a 1-Mbps link is the feasible successor. The Chicago router also has two paths to the San Francisco LAN, but they have the same distance; the minimum bandwidth is 64 kbps over both paths and the delays across the links are the same.

Variance Rule 1 is thus satisfied. Both routers that have to do load sharing have paths going to successors and/or feasible successors over links where the traffic should be load-shared.

Figure 2-22 *Simple Network with Unequal Speed Links*

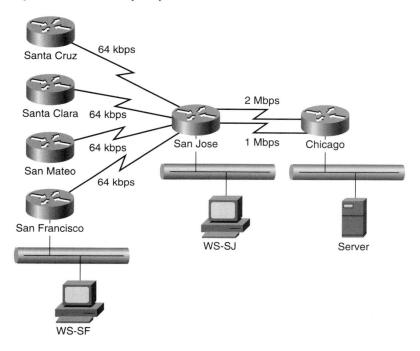

Variance Rule 2—Verification:

The traffic from San Francisco and San Jose toward the Chicago server load-share in the proper ratio; the same is also true for the return traffic from the Chicago server toward the San Jose workstation. The traffic from the Chicago server toward the San Francisco workstation load-share equally across the links because both paths from Chicago toward San Francisco have the same cost. The traffic from Chicago toward San Francisco therefore places too high a load on the lower-speed link. If the number of San Francisco-type offices connected to the San Jose router is high enough and most of the traffic goes from Chicago toward those offices, the 1-Mbps link becomes saturated, while the 2-Mbps link is only 50 percent used.

Variance Rules 3 and 4 do not apply in this particular design.

Based on the previous facts, the design in Figure 2-22 provides load balancing between unequal speed links, but not completely within the required specifications.

Exercise 2-2

How could you modify the EIGRP design in Figure 2-19 to ensure proportional load balancing from Chicago toward all destinations in the San Jose area?

Exercise 2-3

The customer validated load balancing in an environment where the majority of the traffic flowed from the Chicago server toward the remote locations. A new remote backup application was deployed a few months later where the majority of the traffic flowed from remote offices toward the Chicago server. To the customer's surprise, all the traffic from San Jose toward Chicago uses only one of the parallel links. Why?

After implementing the load balancing between Chicago and San Jose, the customer discovered that the slow-speed links in San Jose are saturated over the peak usage periods. The customer decided to upgrade the leased lines to 128 kbps and installed ISDN into all the offices in that area. ISDN is supposed to be used in the dial-backup mode with remote offices calling the San Jose office (dial-in). Unequal-cost load balancing is to be used between the 64-kbps leased line and one ISDN B-channel dial-up connection and the desired traffic ratio between the leased line and ISDN connection is 2:1. The target network diagram is shown in Figure 2-23.

This network conforms to all applicable variance rules for load balancing between remote offices in the Bay area and the San Jose site as follows:

Variance Rule 1—Verification:

The San Jose router has two paths to a remote LAN. The best path to the remote LAN is over the 128-kbps leased line, and the remote router over the ISDN dial-up connection is a feasible successor. The same conclusion can also be reached for paths to the Chicago LAN as seen from the remote office router.

Figure 2-23 *ISDN Used for Load Sharing in Peak Periods*

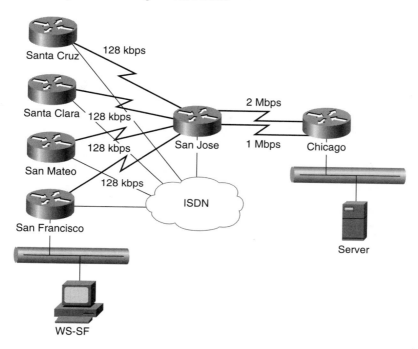

Variance Rule 2—Verification:

In both directions, the successor is reachable over the leased line and the feasible successor is reachable over the ISDN dial-up connection. The delay from Chicago to the remote office in the Bay area is the same over both links, and the minimum bandwidths that dictate the overall value of the composite metric are in the desired 2:1 ratio, yielding an optimal, load-balancing ratio.

Finally, the customer wanted increased reliability in the San Jose site and installed an extra router to handle incoming ISDN calls from remote offices (see Figure 2-24). The San Jose routers link via a back-to-back Ethernet connection.

Figure 2-24 *San Jose Site Redesign*

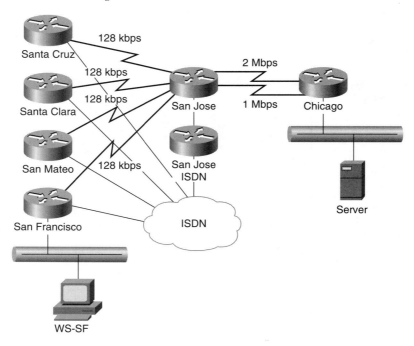

After installing the new router and reconfiguring the routing in the San Jose site, load balancing no longer worked as expected.

Exercise 2-4

How exactly does the load balancing between the San Jose site and remote sites in the Bay area work after the redesign in Figure 2-24? Why?

Exercise 2-5

How would you fix the design in Figure 2-24 to achieve desired load balancing as close to the optimal 2:1 ratio as possible?

Summary

After the details of EIGRP internals are revealed, it's always tempting to compare EIGRP with other routing protocols, particularly with its main competitor: OSPF. One true statement you can make when comparing EIGRP with OSPF is that both perform well in a properly designed network. However, when comparing the details of both protocols, several technical advantages exist in one or the other (in no particular order):

- EIGRP supports the running of several EIGRP processes over a common shared media due to the fact that the AS number is included in every EIGRP packet; OSPF supports only one OSPF process in a shared media environment. EIGRP by itself therefore allows implementation of simple VPNs. OSPF has no similar functionality.

NOTE   With the advanced VPN technologies available in Cisco IOS, using multiple EIGRP processes over the same transmission media is almost never required anymore.

- OSPF only supports equal-cost load balancing; EIGRP supports unequal-cost, proportional load balancing.

- OSPF propagates every change in the network to every router within an area; EIGRP supports bounded updates with proper network design.

- OSPF clearly has a more robust hello protocol because it verifies two-way reachability before attempting to form adjacency, but EIGRP's hello protocol is more adaptable to environments where neighbors over a common subnet have different timing requirements.

- EIGRP flooding is more distributed in environments where several routers share a common LAN because every router is responsible for distribution of its own information. In OSPF, the designated router is a potential bottleneck.

- OSPF can work well in environments where some routers cannot cope with the amount of changes in the network; these routers might misroute the traffic, but the rest of the network is not affected. In EIGRP a single misbehaving or overloaded router can bring the whole network to a meltdown due to SIA events.

- EIGRP transport protocol is an order of magnitude better in adapting to varying neighbor response times and lossy links than OSPF. IOS implementation of EIGRP also gives the network operator a better overview of neighbor responsiveness than the OSPF-related show commands.

- Although tracing SIA events is a difficult undertaking, at least the EIGRP **show** commands enable you step-by-step identification of potential bottlenecks (when troubleshooting) finally leading to the offending router. OSPF lacks any similar mechanism.

CHAPTER 3

IPX EIGRP

Enhanced Interior Gateway Routing Protocol (EIGRP) supports three protocol families: IP, IPX, and AppleTalk. You saw all the details of IP EIGRP in Chapter 1, "EIGRP Concepts and Technology," and Chapter 2, "Advanced EIGRP Concepts, Data Structures, and Protocols," and you will get the same level of details on IPX EIGRP implementation in this chapter. All three EIGRP implementations share common algorithms, protocols, and packet formats. They also share a user interface (IOS **show** commands) and configuration commands as far as possible, making it easy for any network engineer familiar with one protocol family (for example, TCP/IP) to design and implement EIGRP networks for other protocol families (for example, IPX).

Because there are significant differences between various protocol families, for example, in layer-3 addressing, naming, and directory services supported by the protocol family, and so on, it's not surprising that EIGRP implementations differ slightly between various protocol families. This chapter focuses mainly on differences between the IP and IPX implementation of EIGRP, which are as follows:

- **Automatic route redistribution between various IPX routing protocols**—IP redistribution must always be configured manually. The only exception is the redistribution between IGRP and EIGRP with the same Autonomous System number.

- **Metric integration of various IPX routing protocols**—IP routing protocols usually have completely inconsistent and incomparable metrics. The exception is redistribution between (E)IGRP processes.

- **Naming and directory services**—These services are implemented by Service Advertisement Protocol (SAP) in the IPX world and have to be tightly integrated with IPX EIGRP. No similar integration of naming/directory services and routing protocols exists in the IP protocol suite.

All the other features of IP EIGRP are retained in the IPX implementation. The most notable features are as follows:

- The vector and composite metrics and route selection rules.

- The DUAL algorithm is exactly the same.

- The hello and transport protocols are the same.

- Topology database contents and associated **show** commands are basically the same. The only difference is the external metric part of an external EIGRP route.

Due to protocol differences between IP and IPX as well as differing customer requirements, slight adaptations of IP EIGRP mechanisms appear in the IPX implementation:

- You cannot specify the K-values in the IPX implementation. K-values are fixed in IPX EIGRP, leading to the formula for vector-to-composite metric conversion shown in Equation 3-1.

Equation 3-1

$$CompositeMetric = BW + DLY$$

where

$$BW = \frac{10Gbps}{\min Bandwidth}$$

$$DLY = \frac{\sum delay_{microseconds}}{10}$$

- IPX EIGRP information is exchanged in IPX packets on IPX socket 85BE. The internal packet format is the same as for IP EIGRP.

- IPX EIGRP cannot use multicast addresses because IPX does not support multicasting (or at least didn't support it when IPX EIGRP was designed). All the multicast routing information exchange is performed using the IPX broadcast address.

The last introductory remark to be made about IPX EIGRP concerns its position in the evolution of IPX protocol suite and associated routing protocols. When the IP EIGRP was designed, IP classless routing was a well-established concept, and alternate routing protocols such as OSPF and IS-IS were already in existence. It's not surprising that the IP EIGRP implementation contains all the modern concepts like classless prefixes, route aggregation, complex route redistribution, and so on.

At the same time, the IPX protocol suite didn't even support the default routes, let alone route aggregation, or longest prefix-based routing. It didn't make sense to include these features into the new routing protocol because Novell didn't even consider them at that time. The IPX implementation of EIGRP is consequently quite rudimentary when compared with the IP implementation; it was meant only as a bandwidth-efficient and scalable replacement for IPX's Routing Information Protocol (RIP). Modern routing concepts, such as route aggregation and default routes, were introduced into IPX protocol at a much later time with the introduction of Novell Link State Protocol (NLSP), and IPX EIGRP was never adapted to support them.

IPX EIGRP Configuration and Route Redistribution

IPX EIGRP is configured in approximately the same way as IP EIGRP; a router process is started with a unique Autonomous System number, and the networks over which the IPX EIGRP run are specified. Even the command syntax is almost the same as for IP EIGRP, as specified in Table 3-1.

Table 3-1   *Basic IPX EIGRP Configuration Commands*

Task	Command
Start IPX EIGRP routing process	**ipx router eigrp <as-number>**
Start running IPX EIGRP over an interface	**network <ipx-network-number>**
Start running IPX EIGRP on all numbered IPX interfaces	**network all**

IPX EIGRP runs only on the interfaces that you specified with the **network** statements. Moreover, the IPX network number that you specify in the IPX EIGRP router definition must be specified on the interface itself with the **ipx network** command or it won't appear in the router configuration. This limitation precludes IPX EIGRP usage on IPXWAN links.

NOTE   IPXWAN is a more modern IPX encapsulation method used on point-to-point WAN links. It enables IPX routers to dynamically negotiate the IPX network number or use unnumbered IPX links. IPXWAN also measures round-trip delays when the WAN link is initialized.

You cannot run IPX EIGRP over unnumbered IPXWAN links because you cannot specify IPX network number 0 in the **network** statement. On the other hand, IPX EIGRP seems to work on the numbered IPXWAN links, but only until the router reloads.

Consider, for example, the following scenario: You've configured IPX EIGRP on a numbered IPXWAN link with the configuration commands in Example 3-1.

Example 3-1   *IPX EIGRP Configuration over IPXWAN Interface*

```
ipx internal-network ABCD
!
interface serial 0
 encapsulation ppp
 ipx ipxwan 0 1234
!
ipx router eigrp
 network 1234
```

IPX EIGRP runs correctly over the IPXWAN link. It locates the neighboring router and exchanges the routing information. However, the **network 1234** statement does not appear in the configuration because the IPX network specified in the IPX EIGRP process is not specified with the **ipx network** statement on the interface. The fact that the IPX EIGRP ran over network 1234 is lost after the router reloads.

IPX RIP runs by default on any interface with an IPX network number defined, even though this often results in RIP running in parallel with IPX EIGRP. Because every NetWare file server also acts as an IPX router and normally uses IPX RIP to build its routing table, you cannot remove IPX RIP from the LAN networks or you risk losing IPX connectivity with your file servers. However, concurrent operation of IPX RIP and EIGRP on the WAN interfaces definitely doesn't make sense. It's therefore recommended that you turn off IPX RIP on all WAN links as soon as you configure IPX EIGRP. To do that, you have to use the command sequence specified in Example 3-2.

Example 3-2   *Command Sequence Used to Turn Off IPX RIP on WAN Interfaces*

```
ipx router rip
  no network <WAN-ipx-network-number>
```

Route redistribution between IPX EIGRP and IPX RIP is automatic. Under most circumstances, there is no need to turn the redistribution off or to fine-tune it because the tight integration of IPX RIP metrics into IPX EIGRP assures optimum route selection. If you encounter a scenario where the automatic redistribution proves harmful, you can use the commands in Table 3-2 to turn it off or to filter the routes being redistributed between the two routing protocols.

Table 3-2   *Configuration Commands to Control IPX Route Redistribution*

Task	Command
Stop IPX RIP routes from being redistributed into IPX EIGRP	**ipx router eigrp <as-number>** **no redistribute rip**
Stop IPX EIGRP routes from being redistributed into IPX RIP	**ipx router rip no redistribute eigrp <as-number>**
Filter routes being redistributed from IPX RIP into IPX EIGRP	**ipx router eigrp <as-number> distribute-list out <ACL> rip**
Filter routes being redistributed from IPX EIGRP into IPX RIP	**ipx router rip distribute-list out <ACL> eigrp <as>**

NOTE   The IOS implementation of the IPX routing protocols lacks most of the advanced features found in the IP routing protocol implementations; it has no route maps, administrative distances, or default metrics.

Integration of IPX RIP Metrics into IPX EIGRP and IPX Route Selection

Using several concurrent routing protocols with incompatible metrics and automatic redistribution between them is usually a direct path to disaster due to the complexity and unexpected side effects of such a design. The designers of IPX EIGRP thus had to take every possible precaution to avoid all the side effects of running IPX RIP and IPX EIGRP concurrently in an IPX network. They deployed several techniques that deviate slightly from what you'd expect to see in an IP environment, but the end result is a stable implementation that enables you to deploy IPX RIP and IPX EIGRP in any combination without worrying about the complexity of the design. To understand these techniques and their results, you have to understand the details of IPX RIP routing.

IPX RIP Refresher

IPX RIP is a traditional distance-vector protocol modeled after IP RIP. All the routes known to a router are advertised to all its neighbors every 60 seconds and the best routes received are stored in the local routing table. IPX RIP deviates from IP RIP in its route selection rules; the *hop count* used in IP RIP has been augmented by *delays* (also called *ticks*), which take precedence over the hop count. Routes with lower cumulative delays are considered better, and the hop count is used only as a tiebreaker when the delay of two routes is the same.

The default value of the IPX delay is computed from the value specified in the interface **delay** configuration command (the same value is also used by EIGRP), using the formula in Equation 3-2.

Equation 3-2

$$delay_{IPX} = \text{int}\left(\frac{delay_{Interface} + 333}{334}\right)$$

If you don't specify the interface delay using the **delay** command, the IPX delay takes a default value as outlined in Table 3-3.

Table 3-3   *Default Values of an IPX Delay*

Interface Type	Default Value of IPX Delay
LAN interface	1
WAN interface (regardless of interface type and speed)	6

You can also specify the IPX delay manually by using the **ipx delay** interface configuration command or you can use the IPXWAN protocol to measure the delay dynamically before the link is put into operation.

Whenever an IPX router receives an IPX RIP update through one of its interfaces, it adjusts the metrics in the incoming update with the interface values following the formulas in Equation 3-3.

Equation 3-3

$$hopcount_{new} = hopcount_{received} + 1$$

$$delay_{new} = delay_{received} + delay_{incoming\_interface}$$

Redistribution between IPX RIP and IPX EIGRP

Any Cisco router running both IPX RIP and IPX EIGRP performs automatic redistribution between these two protocols unless you disable the redistribution with one of the commands from Table 3-2. IPX RIP routes are redistributed into IPX EIGRP as external EIGRP routes, and the IPX RIP metric is copied into the external data portion of the EIGRP route. The detailed IPX EIGRP and IPX RIP metrics of a route can be displayed with the **show ipx eigrp topology <network>** command, as shown in Example 3-3.

Example 3-3   *Detailed Display of an External IPX EIGRP Route*

```
Router>show ipx eigrp topology 12345
IPX-EIGRP topology entry for 12345
 State is Passive, Query origin flag is 1, 1 Successor(s)
 Routing Descriptor Blocks:
 Next hop is
   FFF40001.0000.0003.0000 (Serial1), from FF40001.0000.0003.0000
 Composite metric is (291456000/290944000), Send flag is 0x0,
 Route is External
  Vector metric:
   Minimum bandwidth is 9 Kbit
   Total delay is 975000 microseconds
   Reliability is 255/255
   Load is 1/255
   Minimum MTU is 1500
   Hop count is 2
  External data:
   Originating router is 0060.7015.5daa
   External protocol is RIP, metric is 2, delay 49
   Administrator tag is 0 (0x00000000)
   Flag is 0x00000000
```

As you can see from Example 3-3, an IPX EIGRP route contains almost exactly the same parameters as an IP EIGRP route; the only difference is in the External data portion. The external data parameters have the meanings explained in Table 3-4.

Table 3-4   *External Data Parameters of an IPX EIGRP Route*

Parameter	Meaning
Originating router	MAC address of the router that redistributed external route into EIGRP. This address can also be set with the **ipx routing** command.
External protocol	External route type—RIP, EIGRP, static, or NLSP.
External protocol metric	RIP hop count and delay of the redistributed route
Administrator tag	The field cannot be set or used.
Flag	The field cannot be set or used.

When an external IPX EIGRP route derived from IPX RIP is propagated through the IPX EIGRP network, its vector metric is adjusted according to EIGRP vector metric adjustment rules and the *delay* part of the External protocol metric is adjusted as well, as shown in Equation 3-4.

Equation 3-4

$$EIGRPDelay_{New} = EIGRPDelay_{Received} + Delay_{Interface}$$
$$Bandwidth_{New} = \min(Bandwidth_{Received}, Bandwidth_{Interface})$$
$$MTU_{New} = \min(MTU_{Received}, MTU_{Interface})$$
$$HopCount_{New} = HopCount_{Received} + 1$$
$$IPXDelay_{New} = IPXDelay_{Received} + IPXDelay_{Interface}$$

The net result of the rules in Equation 3-4 is that an IPX EIGRP route always contains the same IPX delay as an IPX RIP route propagated along the same path would have. This property is extremely important because the IPX delay is used within IPX hosts (file servers and workstations) to calculate transport layer timeouts.

Finally, as the IPX EIGRP route is redistributed back into IPX RIP, the IPX delay field of the RIP route is set to the IPX delay value in the External protocol metric field, and the RIP hop count is set to the RIP hop count in the original redistribution point incremented by one. These transformations are summarized in Equation 3-5.

Equation 3-5

$$IPXDelay_{RIP} = IPXDelay_{EIGRP}$$
$$IPXHopCount_{RIP} = IPXHopCount_{EIGRP} + 1$$

To ensure optimum routing and prevent routing loops in the mixed IPX EIGRP/IPX RIP network, two additional rules are enforced:

- IPX EIGRP routes are always preferred over IPX RIP routes unless they have a higher IPX hop count than the IPX RIP routes. (In IP terms, you could say that IPX EIGRP has a lower administrative distance than IPX RIP.)
- The router redistributes only the routes that are used to forward the data.

Sample Redistribution Scenarios

In this section, you learn how the rules from the previous two sections ensure that all the routers in a mixed IPX RIP/IPX EIGRP network always select the optimum routes. The following scenarios are evaluated:

- IPX RIP and IPX EIGRP running concurrently over all links
- IPX RIP running only on the LAN interfaces and IPX EIGRP on all links
- A misconfigured network where the IPX EIGRP is running on high-speed WAN interfaces and IPX RIP is running on a backdoor, low-speed WAN link
- A misconfigured network where the IPX EIGRP domain is discontinuous

Each scenario is evaluated in a network that hasn't been tuned for optimal IPX operation; the IPX interface delay is the default (1 for LAN interfaces, 6 for WAN interfaces), and only the bandwidths on the WAN links have been set.

Scenario 1—Concurrent IPX RIP and IPX EIGRP Operation

All routers in the network run IPX RIP and IPX EIGRP on all interfaces as displayed in Figure 3-1.

Figure 3-1   *IPX RIP and IPX EIGRP Are Running Everywhere*

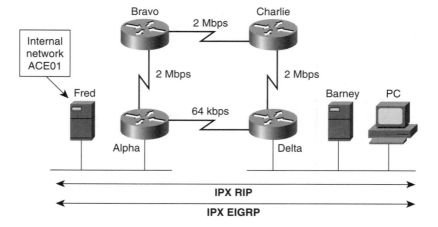

The internal network of file server Fred is propagated to file server Barney and the remote PC in several steps:

1 Fred announces network ACE01 to Alpha via IPX RIP broadcast; RIP hop count = 1.

2 Alpha propagates information about network ACE01 via IPX RIP to Bravo and Delta; RIP hop count = 2.

3 Alpha redistributes the received RIP information into EIGRP and propagates network ACE01 to Bravo and Delta via EIGRP.

4 Bravo receives the RIP and EIGRP routes for network ACE01. The hop count in the RIP route is 2, whereas the hop count in the EIGRP route is 1, so it uses the EIGRP route. Similar processing happens on Charlie.

5 Delta receives RIP routes from Alpha (with hop count of 2) and Charlie (with hop count of 4). EIGRP routes are also received from Alpha and Charlie, and the route through Charlie has better composite metric. Charlie becomes the IPX EIGRP successor. The IPX hop count in the EIGRP route through Charlie is 1 and the IPX hop count of the best IPX RIP route is 2. Delta therefore selects the EIGRP route through Charlie as the best route, leading to optimum IPX routing.

6 Delta redistributes the IPX EIGRP route received through Charlie to IPX RIP. The delay of the IPX RIP route is the cumulative IPX delay of the path Delta—Charlie—Bravo—Alpha—Fred (leading to proper IPX retransmission timeout), and the IPX hop count of the route is 2. (The original IPX hop count in the redistribution point Alpha was 1, and it always increases by one when the redistribution into IPX RIP is performed.)

Scenario 2—IPX RIP Running on LAN Interfaces Only

In the second scenario, where IPX RIP is running only on LAN interfaces (see Figure 3-2), the route selection process is even simpler because no IPX RIP and IPX EIGRP routes are competing. Alpha redistributes the IPX RIP routes received from Fred into IPX EIGRP, and Delta selects the best IPX EIGRP route going through Charlie and Bravo. Delta then redistributes that route back into IPX RIP. The IPX delay and IPX hop count are the same as in the previous scenario.

Figure 3-2 *Running IPX RIP only on LAN interfaces*

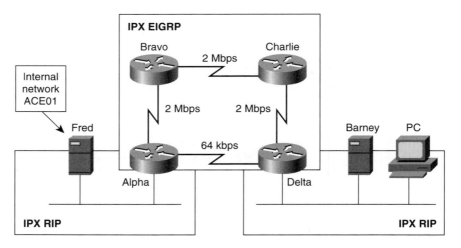

Scenario 3—Running IPX RIP on Some WAN Links

The third scenario represents a misconfigured network that still selects the optimum route. The IPX EIGRP domain is contiguous, but only IPX RIP runs over slow-speed link between Alpha and Delta (see Figure 3-3).

Figure 3-3 *IPX EIGRP Not Running on All WAN Links*

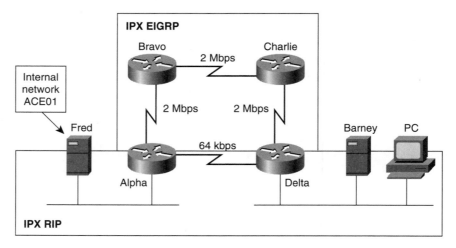

In this scenario, the propagation of network ACE01 from Fred to Barney is performed in the following steps:

1 Alpha receives the IPX RIP update from Fred (IPX hop count = 1). Alpha redistributes it into IPX EIGRP and forwards it to Delta (IPX hop count = 2).

2 Delta receives the IPX EIGRP route through Bravo and Charlie (IPX hop count = 1) and directs the RIP route from Alpha (IPX hop count = 2). The EIGRP route is preferred because it has a lower IPX hop count.

3 Delta redistributes the IPX EIGRP route into IPX RIP. Barney receives the IPX RIP route with an IPX hop count of 2 and an IPX delay of 19 (cumulative delay of LAN interface between Fred and Alpha and three IPX EIGRP WAN links).

Scenario 4—Discontinuous IPX EIGRP Domains

In the last scenario, IPX EIGRP runs only between Alpha and Bravo, and another IPX EIGRP process runs between Charlie and Delta (see Figure 3-4).

Figure 3-4   *Discontinuous IPX EIGRP Domain*

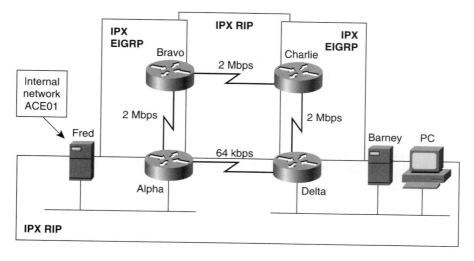

The propagation of network ACE01 advertised by Fred between Alpha and Delta is more complex:

1 Alpha receives the IPX RIP update from Fred (IPX hop count = 1).

2 Alpha redistributes the IPX RIP information into IPX EIGRP and also propagates the IPX RIP information to Delta (hop count = 2).

3 Alpha sends the IPX EIGRP information to Bravo (IPX hop count = 1).

4 Bravo redistributes the IPX EIGRP information received from Alpha into IPX RIP and increases the IPX hop count. The IPX RIP information is sent to Charlie (IPX hop count = 2).

5 Charlie redistributes the received IPX RIP information into IPX EIGRP and propagates the IPX EIGRP information to Delta.

6 Delta received the IPX RIP update with an IPX hop count = 2 and the IPX EIGRP update with the same hop count. The IPX RIP information is considered better, and the IPX EIGRP information is discarded. The IPX RIP information received from Alpha is propagated to Barney.

7 The IPX data flow between PC and Fred goes over the low-speed 64 kbps link.

To ensure optimum IPX routing, the IPX EIGRP processes should always be contiguous. Multiple, sequential redistribution between IPX EIGRP and IPX RIP never leads to routing loops, but it can lead to suboptimal IPX routing.

IPX SAP Integration

Service Advertisement Protocol (SAP) is an integral and important part of the IPX protocol stack. It enables the end-hosts to locate the services and servers they need to access. The protocol itself was designed for small networks with a small number of services and was never meant to scale to large networks.

The SAP protocol is similar to IPX RIP in its design and uses a distance-vector approach to service information dissemination:

- Every server announces its services using periodic SAP updates every 60 seconds. If a service is not announced for a prolonged period of time (by default, 180 seconds), it's considered unreachable.

- Every router announces all services known to it using *periodic* SAP updates sent every 60 seconds.

- All the changes in the network—the appearance of new services or disappearance of existing services—are announced immediately using *flash* updates.

Other messages in the SAP protocol are used to exchange information between workstations and routers or servers, but these are exchanged only on the LAN media and are thus irrelevant to IPX SAP integration into IPX EIGRP.

NOTE   IPX SAP contains no loop prevention mechanism by itself; it doesn't even perform split-horizon checks. All loop prevention is based on IPX routing tables using several sanity checks:

- Information about a service residing on an unreachable network is ignored.

- Information about a service coming from a router that is not the next-hop toward the network on which the service is residing, is ignored.

The periodic SAP updates place a large burden on WAN links in any IPX network. By default, every SAP packet, which is 480 bytes long, can carry up to seven service advertisements. Considering that every Novell file server advertises 3 to 5 services and that every printer and fax server on a LAN also advertises at least one service, the number of services advertised by remote office in a network can approach 10 services per remote LAN. In a network with 200 remote offices, the total number of services that have to be advertised is above 2000. The bandwidth used by periodic SAP packets on every link in a network of that size is calculated in Equation 3-6 and represents nearly 30 percent of the bandwidth of a 64 kbps link. It's evident that a better mechanism for transporting service information is needed in large IPX networks.

Equation 3-6

$$TotalSAPdata_{bytes} = int(\frac{NumberOfServices \times SAPPacketSize}{NumberOfServicesPerPacket})$$

$$= int(\frac{2000 \times 480}{7}) \cong 137000$$

$$SAPbandwidth_{bps} = \frac{TotalSAPdata \times 8}{SAPInterval_{sec}}$$

$$= \frac{137000 \times 8}{60} \cong 19kbps$$

The need for periodic SAP packets arises only from the inherent unreliability of the SAP protocol. If the SAP information exchange were reliable, there would be no need for periodic IPX SAP packets, and the SAP protocol would consume significantly less bandwidth on the WAN links. IPX EIGRP guarantees IPX SAP packet delivery; the IPX SAP protocol itself remains unmodified, but the periodic SAP messages can be suppressed due to the reliability of the underlying transport protocol. The interaction of IPX SAP and IPX EIGRP is best illustrated with the debugging outputs, as demonstrated in Example 3-4.

Example 3-4 *Sample IPX SAP Transaction Using IPX EIGRP as the Transport Protocol*

```
router#debug eigrp packet ipxsap ack
router#debug ipx sap activity

... IPX SAP packet received over Serial 1 announcing that service FileServer became
    unreachable ...
EIGRP: Received IPXSAP on Serial1 nbr FFF40001.0000.0003.0000
 AS 11, Flags 0x0, Seq 408/478 idbQ 0/0 iidbQ un/rely 0/0 peerQ un/rely 0/0
EIGRP: Enqueuing ACK on Serial1 nbr FFF40001.0000.0003.0000
 Ack seq 408 iidbQ un/rely 0/0 peerQ un/rely 1/0
IPXEIGRP: Received EIGRP SAP from FFF40001.0000.0003.0000
IPXSAP: Response (in) type 0x2 len 96 src:FFF40001.0000.0003.0000
 dest:FFF40001.0000.0000.0004(85BE)
 type 0x4, "FileServer", 22.0000.0000.0002(437), 16 hops
IPXSAP: type 4 server "FileServer" poison received from FFF40001.0000.0003.0000
EIGRP: Sending ACK on Serial1 nbr FFF40001.0000.0003.0000
 AS 11, Flags 0x0, Seq 0/408 idbQ 0/0 iidbQ un/rely 0/0 peerQ un/rely 1/0

... Alternate path was found, new information sent over all interfaces in a flash
update. IPX EIGRP runs only over Serial 1, Serial 0 uses IPX SAP protocol ...
IPXSAP: positing update to FFF40000.ffff.ffff.ffff via Serial0 (flash)
IPXSAP: positing update to FFF40001.ffff.ffff.ffff via Serial1 (flash)
IPXSAP: Update type 0x2 len 96 src:ABCD.0000.0c46.d9ec
dest:ABCD.ffff.ffff.ffff(452)
 type 0x4, "FileServer", 22.0000.0000.0002(437), 16 hops
EIGRP: Enqueuing IPXSAP on Serial1
 AS 0, Flags 0x0, Seq 479/0 idbQ 0/0 iidbQ un/rely 0/1 serno 98-98
EIGRP: Enqueuing IPXSAP on Serial1 nbr FFF40001.0000.0003.0000
 AS 0, Flags 0x0, Seq 479/0 idbQ 0/0 iidbQ un/rely 0/0 peerQ un/rely 0/0 serno 98-98
EIGRP: Sending IPXSAP on Serial1 nbr FFF40001.0000.0003.0000
 AS 11, Flags 0x0, Seq 479/408 idbQ 0/0 iidbQ un/rely 0/0 peerQ un/rely 0/1
serno 98-98
EIGRP: Received ACK on Serial1 nbr FFF40001.0000.0003.0000
 AS 11, Flags 0x0, Seq 0/479 idbQ 0/0 iidbQ un/rely 0/0 peerQ un/rely 0/1
```

The periodic SAP messages were primarily designed to overcome the unreliable transport mechanism, but they also serve two additional purposes:

- They initially populate the SAP tables of newly started routers.

- Under some conditions, they enable the discovery of alternate paths toward services that became inaccessible.

IPX EIGRP has a special table, called the *backup SAP table,* to emulate the behavior of the periodic SAP protocol. Whenever an incoming SAP update is received, the information in the update is always stored in the *backup SAP table*. Sanity checks are performed on the received information; the network specified in the SAP advertisement has to be reachable through the neighbor that sent the SAP update. Only the information that passes the sanity checks is considered for import into the main SAP table. The main SAP table contains only the best service advertisements that have passed the sanity checks. The whole process is illustrated in Figure 3-5.

Figure 3-5   *Incoming IPX EIGRP SAP Update Processing*

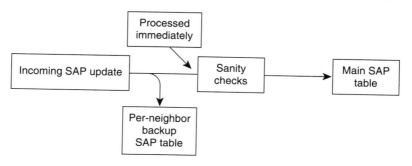

You can display the per-neighbor backup SAP table with the **show ipx eigrp neighbor server** command as illustrated in Example 3-5.

Example 3-5   *SAP Backup Table Display*

```
Router>show ipx eigrp neighbor server
IPX EIGRP Neighbors for process 11
H       Address          Interface          Hold Uptime   SRTT  RTO     Q  Seq
                         (sec)              (ms)  Cnt Num
1       FFF40000.0000.0000.0002 Se0              11 00:01:22 879          5000 0 219
Server table for this peer:
      Type Name           Address                Port Hops
        4 FileServer       22.0000.0000.0002:0437 4
        4 Top2600          1.0000.0000.0001:0837 3
0       FFF40001.0000.0003.0000 Se1              13 00:52:52 31           200 0 423
Server table for this peer:
      Type Name           Address                Port Hops
        4 FileServer       22.0000.0000.0002:0437 2
        4 Top2600          1.0000.0000.0001:0837 2
```

Whenever the primary path to a service in the main SAP table is lost, the EIGRP neighbor is lost due to topology changes, and so on, and the backup table is scanned to find alternate information about the lost services. This process is illustrated in Figure 3-6.

Figure 3-6   *Information Retrieval from Backup SAP Table*

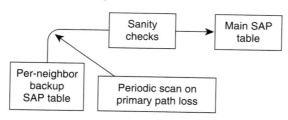

Backward Compatibility of IPX EIGRP and IPX SAP

The IPX SAP protocol distributes service reachability information between the servers and the routers, but it's also used by the workstations to find the desired services. Novell dedicated several special IPX SAP packet types to service information search purposes; however, several custom applications do not use these packets but rely on listening to IPX SAP updates to find the services they need. These applications rely on IPX SAP protocol being present on the LAN where the workstations are to find the servers they need.

It's therefore necessary to retain the original IPX SAP protocol on the LAN networks, and it's also desirable to avoid periodic IPX SAP messages on the WAN networks to minimize bandwidth usage. IPX EIGRP defaults were thus chosen as follows:

- Periodic IPX SAP messages are always sent over LAN media regardless of whether EIGRP neighbors are reachable over the LAN.

- Periodic IPX SAP messages are suppressed on the WAN links as soon as an EIGRP neighbor is discovered over that WAN interface.

Although these defaults satisfy most design scenarios, you might find a few exceptions where you want to disable periodic SAP messages on LAN media or enable periodic SAP messages on WAN media. The commands you use to fine-tune the protocols used to deliver SAP information are specified in Table 3-5.

Table 3-5   *Commands to Fine-Tune SAP Information Delivery*

Command	Purpose
interface ethernet 0 **ipx sap-incremental eigrp <as>**	Stop periodic IPX SAP messages on LAN media as soon as an EIGRP neighbor in EIGRP process <as> is discovered
interface serial 0 **no ipx sap-incremental eigrp <as>**	Send periodic IPX SAP messages on WAN media even though there are EIGRP neighbors in EIGRP process <as> reachable over the specified WAN interface
interface serial 0 **ipx sap-incremental eigrp <as> rsup-only**	Use EIGRP only for incremental SAP transport. Suppress periodic SAP messages as soon as there is an EIGRP neighbor in EIGRP process <as> reachable through a specified interface, but do not accept any EIGRP routing updates through the specified interface

In several scenarios, the IPX EIGRP SAP processing needs fine-tuning.

Scenario 1—Transit-Only IPX LAN

In a network where several routers are connected to a common transit-only LAN (a LAN segment which has no servers or hosts connected to it), suppression of periodic IPX SAP updates on the transit LAN might reduce the CPU load on the routers connected to that LAN. All the routers connected to the transit LAN should run EIGRP. You should configure periodic IPX SAP suppression on all routers with the **ipx sap-incremental eigrp** configuration command.

Scenario 2—Mixed WAN Environment

When you run IPX over a multipoint Frame-Relay connection, and some of the remote routers do not support IPX EIGRP, you have to enable periodic IPX SAP propagation manually using the **no ipx sap-incremental eigrp** command. Typically such situations include Frame Relay networks where the remote routers do not support IPX EIGRP (for example, very old Cisco IOS releases or third-party routers) or do not have IPX EIGRP configured.

Scenario 3—Using IPX EIGRP only to Suppress Periodic IPX SAP Update

In very rare scenarios, you might want to use IPX EIGRP to suppress periodic IPX SAP updates, but you want to retain the IPX routing structure as computed by IPX RIP. In these cases, IPX EIGRP should not be used for route selection because it might select different paths than IPX RIP, but only for IPX SAP transport. The command to use on the WAN interfaces is **ipx sap-incremental eigrp rsup-only**.

Summary

IPX EIGRP's implementation is very similar to IP EIGRP; the user interface, core algorithms, and protocols are the same, giving you a consistent configuration and management interface. However, several differences related to IPX-specific details do exist:

- Redistribution between IPX EIGRP and IPX RIP is automatic.
- External protocol metric in IPX EIGRP route is adjusted when the route is propagated between IPX EIGRP neighbors.
- IPX routes received from various IPX routing protocols are compared based on their IPX hop count, not on the administrative distance as in IP.
- IPX SAP is tightly integrated into IPX EIGRP to suppress periodic IPX SAP updates and reduce WAN bandwidth utilization.

The IOS implementation of IPX routing protocols is also less flexible than the IP routing implementation. It has no route maps, administrative distances, or routing protocol tags that you can use to control redistribution. Anyhow, the tools available in the IPX world are flexible enough to provide you with a comprehensive toolbox for scalable internetwork design, as you will see in the following chapters.

CHAPTER 4

AppleTalk EIGRP

AppleTalk is the third protocol family supported by EIGRP. You have seen the details of IP EIGRP in Chapter 2, "Advanced EIGRP Concepts, Data Structures, and Protocols," and the differences between IP EIGRP and IPX EIGRP in Chapter 3, "IPX EIGRP." In this chapter, you will see the differences between AppleTalk EIGRP and IP EIGRP.

Although the three EIGRP implementations share common algorithms, protocols, and packet formats, the behavior of AppleTalk EIGRP deviates from the common behavior you saw in IP and IPX protocol families. To start with, the Autonomous System number used in IP EIGRP and IPX EIGRP is replaced with router-ID in AppleTalk, preventing the network designer from deploying several parallel instances of AppleTalk EIGRP in the network. This is also counterintuitive to IP EIGRP and IPX EIGRP users. In the IP and IPX world, the EIGRP routing process number has to *match* between the neighbors; whereas in AppleTalk, the EIGRP router-ID must be *unique*. This also influenced the CLI interface in Cisco IOS. In the IP and IPX world, the EIGRP parameters are configured in the **router eigrp** subconfiguration mode; in AppleTalk EIGRP, they are specified in global configuration mode. The IOS show commands for AppleTalk EIGRP, on the other hand, retain their similarity to IP EIGRP **show** commands, giving the network operator a consistent view of all three EIGRP implementations.

Significant differences exist between AppleTalk and IP protocol families, ranging from address allocation and routing protocol support to naming and directory services. As you might expect, there are several differences between IP EIGRP and AppleTalk EIGRP implementations. Some of these differences are as follows:

- **Automatic route redistribution between various AppleTalk routing protocols—** IP redistribution always has to be configured manually.

- **Metric integration of various AppleTalk routing protocols—**Almost all IP routing protocols have completely inconsistent and incomparable metrics.

All the other features of EIGRP are shared across all three protocol families. The most notable are as follows:

- The vector and composite metrics and route selection rules are the same.

- The DUAL algorithm is the same.
- The hello and reliable transport protocols are very similar.
- The topology database contents and associated **show** commands are almost the same, the only difference being the external metric part of an external EIGRP route.

Similar to IPX EIGRP, AppleTalk EIGRP offers you fewer network design options. For example, you cannot specify the K-values in AppleTalk EIGRP. K-values are fixed, leading to the formula for vector-to-composite metric conversion shown in Equation 4-1.

Equation 4-1

$$CompositeMetric \ = \ BW + DLY$$

where

$$BW \ = \ \frac{10\,Gbps}{\min Bandwidth}$$

$$DLY \ = \ \frac{\sum delay_{microseconds}}{10}$$

AppleTalk EIGRP also uses slightly different transport mechanisms than IP EIGRP:

- AppleTalk EIGRP information is exchanged in AppleTalk packets. The internal packet format is the same as for IP EIGRP.
- AppleTalk EIGRP uses a broadcast, not a multicast address to send routing updates.

AppleTalk EIGRP Configuration and Route Redistribution

AppleTalk EIGRP configuration is completely different from IP EIGRP or IPX EIGRP configuration:

- EIGRP routing is configured with the **appletalk routing** command and a unique router-ID has to be specified during configuration.
- Other AppleTalk routing protocols are enabled or disabled on the individual interface.

Table 4-1 specifies the commands to configure AppleTalk EIGRP.

Table 4-1   *Basic AppleTalk EIGRP Configuration Commands*

Task	Command
Start AppleTalk EIGRP routing process	**appletalk routing eigrp <router-id>**
Stop AppleTalk EIGRP routing process	**no appletalk routing eigrp <router-id>**
Start running AppleTalk EIGRP over an interface	**interface <type> <number>** **appletalk protocol eigrp**
Stop running AppleTalk EIGRP over an interface	**interface <type> <number>** **no appletalk protocol eigrp**
Stop running AppleTalk RTMP over an interface	**interface <type> <number>** **no appletalk protocol rtmp**

NOTE   There must be at least one AppleTalk routing protocol running on an interface where AppleTalk is configured at all times. If you want to disable RTMP on an interface, you must enable EIGRP first and then disable RTMP.

WARNING   When disabling AppleTalk EIGRP routing with the **no appletalk routing eigrp** command, all interfaces that run AppleTalk EIGRP as the only AppleTalk routing protocol lose their AppleTalk configuration. If you want to disable AppleTalk EIGRP and revert back to using RTMP instead on specific interfaces, enable RTMP on each interface using the **appletalk protocol rtmp** command before disabling AppleTalk EIGRP with the **no appletalk routing eigrp** command.

AppleTalk EIGRP is normally (by default) run in parallel with RTMP (the default AppleTalk routing protocol) on an interface. RTMP is used by AppleTalk hosts to discover routers and cable ranges assigned to the LAN; it must always be enabled on LAN interfaces where AppleTalk hosts are attached. Concurrent operation of RTMP and AppleTalk EIGRP on WAN interfaces definitely doesn't make sense because the main design goal of AppleTalk EIGRP was to reduce high bandwidth usage imposed on the WAN links by RTMP. It's therefore recommended that you turn off RTMP (using the command sequence specified in Example 4-1) on the WAN links configured for AppleTalk routing as soon as you enable AppleTalk EIGRP.

Example 4-1   *Command Sequence Used to Turn Off RTMP on WAN Interfaces*

```
interface serial <number>
appletalk protocol eigrp
no appletalk protocol rtmp
```

Route redistribution between AppleTalk EIGRP and RTMP is automatic. Under most circumstances, there is no need to turn the redistribution off because the translation of RTMP metrics into EIGRP metrics at the redistribution points assures optimal route selection. Should you encounter a scenario where automatic redistribution proves harmful, you can use the commands in Table 4-2 to turn it off.

Table 4-2   *Configuration Commands to Control AppleTalk Route Redistribution*

Task	Command
Stop automatic redistribution between AppleTalk routing protocols	**no appletalk route-redistribution**
Re-enable automatic route redistribution between AppleTalk routing protocols	**appletalk route-redistribution**

NOTE   IOS implementation of AppleTalk routing is even more rudimentary than the IPX implementation; there are no redistribution filters, per-protocol filters, route maps, administrative distances, default metrics, and so on.

Integration of RTMP and AppleTalk EIGRP and AppleTalk Route Selection

Automatic two-way route redistribution between routing protocols with incompatible metrics is usually complex and prone to unexpected and undesired side effects. The designers of AppleTalk EIGRP had to take every possible precaution to avoid all the side effects of running RTMP and AppleTalk EIGRP concurrently in an AppleTalk network. They deployed several techniques similar to IP administrative distance resulting in a stable implementation that enables you to deploy RTMP and AppleTalk EIGRP in almost any combination without worrying about the complexity of the design.

RTMP Refresher

RTMP is a traditional distance-vector protocol modeled after IP RIP. All the routes (cable ranges) known to a router are advertised to all of its neighbors every 10 seconds, and the best routes received from all neighbors are stored in the local routing tables. RTMP uses the hop count as the only route selection rule; the route with the lowest hop count is considered the best.

NOTE	You can change RTMP timers with the **appletalk timers** global configuration command. The command applies to all interfaces on the router and the same timer values have to be configured on all routers in an AppleTalk network. Some vendors' devices do not support configurable RTMP timers, making this functionality unusable in networks where those devices are deployed.

RTMP has additional functionality beyond exchanging routes between the adjacent routers. It's used by the AppleTalk hosts to discover adjacent routers and cable ranges assigned to the LAN to which the host is attached.

NOTE	In environments where AppleTalk EIGRP is deployed and the only routing devices in the network are Cisco routers, you can save bandwidth and router CPU by using RTMP only for advertising information to AppleTalk hosts. Use the interface configuration command, **appletalk rtmp-stub**, in these cases to prevent RTMP from distributing routing information.

Redistribution between RTMP and AppleTalk EIGRP

A router running AppleTalk EIGRP performs automatic redistribution between RTMP and AppleTalk EIGRP unless you disable it with one of the commands from Table 4-3. RTMP routes are redistributed into AppleTalk EIGRP as external EIGRP routes and the RTMP hop count is copied into the hop count field of EIGRP vector metric. The bandwidth portion of the EIGRP vector metric is set to 9.6 kbps for redistributed RTMP routes, so routers prefer native AppleTalk EIGRP routes under most scenarios. You can display the detailed AppleTalk EIGRP metric, including the hop count, with the **show appletalk eigrp topology <cable-range>** command, as shown in Example 4-2.

Example 4-2   *Detailed Display of an External AppleTalk EIGRP Route*

```
Router>show appletalk eigrp topology 100-100
AppleTalk-EIGRP topology entry for 100-100
 State is Passive, Query origin flag is 1, 1 Successor(s)
 Routing Descriptor Blocks:
4080.83 (Serial0), from 4080.83
      Composite metric is (2198016/53760), Send flag is 0x0, Route is Internal
      Vector metric:
      Minimum bandwidth is 1544 Kbit
      Total delay is 21100000 nanoseconds
      Reliability is 255/255
      Load is 1/255
      Minimum MTU is 1500
      Hop count is 2
```

As you can see from Example 4-2, an AppleTalk EIGRP route contains the same parameters as an IP EIGRP route, apart from the external data portion, which is not present in external AppleTalk EIGRP routes.

When an AppleTalk route is propagated through an AppleTalk EIGRP network, its vector metric is adjusted according to EIGRP vector metric adjustment rules. The hop-count part of the vector is also adjusted, as shown in Equation 4-2, resulting in a correct hop count that can be exported in RTMP at any redistribution point.

Equation 4-2

$$Delay_{New} = Delay_{Received} + Delay_{Interface}$$

$$Bandwidth_{New} = \min(Bandwidth_{Received}, Bandwidth_{Interface})$$

$$MTU_{New} = \min(MTU_{Received}, MTU_{Interface})$$

$$HopCount_{New} = HopCount_{Received} + 1$$

To ensure optimal routing and prevent routing loops in a mixed RTMP/AppleTalk EIGRP network, route selection rules similar to IP administrative distances are implemented. The AppleTalk routes are preferred in the following order:

- Static AppleTalk routes configured with the **appletalk static cable-range** command
- Internal AppleTalk EIGRP routes (routes that have never passed through RTMP)
- External AppleTalk EIGRP routes (routes that were propagated by RTMP somewhere along the routing path)
- RTMP routes (routes that were only propagated by RTMP)
- Floating static AppleTalk routes configured with the **appletalk static cable-range . . . floating** command.

NOTE   Due to RTMP—AppleTalk EIGRP redistribution rules, a route that was carried in AppleTalk EIGRP somewhere in the network but arrived at the current router through RTMP is indistinguishable from a route that was carried by RTMP all the way from the source to the current router.

Sample Redistribution Scenarios

In this section, you'll see how the rules from the previous section ensure that all the routers in a mixed RTMP/AppleTalk EIGRP network always select the optimal route. The following scenarios are evaluated:

- RTMP and AppleTalk EIGRP running concurrently over all links
- RTMP running only on the LAN interfaces and AppleTalk EIGRP on all links
- A misconfigured network where the AppleTalk EIGRP is running on high-speed WAN interfaces and RTMP is running on a backdoor, low-speed WAN link
- A misconfigured network where the AppleTalk EIGRP domain is discontinuous

Scenario 1—Concurrent RTMP and AppleTalk Operation

All routers in the network run RTMP and AppleTalk EIGRP on all interfaces, as displayed in Figure 4-1.

Figure 4-1   *Scenario 1—RTMP and AppleTalk EIGRP Are Running Everywhere*

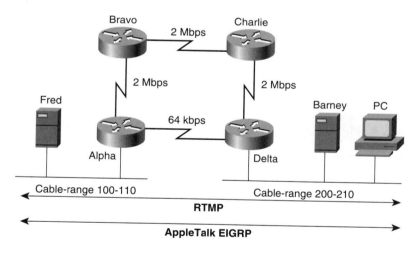

The cable range on the LAN interface attached to router Alpha is propagated to file server Barney and the remote PC in several steps:

Step 1   Alpha propagates information about cable range 100-110 via RTMP to Bravo and Delta (RTMP hop count = 1).

Step 2   AppleTalk EIGRP is running on the LAN interface of router Alpha.
Cable-range 100-110 is therefore inserted in Alpha's EIGRP topology
database and propagated to Bravo and Delta via EIGRP with a hop count
of 1.

Step 3   Bravo receives the RTMP and EIGRP information about the cable-range
100-110, so it uses the EIGRP route. Similar processing happens on
Charlie.

Step 4   Delta receives RTMP and EIGRP routes from Alpha (with a hop count of
1) and Charlie (with a hop count of 3). EIGRP routes are preferred over
RTMP routes and the EIGRP route through Charlie has better composite
metric. Charlie becomes the AppleTalk EIGRP successor, and Delta
selects the EIGRP route through Charlie as the best route, leading to
optimal AppleTalk routing.

Step 5   Delta redistributes the AppleTalk EIGRP route received through Charlie
to RTMP. The final RTMP hop count is 4, making it indistinguishable
from a native RTMP route coming through the same set of routers.

Scenario 2—RTMP Running on LAN Interfaces Only

In the second scenario, where RTMP is running only on LAN interfaces (see Figure 4-2),
the route selection process is even simpler because there are no competing RTMP and
AppleTalk EIGRP routes. Alpha redistributes RTMP routes for cable range 2-3 received
from Fred into AppleTalk EIGRP, and Delta selects the best AppleTalk EIGRP route going
through Charlie and Bravo. That route is redistributed back into RTMP resulting in the
proper RTMP hop count.

Figure 4-2   *Scenario 2—Running only RTMP on LAN Interfaces*

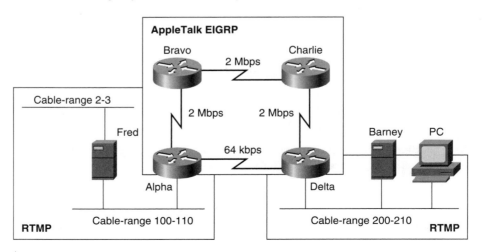

Scenario 3—Running RTMP on Some WAN Links

The third scenario represents a misconfigured network that still selects the optimal route; the AppleTalk EIGRP domain is contiguous, but only RTMP is running over the slow-speed link between Alpha and Delta (see Figure 4-3).

Figure 4-3   *Scenario 3—AppleTalk EIGRP Not Running on All WAN Links*

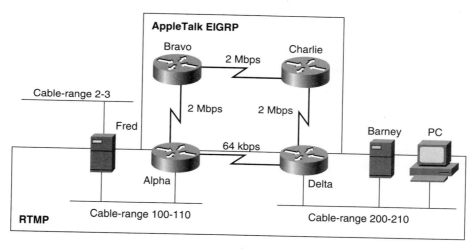

In this scenario, the propagation of cable-range 2-3 from Fred to Barney is done in the following steps:

Step 1   Alpha receives RTMP update from Fred (hop count = 1). Alpha redistributes it into AppleTalk EIGRP and forwards it to Delta through RTMP with a hop count of 2.

Step 2   Delta receives the AppleTalk EIGRP route through Bravo and Charlie and the RTMP route from Alpha. The EIGRP route is preferred over the RTMP route.

Step 3   Delta redistributes the AppleTalk EIGRP route into RTMP. Barney receives the RTMP route with the hop count of 5.

Scenario 4—Discontinuous AppleTalk EIGRP Domain

In the last scenario, AppleTalk EIGRP runs only between Alpha and Bravo and between Charlie and Delta (see Figure 4-4).

Figure 4-4   *Discontinuous AppleTalk EIGRP Domain*

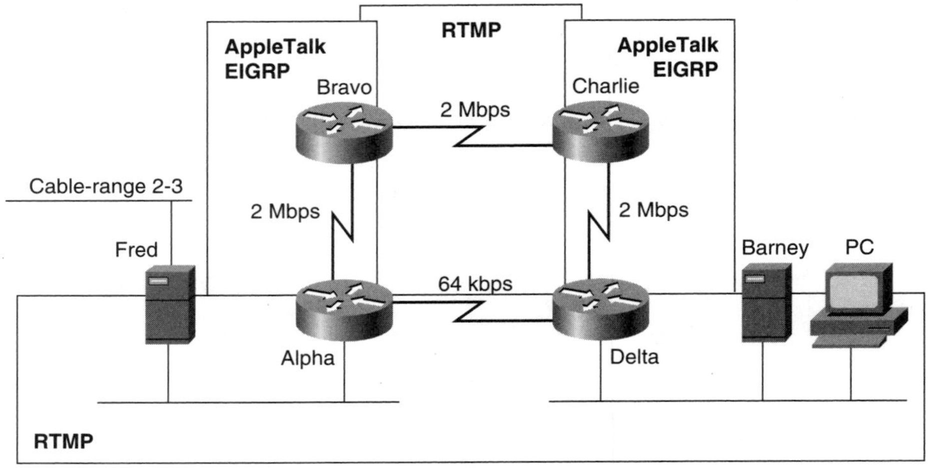

The propagation of cable-range 2-3 advertised by Fred between Alpha and Delta is more complex:

Step 1   Alpha receives RTMP update from Fred with a hop count of 1.

Step 2   Alpha redistributes the RTMP information into AppleTalk EIGRP and also propagates RTMP information to Delta with a hop count of 2.

Step 3   Alpha sends AppleTalk EIGRP information to Bravo.

Step 4   Bravo redistributes AppleTalk EIGRP information received from Alpha into RTMP. The RTMP information is sent to Charlie with a hop count of 3.

From this moment on, there are two possible scenarios, based on the exact timing of the RTMP and EIGRP events:

• Delta redistributes RTMP information received from Alpha into AppleTalk EIGRP and then to Charlie. Charlie prefers the AppleTalk EIGRP route from Delta over the RTMP route from Bravo, resulting in suboptimal routing.

• Charlie receives the RTMP information from Bravo before Delta redistributed RTMP information from Alpha into AppleTalk EIGRP. The RTMP information from Bravo is the best route Charlie has at that moment, so Charlie redistributes it into AppleTalk EIGRP and then sends it to Delta. Router Delta is faced with an AppleTalk EIGRP route and an RTMP route. AppleTalk EIGRP route is preferred resulting in optimal routing.

In conclusion, to ensure optimal AppleTalk routing under all circumstances, the AppleTalk EIGRP process must always be contiguous. Multiple, sequential redistribution between RTMP and AppleTalk EIGRP never leads to routing loops, but it might lead to suboptimal AppleTalk routing.

Summary

AppleTalk EIGRP implementation is similar to the other two EIGRP implementations; the network operator user interface (**show** commands), core algorithms, and protocols are the same, giving you a consistent management interface. The differences related to AppleTalk protocol suite details or specifics of AppleTalk EIGRP implementation are as follows:

- AppleTalk EIGRP does not support multiple instances of AppleTalk EIGRP in the same router or multiple AppleTalk EIGRP instances running over the same, shared media.

- AppleTalk EIGRP's associated routing process parameters are configured globally on the router, whereas similar IP EIGRP or IPX EIGRP parameters are configured under the **router eigrp** router configuration mode for IP EIGRP and IPX EIGRP.

- The EIGRP Autonomous System number is replaced with router-ID in AppleTalk EIGRP. The router-IDs have to be unique throughout the AppleTalk EIGRP network, whereas the Autonomous System number must match between all the routers running the same instance of IP or IPX EIGRP.

- Redistribution between RTMP and AppleTalk EIGRP is automatic.

- No external data portion of the AppleTalk EIGRP route exists when an RTMP route is redistributed into AppleTalk EIGRP. The hop-count variable of the EIGRP vector metric is used to transport RTMP hop count through the AppleTalk EIGRP domain.

- AppleTalk EIGRP routes are always preferred over RTMP routes.

The IOS implementation of the AppleTalk routing protocols is also less flexible than the IP routing implementations; no route maps, route filters, administrative distances, or routing protocol tags exist for you to control redistribution. Your choices in AppleTalk network design are thus more limited.

Designing Enterprise EIGRP Networks

CHAPTER 5

Scalability Issues in Large Enterprise Networks

Many customers who deploy EIGRP in their small networks are surprised to learn that EIGRP cannot scale forever without the network's design being taken into account. Quite a few of these networks have no network management whatsoever (or network management might be limited to monitoring link up/down status), so the starting symptoms of potential network meltdown are often overlooked, and the network manager reacts only when it's too late—when the network is gone and the phones start to ring.

This chapter introduces the EIGRP scalability issues by presenting a poorly designed network that grew until it melted down. The concept of *query boundaries*, which is crucial to EIGRP scalability, is also defined, and the chapter finishes by defining a poorly performing benchmark network that will be used throughout the scalability part of this book to show how different scalability tools can improve the stability of EIGRP networks.

Case Study 1—Large Enterprise Network Experiencing Meltdown Situations

For more information on this case study, please visit www.ciscopress.com/eigrp.

DUAL-Mart is a large department store chain with outlets throughout the United States. It based its communications on PC-to-PC communication over dial-up links. Installation of client-server applications (Microsoft Exchange and SAP/R3) that did not support this type of connectivity forced it to implement a routed network. The company was warned that some applications would hang up the client computer when the session with the server was lost, so it wanted to implement a routing protocol with fast convergence (ruling out RIP). It chose EIGRP as the routing protocol in its network because it seemed to be the easiest to implement and it offered the fast convergence that some applications required.

The initial pilot network, as shown in Figure 5-1, was extremely easy to set up and operate. After reading a couple of books and white papers from various vendors, DUAL-Mart decided to use the following approach:

- Frame Relay was used for WAN connectivity connecting each remote office with the central site through a Frame Relay permanent virtual circuit (PVC).

- A single router was used in the central site.

- Private IP address space was used. It decided to use network 10.0.0.0/8 subnetted to /24.

Figure 5-1 *DUAL-Mart Initial Pilot Network*

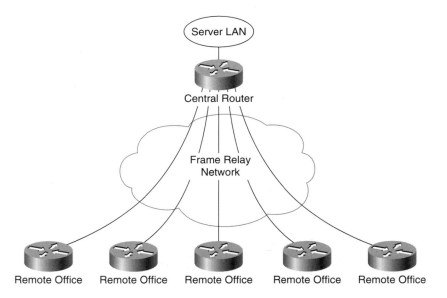

The addressing scheme was not documented because no one felt that was needed. IP subnets were sequentially assigned to new branches as they were connected.

The pilot network was a huge success. After sorting out the organizational problems and bugs in the new applications, the deployment was very smooth, and the network was never seen as an obstacle. The project manager responsible for pilot network setup was promoted, and the CIO decided on a quick large-scale rollout.

Unfortunately, the production rollout was not as successful as the initial pilot. In the first few weeks, everything worked well. After a while, however, users in different branch offices experienced unexplained outages that could not be related to Frame Relay link failures between their locations and the central site. It seemed that these outages started to happen after a few sites in remote locations were connected. These sites were connected to the DUAL-Mart network with low-speed links with no bandwidth guarantees (Committed Information Rate of the PVC was set to zero) due to the very low requirements of these locations.

Nobody correlated the outages the users experienced with the link flaps at the newly connected location until one of the locations started to experience a long series of link flaps resulting in complete network meltdown. The network management station logged these flaps and the correlation was so obvious that no one could deny the connection between these two events.

A task force was formed to solve the problem, and it tried a few obvious things:

- An additional central router was added to relieve the first router that had more than 200 remote sites connected to it at that time. The stability of the new network (shown in Figure 5-2) temporarily improved but got worse after some more locations were added.

Figure 5-2   *DUAL-Mart Network with Two Central Routers*

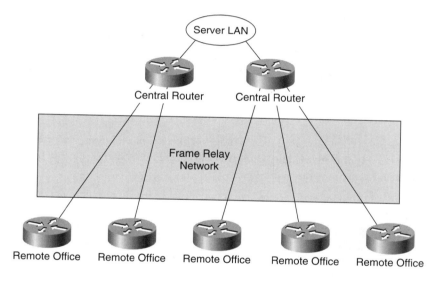

- Distribution-layer routers were introduced in the large regions to give the network some hierarchical structure. After spending over a hundred thousand dollars for the additional equipment and even more for changing the Frame Relay connections and router configurations, the task force was faced with defeat; the stability of the network in Figure 5-3 did not improve.

Finally, the CIO insisted on bringing in external help. A professional services company was engaged, and on the first visit, its consultant pointed out several items that should have been obvious:

- Every large network must have a hierarchical structure.
- This structure must be supported by a good addressing scheme.
- Every modern routing protocol must have tools that can use the hierarchical structure and corresponding addressing scheme to make the network scalable and stable.

Figure 5-3 *DUAL-Mart Network after Introduction of Distribution Routers*

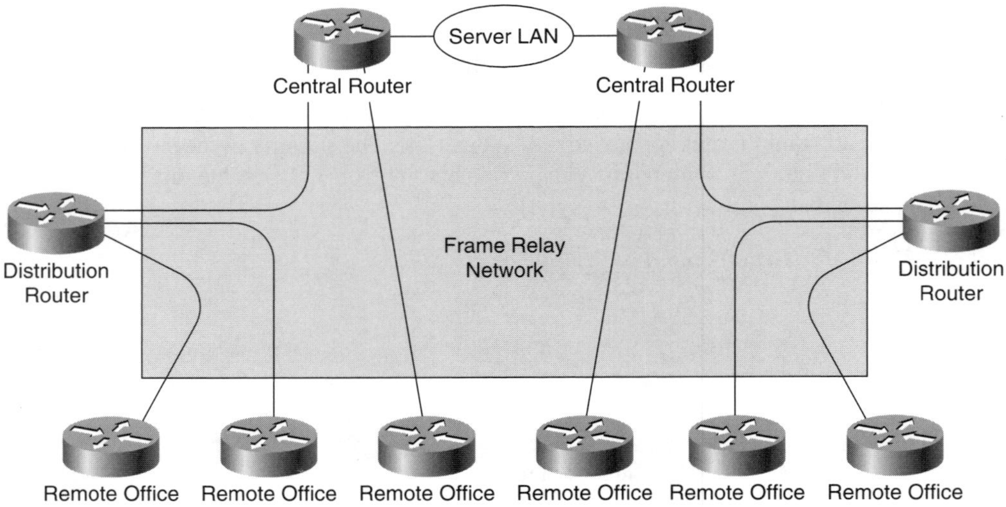

The consultant also used technical terms like *summarization*, *route filters*, and *default routes* and tried to explain to DUAL-Mart designers that they have to be used to implement query boundaries in EIGRP.

After a thorough network redesign, which included hierarchical network restructuring, IP readdressing, and the introduction of redundancy features, costing DUAL-Mart even more in additional hardware, services, lost revenue, and so on, DUAL-Mart had a stable hierarchical network, as shown in Figure 5-4. The network has since been expanded from 200 locations to well over 3000 locations, and DUAL-Mart never again experienced the meltdown that marked its initial large-scale deployment.

Figure 5-4 *DUAL-Mart Hierarchical Network*

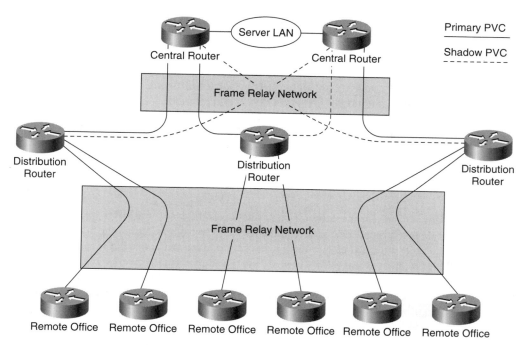

Server LAN	Primary PVC
Central Router	Shadow PVC
Central Router	
Frame Relay Network	
Distribution Router	
Distribution Router	
Distribution Router	
Frame Relay Network	
Remote Office Remote Office Remote Office Remote Office Remote Office Remote Office	

NOTE   The DUAL-Mart case study illustrates the typical scenarios I've seen in many enterprise and service provider networks. All these networks started small, and their growth was largely uncontrolled because the original network designers were busy doing something else and the network operators were not trained to detect the symptoms of potential EIGRP problems.

Most of these networks operated well for a while. (EIGRP is able to take a lot of abuse before breaking.) However, the introduction of a new element would unexpectedly push the network over the edge. The new element could be anything from adding more locations or adding locations with flapping connections to the central site to introducing roaming users accessing the network through ISDN dial-up connections.

Why Did DUAL-Mart Fail?

Several things went wrong in DUAL-Mart, from lack of network design to lack of thorough network monitoring and feedback processes, but only the EIGRP-related mistakes are covered here.

DUAL-Mart experienced one of the less-understood features of EIGRP; all the routers running EIGRP are very tightly coupled through the diffusing computation mechanism. For example, when a remote LAN is lost due to a link failure, all the remaining routers in the network have to agree that there is no alternate path to that LAN. Each router receives a query packet and replies with a reply packet. The router originating the diffusing computation must wait until all the replies come back before deciding that the route is really lost. The tight coupling of all the routers also implies that a single bottleneck (oversubscribed link, overloaded router, and so on) can bring the whole network to its knees.

The direct cause for the network meltdown in all these scenarios is a *Stuck-in-Active (SIA)* event. When a router doesn't receive a response to a query within the active timer period (the default value is three minutes), it assumes that the router that isn't responding has failed and clears the adjacency. This loss of an adjacency normally results in even more lost routes, more queries, and possibly more SIA events could happen somewhere else in the network. The chain reaction triggered by the first SIA event could eventually bring the network down.

NOTE   Some engineers might suggest that the SIA scenario described previously can be avoided by increasing the SIA timer value. I forcefully disagree with this idea. An SIA signals that your network is unable to converge within three minutes, which is probably unacceptable for most applications. If you are willing to accept three-minute convergence, you could easily use RIP.

SIAs are therefore not something that should be prevented by extending the timeout value; instead, they tell you that something is fundamentally wrong with your network. Whenever you experience an SIA, you have to use scalability tools to introduce more query boundaries and reduce the number of routes carried by individual routers. Extending (or even disabling) the SIA timer is just a temporary cosmetic measure that does not solve the problem but only prolongs the headache (allowing it to grow bigger before it becomes unbearable).

The initial DUAL-Mart network shown in Figure 5-1 experienced SIAs due to a large number of neighbors of the central router. Following a Frame Relay DLCI flap, the central router queried all the remaining remote locations about whether they had an alternate path to the lost remote office. Under the heavy load placed on the Frame Relay connection by a large number of query packets, these packets were lost due to congestion (resulting in EIGRP retransmissions) or delayed by the EIGRP pacing in the central router.

NOTE   Proper EIGRP configuration on Frame Relay interfaces can significantly diminish the bursts placed on the Frame Relay network by EIGRP process. Please refer to Chapters 12, "Switched WAN Networks and Their Impact on EIGRP," and 13, "Running EIGRP over WAN Networks," for more details.

However, because the DUAL algorithm is not aware of any underlying transport protocol problems, it triggers SIA events even when the bottleneck is the outgoing interface of the local router. In the DUAL-Mart network, the SIA resulted in adjacency loss with a random remote office. Users in that remote office experienced connectivity loss during the rebuilding of the EIGRP adjacency even when the Frame Relay link connecting them to the rest of the network worked flawlessly.

The second central router that was introduced to reduce the load of the first router (refer to Figure 5-2) reduced the number of neighbors, making the SIA less probable. However, when the number of remote offices increased again, the situation only got worse. The SIA occurred between the central router and the remote office or between the central routers, as shown in Figure 5-5.

Let's work through one possible scenario to see why this is. Assume that Alpha detects a lost route and starts a diffusing computation, querying all its remote neighbors as well as the other central router (Beta). Beta would further query all its remote neighbors. (These query packets are marked *R-Query* in Figure 5-5.) Given that one of Beta's neighbors doesn't ever answer the query with a reply, due to a slight delay between the start of the diffusing computation on Alpha and the moment Beta receives the query and starts processing it, the SIA timeout is likely to expire on Alpha first. Alpha then clears its adjacency with Beta resulting in loss of approximately half the routes in the network.

NOTE   The SIA time has some jitter, so it is possible for some router, other than the router that started the diffusing computation, to experience SIA first. In our scenario, the odds favor Alpha, but it's not certain that the SIA event will happen on router Alpha every time.

Figure 5-5 *Stuck-in-Active between Core Routers in DUAL-Mart Network*

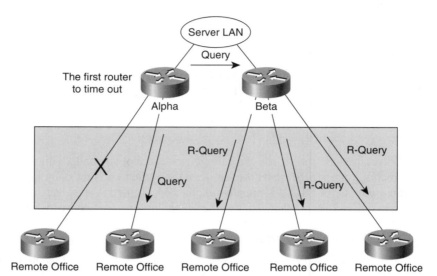

Introduction of distribution routers into the DUAL-Mart network was a good idea; the only mistake the team made was that it did not introduce distribution routers throughout the whole network. Some remote offices still linked to the central routers. The links to these remote offices continued to represent bottlenecks that could cause SIA events after the number of remote locations increased again. Assuming that the links to remote offices were the only bottleneck in the network in Figure 5-6 and could thus become congested during diffusing computation, the SIA might occur in one of two places:

- The SIA could happen between the distribution and core router in case the link to a remote office connected to a distribution router failed.

- The SIA could also happen between the core routers (or the core and distribution router) if the link to a remote office directly connected to the core router failed. (This scenario is illustrated in Figure 5-6.)

Figure 5-6   *SIA Event Occurs on the Central Router if the Link between Central Router and Remote Office Fails*

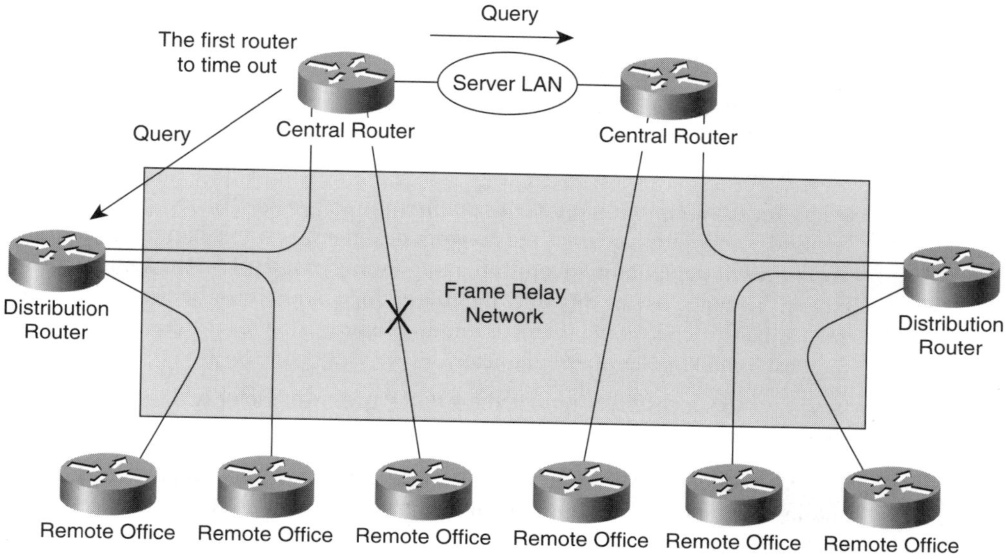

Case Study Summary

To conclude this case study, let's summarize the lessons learned from the DUAL-Mart fiasco:

- Every network that could potentially grow (and they all will) must be carefully designed with the growth in mind.

- The network structure must be hierarchical, and the network-addressing scheme must support the use of scalability tools, such as address summarization and default routes.

- The network must be monitored during extensive growth or the introduction of new services, such as dial-up connectivity, and the network design must eventually be adapted to keep it stable and scalable.

Query Boundaries—What They Are and Why They Are Useful

The discussions in the previous section pointed out the major design requirement for large EIGRP networks: Reduce the number of route flaps and the diffused computation diameter (for example, the number of routers involved in diffused computation). Based on rules in

"Diffusing Computation" in Chapter 1, "EIGRP Concepts and Technology," only a few ways to limit the query propagation potentially resulting in smaller query diameter exist:

- *Query received when the route is already active.* This rule is not applicable to query diameter reduction.

- *Query received from the only successor with the router having no other EIGRP neighbor.* This rule limits the logical network topology to star-like shape, which is not a viable implementation option in networks that require built-in redundancy.

- *Query received but the route is not in topology database.* This property of EIGRP diffused computation enables the network designer to establish query boundaries that stop diffused computation from spreading throughout the EIGRP autonomous system. To make use of this rule, the route propagation must be limited by mechanisms such as route filters or route summarization resulting in smaller topology databases and smaller query diameters.

Only two ways to successfully reduce the EIGRP query diameter resulting in reduced convergence time and prevention of SIA events exist:

- You can reduce overall EIGRP AS size (resulting in hard boundaries that EIGRP queries cannot cross) by introducing additional routing protocols like RIP in the access layer or Border Gateway Protocol (BGP) in the network core. This approach can be efficiently implemented in large networks with good multilayer structure, as you will see in Chapter 9, "Integrating EIGRP with Other Enterprise Routing Protocols."

- You can establish query boundaries by using tools, such as route summarization, route filters, and default routes. These tools and the query boundaries they establish are discussed in Part II, "Designing Enterprise EIGRP Networks," together with appropriate design guidelines.

Monitoring the Stability of Your EIGRP Network

One of the summary conclusions of the DUAL-Mart case study was that network performance must be constantly monitored to discover potential symptoms of EIGRP overload well before the EIGRP is pushed beyond its limits.

To monitor EIGRP performance in your network to find out whether you might be faced with EIGRP meltdown problems in the future, you can use the following tools:

- Use the *syslog* or any other logging tool, such as Resource Manager Essentials (RME), to discover an SIA event as soon as it occurs.

- Monitor the EIGRP traffic with **show ip eigrp traffic** command on your core routers. If the number of queries per second is high, chances are that some remote router will not be able to cope with all the queries. The relevant fields in command printout are highlighted in Example 5-1.

Example 5-1 *show ip eigrp traffic Printout*

```
router#show ip eigrp traffic
IP-EIGRP Traffic Statistics for process 109
  Hellos sent/received: 8407089/6214188
  Updates sent/received: 2032447/1960578
  Queries sent/received: 668047/707959
  Replies sent/received: 717771/673734
  Acks sent/received: 3286950/3142927
  Input queue high water mark 10, 0 drops
```

It's important to note that there is no right value for the number of queries a router sends or receives. The only relevant value for a network is a long-term average when the network is stable. If the number of queries in a certain time interval rises well above that average value, the network might be facing instabilities that could potentially result in EIGRP problems. If, on the other hand, the number of queries and replies per minute stays constantly high, the network never reaches a stable state, which also indicates a potential problem.

- Monitor the number of active routes and the time they stay in active state with the **show ip eigrp topology active** command. The relevant fields in the command printout are highlighted in Example 5-2. A high number of active routes indicate an unstable network, and active routes that stay active for a long time indicate that the network is converging slowly, potentially resulting in Stuck-in-Active routes.

Example 5-2 *show ip eigrp topology active Printout*

```
router#show ip eigrp topology active
IP-EIGRP Topology Table for process 1

Codes: P - Passive, A - Active, U - Update, Q - Query, R - Reply, r - Reply status

A 10.2.0.0/16, 0 successors, FD is 40793600, Q
    1 replies, active 00:01:45, query-origin: Local origin
        via 10.4.0.1 (Infinity/Infinity), Ethernet0
    Remaining replies:
        via 10.5.0.4, r, Serial0
```

Case Study 2—Diffused Computation in Hierarchical Networks

For more information on this case study, please visit www.ciscopress.com/eigrp.

The hierarchical DUAL-Mart network, as shown in Figure 5-7, is used here to benchmark the effects of various scalability tools on stability of the network. In this case study, no scalability tools are used to establish the baseline behavior.

Figure 5-7   *Hierarchical DUAL-Mart Network*

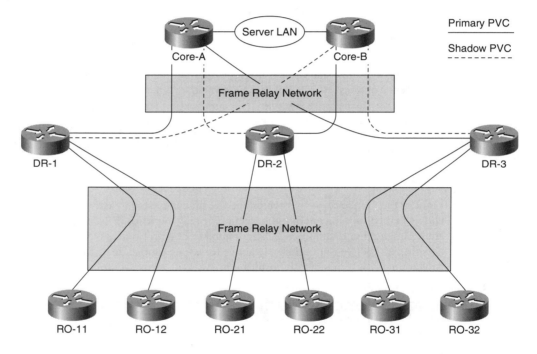

NOTE	Good network design separates the LAN on which the transit traffic is exchanged from the LAN on which the central servers are placed. Because most of the traffic in the DUAL-Mart network is exchanged between the remote offices and the central site due to the client-server nature of the applications, no need for a separate transit traffic LAN exists.

The network uses a good IP addressing scheme that is adapted to its hierarchical structure. The parts of the addressing scheme relevant for our case study are shown in Table 5-1. (WAN links and loopback interfaces are ignored.)

Table 5-1   *IP Addressing Scheme in DUAL-Mart Network*

Router Name	LAN IP Subnet
Core-A, Core-B	10.0.1.0/24
DR-x (x being the region number)	10.x.0.0/24
RO-xy (x being the region number, y being the office number within region)	10.x.y.0/24

The DUAL-Mart network uses only Frame Relay for its WAN transport. The connections between distribution sites and the core site are redundant using *shadow PVCs* offered by the service provider. Primary PVCs of odd-numbered distribution routers connect to Core-A with shadow PVCs connected to Core-B. Primary PVCs of even-numbered distribution routers connect to Core-B with shadow PVCs connected to Core-A.

NOTE

A shadow PVC is a feature offered by some Frame Relay service providers where the customers get two PVCs for the price of one under the condition that the shadow PVC is used marginally (for routing traffic only) when the primary PVC is available. If the customers exceed the traffic limit on the shadow PVC while the primary PVC is available, they are charged for two PVCs. It's therefore very important that the routing works correctly and the routers avoid sending any unnecessary data over the shadow PVCs.

The Committed Information Rate (CIR) of the primary PVC is 512 kbps; the CIR of the shadow PVC is 256 kbps. PVCs between distribution routers and remote offices have a CIR of 64 kbps. All the Frame Relay links in the network are configured over point-to-point subinterfaces. The bandwidth set on Frame Relay subinterfaces is set to CIR value. The delay on most subinterfaces was left at the default value of 20,000 microseconds. The delay on the shadow PVC subinterfaces had to be increased to 40,000 microseconds for proper routing.

Exercise 5-1

The DUAL-Mart network was initially implemented by setting the proper bandwidth on the Frame Relay subinterfaces. During the functional tests, it was discovered that the traffic from the distribution router toward the server LAN flows only over the primary PVC, whereas the return traffic from the servers to the remote offices might also flow over the shadow PVC. The return traffic toward the clients on the distribution site LAN always flew over the primary PVC. The shadow PVC usage was even more pronounced when the traffic flows between the remote sites connected to different distribution routers were examined.

Why did the return traffic flow over shadow PVC? Why were only the remote offices affected? Why did the increased delay on the shadow PVC subinterface solve the problem?

To establish baseline EIGRP behavior in the DUAL-Mart network, let's examine three typical failures:

- The PVC between distribution router and remote office fails.
- The shadow PVC fails while the primary PVC is active.
- The primary PVC fails and the traffic is rerouted over the shadow PVC.

All failures will only be evaluated in region 1. The behavior of all the other odd-numbered regions is identical. To get the behavior of the even-numbered regions, just change Core-A and Core-B in the evaluations.

EIGRP behavior depends heavily on successors and feasible successors. All the relevant successors and feasible successors for various destinations are summarized in Table 5-2.

Table 5-2 *Successors and Feasible Successors in DUAL-Mart Network*

From Router	To LAN	Successor	Feasible Successor
Core-A	RO-1x	DR-1	none
Core-B	RO-1x	Core-A	DR-1
DR-1	RO-1x	RO-1x	none
DR-1	Server LAN	Core-A	Core-B
DR-1	DR-x	Core-A	Core-B
DR-1	RO-xy (x > 1)	Core-A	Core-B
DR-x (x > 1, x odd)	DR-1, RO-1x	Core-A	Core-B
DR-x (x > 1, x even)	DR-1, RO-1x	Core-B	Core-A

Exercise 5-2

The reader is kindly invited to verify the contents of Table 5-2.

Remote Office PVC Failure

This scenario seems to be the easiest one to simulate. The expected result is that all the routers in the network become involved in the diffusing computation and agree that no route to the remote subnet exists. However, the redundancy between the distribution and core routers gives rise to interesting phenomena that make this scenario worth examining step-by-step.

1 When the PVC between DR-1 and RO-11 fails, DR-1 loses its successor for the subnet 10.1.1.0/24. DR-1 doesn't have a feasible successor, so the route becomes active and queries are sent to all other remote offices in region 1 as well as Core-A and Core-B (see Figure 5-8). These packets are labeled Q(1) to denote Query packets in Step 1.

Figure 5-8   *Remote Office PVC Failure—Step 1*

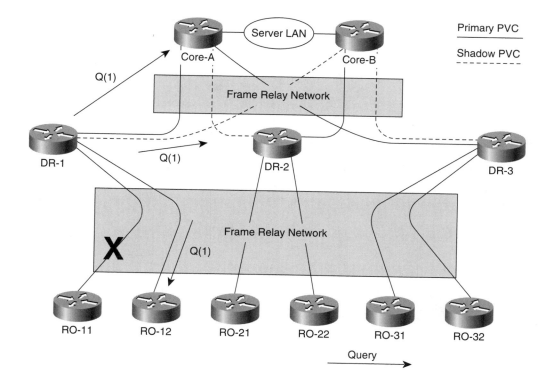

2 Core-A receives the Q(1) packet from its successor for this destination and checks its topology table for an alternate path. Because it has no feasible successor, it marks the route active and generates queries to all its other neighbors. The other remote routers in region 1, RO-1x, also receive the query, Q(1) from their successors, but they have no other neighbors, so they immediately reply that they have no other route toward the lost subnet. Core-B, however, receives the query from a nonsuccessor and replies immediately with an alternate route going through Core-A (see Figure 5-9). The query packets generated in the second step are labeled Q(2), and all the replies are labeled with the metric they carry.

NOTE	The step-by-step evaluation of DUAL behavior in this scenario and all the following scenarios in this chapter depends on the timing of the query and reply packets and therefore represents only the most likely sequence of events. For example, Core-B could receive the query packet from Core-A before it receives the query packet from DR-1.

Figure 5-9   *Remote Office PVC Failure—Step 2*

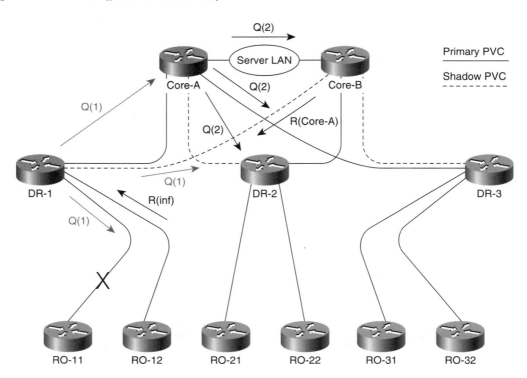

NOTE	After Step 2, the DR-1 might almost conclude that there is an alternate path to subnet of RO-11, but it's still missing a reply from Core-A. The route is therefore still active, and the next hop cannot be changed.

3 Core-B now receives a query packet from its successor. The route becomes active on Core-B, and it sends queries (labeled Q(3)) to all its other neighbors (all the distrib- ution routers, including DR-1). In the meantime, DR-2 through DR-n receive the Q(2) packet and immediately reply. For even-numbered DR routers, Q(2) is received from a nonsuccessor, and the reply carries the metric toward Core-B. The odd-numbered DR routers receive Q(2) from the successor, but they have a feasible successor (Core-B). An update packet is also sent from odd-numbered DR routers toward the remote offices to inform them that the route cost has increased (see Figure 5-10).

Figure 5-10 *Remote Office PVC Failure—Step 3*

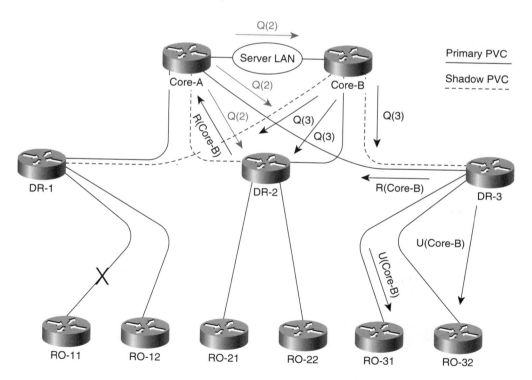

4 When DR-1 receives the query Q(3), it immediately replies with infinite metric because the route is already active and the feasible distance of the route is infinity. All the other DR routers receive Q(3) from the current successor and continue the diffusing computation; queries are sent to all remote offices and Core-A (see Figure 5-11). In the meantime, the remote offices in odd-numbered regions have received the update packet U(Core-B) reporting a cost increase from the successor. They mark the route active, but they have no other neighbors. The active state ends immediately, and the new higher cost is accepted.

Figure 5-11 *Remote Office PVC Failure—Step 4*

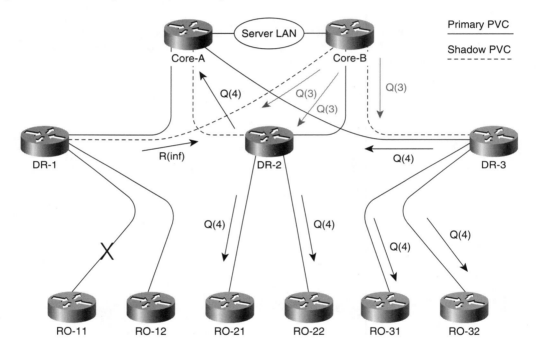

5 All the remote offices receive the Q(4) query packet from their successors, but they have no other neighbors, so they immediately reply with infinite metric and remove this destination from their topology and routing tables. Core-A also replies with an infinite metric because the route is already active and the reported distance is set to infinity (see Figure 5-12).

Figure 5-12 *Remote Office PVC Failure—Step 5*

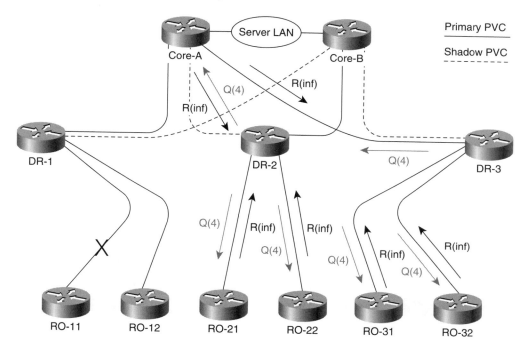

6 The diffusing computation on the DR routers (apart from DR-1) is complete, resulting in the conclusion that subnet 10.1.1.0/24 is unreachable. This result is reported back to the router that triggered the diffusing computation on DR routers—Core-A. The reply packets from the DR routers are shown in Figure 5-13.

7 Core-A has only one outstanding query at this point; Core-B still hasn't replied. When Core-B receives all the replies to its queries, it reports the result (subnet unreachable) to Core-A—the router it received the original query from (refer to Figure 5-9). The diffusing computation is now complete on Core-A; it reports that there is no alternate route to the lost subnet to DR-1 and removes this destination from its topology and routing tables. Core-A's reply to DR-1 allows DR-1 to complete the diffusing computation it started in Figure 5-8.

Figure 5-13 *Remote Office PVC Failure—Step 6*

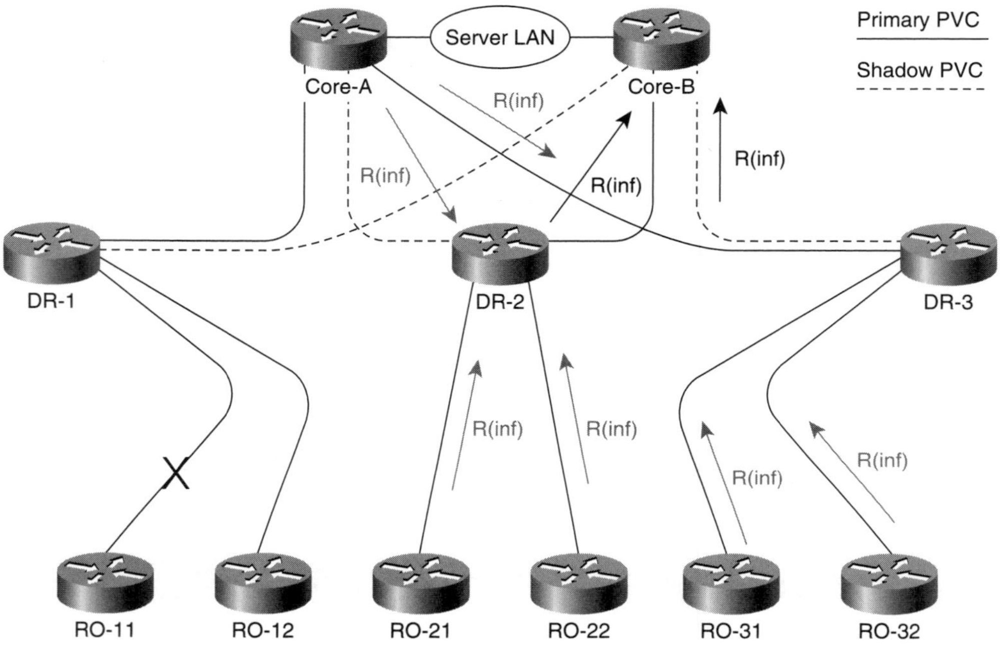

Exercise 5-3

Repeat the EIGRP simulation with different timing assumptions. For example, assume that Core-B received the Q(2) packet from Core-A in Figure 5-9 before it received the Q(1) packet from DR-1.

As it turns out, the simple nonredundant PVC failure to a remote office involves all routers in the DUAL-Mart network in the diffusing computation, as was expected. The unexpected side effects are some intermediate results that also result in data traffic unnecessarily being shifted to shadow PVCs (for example, traffic from odd-numbered regions toward RO-11 in the interval between Figure 5-10 to Figure 5-11).

Shadow PVC Failure

Shadow PVC failure between DR-1 and Core-B is the easiest failure scenario (see Figure 5-14). Both DR-1 and Core-B notice a neighbor failure due to hold time expirations or a subinterface going down, but the neighbor is not a successor for any route. The paths learned from the lost neighbor are silently deleted from the topology database, and no other routers are involved.

Figure 5-14 *Shadow PVC Failure*

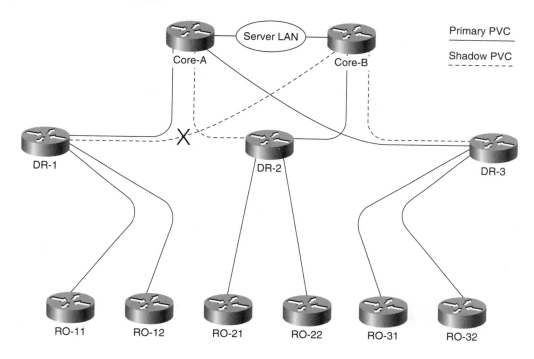

Primary PVC Failure with Traffic Rerouting

PVC failure between DR-1 and Core-A (see Figure 5-15) does not present a serious problem for DR-1 because it has a feasible successor for all the routes for which Core-A was a successor. Core-B is immediately selected as the new successor, and a large number of updates are sent to all remote offices because the EIGRP metric for all destinations in the network increased. These updates trigger a diffusing computation on all remote office routers in region 1, but as they have no other neighbors to query, the diffused computation is immediately terminated. In any event, a large number of updates are sent to the remote offices because this is a big network, unnecessarily loading the low-speed Frame Relay connections between DR-1 and remote office routers.

Figure 5-15   *Primary PVC Failure and the Resulting Action on DR-1*

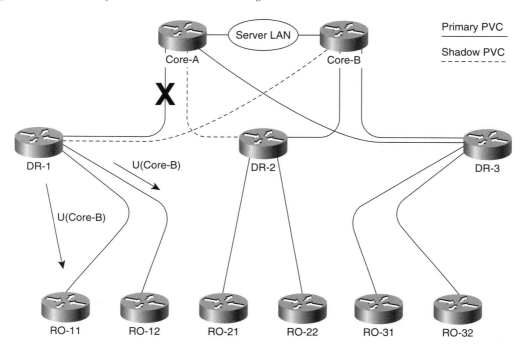

The situation is more complex at the core site:

1 Core-A loses its successor for all the remote offices and DR LANs in region 1, and it has no feasible successor. Core-A marks each of the routes as active and starts a diffusing computation for each of them. Queries (labeled Q(1)) are sent to Core-B and all other distribution routers (see Figure 5-16).

2 Core-B receives Q(1) from the successor, but because it has a feasible successor for all of the queried routes, it can reply immediately. It also sends an update reporting increased EIGRP metric to all the distribution routers.

3 Even-numbered DR routers (DR-2 in Figure 5-16) receive Q(1) queries from a nonsuccessor. They delete the entry previously received from Core-A from their topology databases and reply with their best route through Core-B.

4 Odd-numbered DR-routers, however, receive Q(1) from their successors. They have a feasible successor for every queried route (Core-B), so they select Core-B as their new successor and reply with the new best route. They also send updates reporting metric increases for a large number of routes to each of the remote offices connected to them. Figure 5-17 shows steps 2–4.

Figure 5-16   *Primary PVC Failure—Step 1*

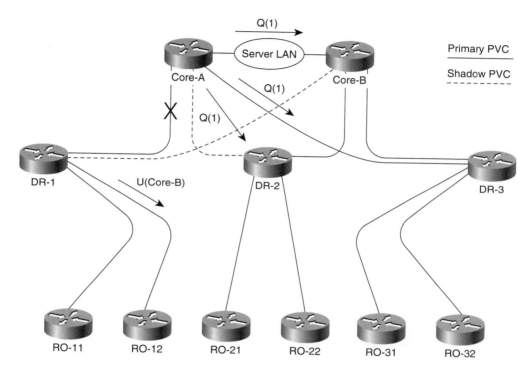

NOTE   From this moment until the network converges, the traffic from odd-numbered regions toward region 1 flows over two shadow PVCs: one that is allowed to be used (region 1) and another one that should have been avoided.

5 Core-A received all the replies to its query; it can now select the best route that goes through Core-B. Because the successor and the interface through which the successor is reachable have both changed, Core-A reports a new metric for all the affected routes to all DR routers. An update noting this destination is unreachable through Core-A and is sent toward Core-B.

Figure 5-17   *Primary PVC Failure—Steps 2–4*

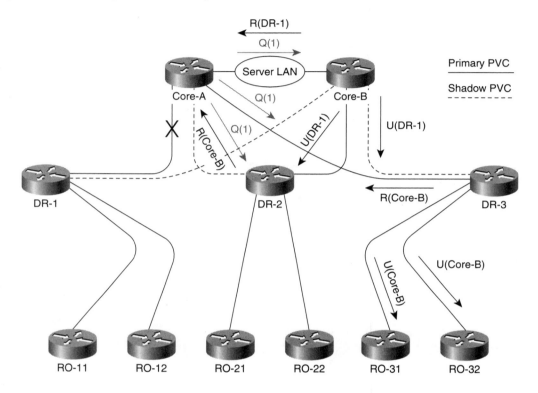

6 All the DR routers receive several update packets from Core-B reporting metric increases for all routes in region 1. The updates come from the current successor and have no feasible successor, so they start a diffusing computation in their regions. All the remote offices are queried for potential better paths toward all the routes in region 1 (see Figure 5-18).

7 Meanwhile, remote offices in the odd-numbered regions are busy processing the metric increase reported by the DR router (for example, DR-3 in Figure 5-17). They start a diffusing computation for each one of the routes in region 1, but it ends immediately because they have no other neighbors to query.

Figure 5-18   *Primary PVC Failure—Steps 5–7*

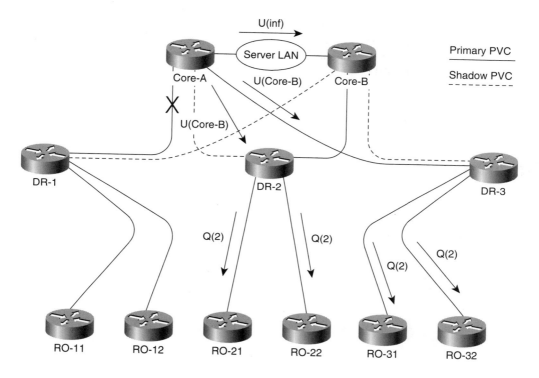

8 The DUAL-Mart network has, by now, almost converged. The core routers have converged. All the remote offices receive Q(2) packets and reply with infinite metric, ending the diffusing computation on all the distribution routers. The distribution routers also receive updates from Core-A, which are ignored on even-numbered DR routers because the path offered by Core-B is better. For the odd-numbered DR routers, the path through Core-A is still better than the direct path to Core-B going over the shadow PVC, so they select a new successor and inform the remote offices that the cost toward all destinations in region 1 has decreased.

Exercise 5-4

Compute the EIGRP metric that Core-A reports to DR routers for RO-11 and DR-1 LAN. Compute the EIGRP metric for these destinations on DR-2 and DR-3 and verify that they select the paths over primary PVCs.

The primary PVC failure simulation presents an extremely valuable lesson: Even though redundant paths exist in the network, a diffusing computation for a large number of routes is performed on nearly all routers in the network (apart from routers in region 1). Additionally, for a brief time period, the traffic from odd-numbered regions toward region 1 flows over a suboptimal path. This simulation therefore illustrates the true danger of nonscalable EIGRP implementation: Large numbers of routers, most of them reachable over low-speed links, have to agree on optimum path toward a large number of destinations. No wonder DUAL-Mart experienced SIA events when its network grew larger and larger, resulting in more and more query packets being sent over low-speed Frame Relay PVCs.

Summary

Every large network deploying any interior routing protocol requires careful design, backed up with a good addressing scheme that allows efficient summarization, and networks implemented with EIGRP are no exception. Although EIGRP is sometimes presented as a routing protocol that requires no network design, that is not true in reality.

EIGRP-specific network design should focus on query boundaries that limit the diameter of diffusing computations. Several scalability tools are available for EIGRP designers, including summarization, route filters, default routes, and combinations of EIGRP with other routing protocols such as RIP or BGP.

CHAPTER 6

EIGRP Route Summarization

The case studies in Chapter 5, "Scalability Issues in Large Enterprise Networks," illustrated the need for hierarchical network design and a corresponding IP addressing scheme. In this chapter, you'll see two scalability tools that you can use in hierarchical networks with a good IP addressing scheme: autosummarization, which can be used to implement automatic summarization on major network boundaries, and manual per-interface summarization, which can be used where summarization behavior has to be fine-tuned. But before going into technical details, let's take a look at another case study illustrating the potential summarization drawbacks.

Case Study—Connectivity Loss Following Private IP Address Deployment

For more information on this case study, please visit www.ciscopress.com/eigrp.

GreatCoals mining company has a large WAN network connecting several core sites, housing finance, sales, marketing, and research and development facilities with a widespread network of sites where various operations are performed. The network uses public IP address space because the network designers want to give Internet access to every user of the network. The company received one class B address (131.7.0.0/16) several years ago, which was subnetted, and the subnets were distributed throughout the network. With the addition of a large number of new remote sites, the company started running out of address space, and it is trying to recover the public IP addresses assigned to WAN links. One possibility was to replace the public IP addresses used on the WAN links with private IP addresses from the class B network 172.16.0.0/16. The solution seemed risky at first, but because the company uses EIGRP, the network designers argued that EIGRP supports variable-length subnet masks (VLSMs) and discontiguous networks, so the IT manager approved the solution. The first test was to be performed on a core WAN link connecting the research and development facility in Houston with the company headquarters in Austin, as shown in Figure 6-1.

Figure 6-1 *GreatCoals Network*

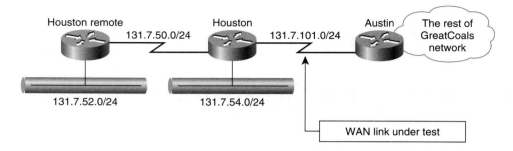

Changing the IP subnet on the WAN link between Houston and Austin from 131.7.101.0/24 to 172.16.1.4/30 turned out to be an extremely easy task and the engineers were starting to celebrate when the phones started to ring. A quick troubleshooting session revealed that the connectivity between Houston and the rest of the network was lost. Digging deeper, the engineers found that the adjacency between Houston and Austin was established, but it seemed as though no routing updates were being exchanged over the connection. Furthermore, a new route for the whole class B network (131.7.0.0/16) pointing to interface Null 0 was installed on both routers. This route was killing all the traffic that previously flowed over the WAN link. The routing tables and EIGRP printouts of these two routers can be seen in Example 6-1, Example 6-2, and Example 6-3.

Example 6-1 *Detailed EIGRP Neighbor Information on Austin and Houston Routers*

```
Houston#show ip eigrp neighbors 131
IP-EIGRP neighbors for process 131
H   Address              Interface     Hold Uptime    SRTT   RTO  Q  Seq
                                       (sec)          (ms)        Cnt Num
1   131.7.50.2           Se2.1          12 00:00:53   411   2466  0  9
0   172.16.1.6           Se1.1          14 00:01:00  1612   5000  0  25

Austin#show ip eigrp neighbors 131
IP-EIGRP neighbors for process 131
H   Address              Interface     Hold Uptime    SRTT   RTO  Q  Seq
                                       (sec)          (ms)        Cnt Num
0   172.16.1.5           Se0.1          13 00:02:33     0   3000  0  21
1   131.7.22.2           Se0           129 00:06:30    44   1140  0  10
```

Example 6-2 *Routing Table for Network 131.7.0.0/16 on Houston Router*

```
Houston#show ip route 131.7.0.0
Routing entry for 131.7.0.0/16, 5 known subnets
  Attached (3 connections)
  Variably subnetted with 2 masks
  Redistributing via eigrp 131

D        131.7.0.0/16 is a summary, 00:03:25, Null0
D        131.7.52.0/24 [90/40640000] via 131.7.50.2, 00:03:19, Serial2.1
C        131.7.53.0/24 is directly connected, Loopback7
C        131.7.54.0/24 is directly connected, Ethernet0
C        131.7.50.0/24 is directly connected, Serial2.1
```

Example 6-3 *Routing Table for Network 131.7.0.0/16 on Austin Router*

```
Austin#show ip route 131.7.0.0
Routing entry for 131.7.0.0/16, 4 known subnets
  Attached (2 connections)
  Variably subnetted with 2 masks
  Redistributing via eigrp 2, eigrp 131

D        131.7.0.0/16 is a summary, 00:03:00, Null0
C        131.7.20.0/24 is directly connected, Loopback7
C        131.7.22.0/24 is directly connected, Serial0
D        131.7.23.0/24 [90/20640000] via 131.7.22.2, 00:05:08, Serial0
```

A call to Cisco's TAC provided a quick explanation for the unexpected behavior: The GreatCoals' engineers forgot to consider a feature called *autosummarization*. A few minutes and two router configuration commands later, the traffic started to flow between Houston and Austin, and the networking team proved the validity of its concept. The final routing table of Houston router is shown in Example 6-4.

Example 6-4 *Routing Table in Houston Router after the Autosummarization Has Been Turned Off*

```
Houston#sh ip rout 131.7.0.0
Routing entry for 131.7.0.0/24, 6 known subnets
  Attached (3 connections)
  Redistributing via eigrp 131

D        131.7.20.0 [90/46354176] via 172.16.1.6, 00:00:03, Serial1.1
D        131.7.22.0 [90/46738176] via 172.16.1.6, 00:00:03, Serial1.1
D        131.7.52.0 [90/40640000] via 131.7.50.2, 00:00:16, Serial2.1
C        131.7.53.0 is directly connected, Loopback7
C        131.7.54.0 is directly connected, Ethernet0
C        131.7.50.0 is directly connected, Serial2.1
```

Autosummarization

Autosummarization was initially introduced in EIGRP to facilitate smooth migration from Interior Gateway Routing Protocol (IGRP) to EIGRP. This feature gives EIGRP the same classful behavior well known to IGRP users, which can be summarized in the following rule:

> Never announce the subnets of one major network into another major network. Only the major network prefix is announced with the metric of the closest subnet (usually a directly connected interface).

The statement that EIGRP supports VLSM and discontiguous subnets is therefore only partially true; EIGRP always supports variable-length subnets, but support for discontiguous subnets has to be configured manually, as the GreatCoals' engineers found out the hard way.

NOTE   Although autosummarization was a great feature for those initial EIGRP adopters who wanted smooth migration from IGRP to EIGRP, it might be more pain than gain in some of the networks today. Not all networks have a classful addressing scheme where the core would be in one major IP network and each region would have a separate major IP network assigned, making them a natural fit for EIGRP autosummarization.

To enable or disable support for discontiguous networks in EIGRP, use the EIGRP router configuration commands in Table 6-1.

Table 6-1   *Configure Support for Discontiguous Networks in EIGRP*

Router Configuration Command	Meaning
No auto-summary	Enables support for discontiguous networks in EIGRP. No automatic summarization across major network boundaries is performed.
auto-summary (default setting)	Reverts to IGRP compatibility mode where only major networks are announced across network boundaries and the subnets are suppressed.

NOTE   All EIGRP adjacencies are reset when you change the autosummary setting; therefore, this configuration change should be performed with extreme caution.

The precise autosummarization rules are slightly more complex than the simple statement at the beginning of this section.

EIGRP Autosummarization Rule 1

Whenever an EIGRP process has more than one network defined, it creates a summary route for each of the defined networks as soon as at least one of the subnets of that network is in the EIGRP topology table.

EIGRP Autosummarization Rule 2

The summary route created by Rule 1 points to Null 0 interface and has the minimum metric of all the subnets of the network covered by the summary route. The summary route is also inserted into the main IP routing table with an administrative distance of 5 (nonconfigurable).

EIGRP Autosummarization Rule 3

Subnets summarized by Rules 1 and 2 are suppressed when updates are sent to neighbors in different major IP networks; only summary routes are sent.

EIGRP Autosummarization Rule 4

Subnets that do not belong to any of the networks listed in EIGRP process definition are not summarized.

Additional complexity is also introduced by the fact that some routers in an EIGRP network can have autosummary turned on while others can have it turned off.

CAUTION   Rule 3 might produce unexpected behavior when an unnumbered WAN link connects two major networks and the IP addresses used on the WAN link are from different major networks. This design is therefore strongly discouraged.

With the help of EIGRP autosummarization rules, it's easy to explain what happened to GreatCoals' engineers after they made their initial changes to their network as summarized in Figure 6-2.

Figure 6-2 *GreatCoals Network after WAN Subnet Change*

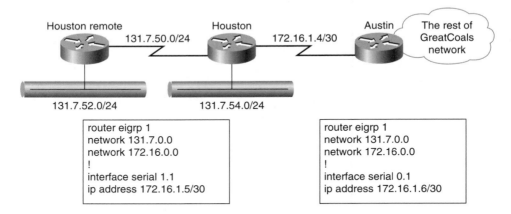

Two networks were defined on both Houston and Austin routers with EIGRP autosummary being configured, by default, on both routers. The summary routes for 131.7.0.0/8 and 172.16.0.0/8 were generated (Rule 1) and inserted into IP routing table (Rule 2). Only the information about network 131.7.0.0/8 was propagated across the WAN link between Houston and Austin (Rule 3) and could be observed in EIGRP topology database on both routers. The relevant entry on router Austin can be seen in Example 6-5.

Example 6-5 *EIGRP Topology Database Entry for Network 131.7.0.0 on Router Austin*

```
Austin#show ip eigrp topology 131.7.0.0 255.255.0.0
IP-EIGRP topology entry for 131.7.0.0/16
  State is Passive, Query origin flag is 1, 1 Successor(s), FD is 128256
  Routing Descriptor Blocks:
  0.0.0.0 (Null0), from 0.0.0.0, Send flag is 0x0
      Composite metric is (128256/0), Route is Internal
      Vector metric:
        Minimum bandwidth is 10000000 Kbit
        Total delay is 5000 microseconds
        Reliability is 255/255
        Load is 1/255
        Minimum MTU is 1514
        Hop count is 0
  172.16.1.5 (Serial0.1), from 172.16.1.5, Send flag is 0x0
      Composite metric is (46354176/128256), Route is Internal
      Vector metric:
        Minimum bandwidth is 56 Kbit
        Total delay is 25000 microseconds
        Reliability is 255/255
        Load is 1/255
        Minimum MTU is 1500
        Hop count is 1
```

The first entry in Example 6-5 is the summary route generated on Austin. The second entry is the summary route generated on Houston and advertised to Austin over the WAN link belonging in network 172.16.0.0.

EIGRP autosummarization Rule 4 will be explained with another example in Figure 6-3.

Figure 6-3   *EIGRP Autosummarization Only Applies to Networks Defined in EIGRP Process*

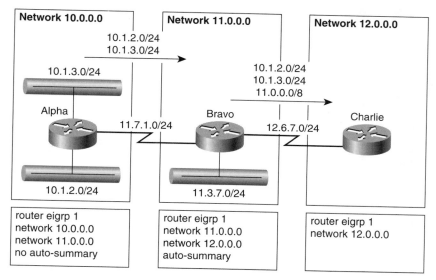

In this network, the network designer chose to turn off autosummary on router Alpha. The subnets of network 10.0.0.0 are therefore propagated to network 11.0.0.0. On the next major network boundary between networks 11.0.0.0 and 12.0.0.0, the subnets of network 11.0.0.0 are summarized into one route (11.0.0.0/8), which is then sent into network 12.0.0.0. Summarization is not performed for subnets of network 10.0.0.0 because that network is not listed in the EIGRP process on Bravo. Subnets of network 10.0.0.0 appear unmodified in network 12.0.0.0.

To enable autosummarization of subnets of network 10.0.0.0 on Bravo, the only change needed is to add **network 10.0.0.0** into the EIGRP process of Bravo using EIGRP configuration command network 10.0.0.0. The command is accepted even though Bravo has no interfaces in network 10.0.0.0 and leads to the results pictured in Figure 6-4.

Figure 6-4   *Autosummarization after Addition of Network 10.0.0.0 in EIGRP Process*

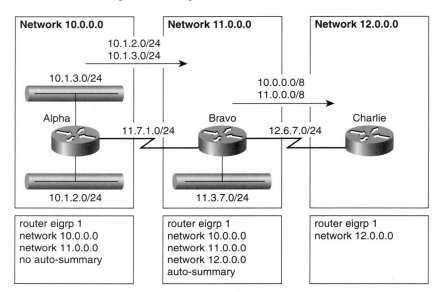

The quick fix shown in Figure 6-4 might be enough for the example network, but it has an interesting side effect: Bravo stops announcing subnets of network 10.0.0.0 even to other routers in network 11.0.0.0 (for example, Delta), as shown in Figure 6-5. The only way to summarize subnets of network 10.0.0.0 over the WAN link between Bravo and Charlie, but not to other neighbors in network 11.0.0.0, is to use per-interface summarization.

NOTE   The behavior described in Figure 6-5 might change in future IOS versions; therefore, you should not base your network design on it. The discussion on cases similar to the one in Figure 6-5 is intended to illustrate the unexpected side effects of autosummarization.

Figure 6-5   *Autosummarized Subnets Are Not Propagated in the Subnet Through Which They Were Received*

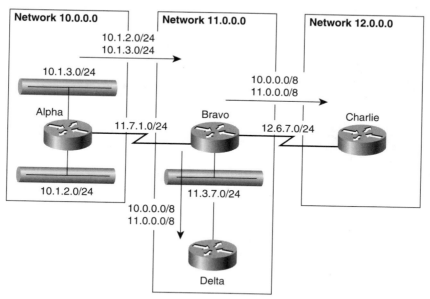

Autosummarization rules are also applied to external routes redistributed into EIGRP, as illustrated by the example in Figure 6-6.

Router Alpha inserts external subnets into the EIGRP process. The subnets are not autosummarized on Alpha because the network 10.0.0.0 is not listed in the EIGRP process on Alpha. Subnets of network 10.0.0.0 are propagated from Alpha to Bravo, where they get summarized, since the network 10.0.0.0 is listed in the EIGRP process on Bravo. Note that the network 10.0.0.0 is listed on Bravo only to enable autosummarization of external routes because Bravo has no interfaces in this network. The summarized routes are then propagated to Charlie, which receives only information about network 10.0.0.0 and not the individual subnets.

Figure 6-6   *External Routes Being Autosummarized*

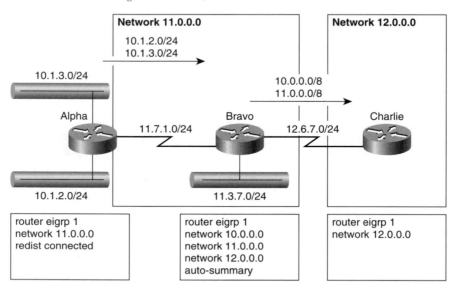

NOTE   As the previous example illustrated, external routes redistributed into EIGRP get autosummarized only under well-controlled circumstances (for example, network 10.0.0.0 being configured in EIGRP process on Bravo to facilitate autosummarization). Usually, they are not autosummarized and are propagated through the EIGRP process.

The autosummarization of networks composed from external subnets only might also change in future IOS versions.

Query Boundaries with Autosummarization

You might feel that autosummarization does more damage than good to your network—and you might be right, depending on your network design. However, it does achieve query boundaries in EIGRP, although not where you would expect to see them.

Let's take an example of an EIGRP network composed of two major IP networks: a class A (10.0.0.0) and a class B (131.7.0.0) as shown in Figure 6-7.

Figure 6-7   *EIGRP Network Composed of Two Major IP Networks*

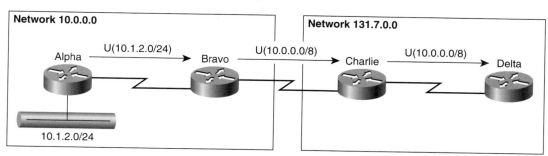

Router Alpha sends information about subnet 10.1.2.0/24 to Bravo, which performs auto-summarization and sends only the information about reachability of network 10.0.0.0/8 to Charlie, which further propagates this information to Delta. One would expect that the queries for subnet 10.1.2.0/24 would be stopped at the same boundary, which turns out not to be the case as illustrated in Figure 6-8.

Figure 6-8   *EIGRP Query Goes over the Summarization Boundary*

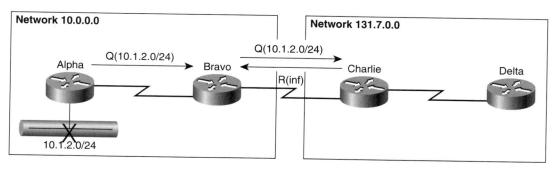

When the subnet 10.1.2.0/24 is lost on router Alpha, it starts diffused EIGRP computation. Router Bravo receives the query from its successor and because there are no feasible successors, it continues the diffused computation. As seen in Figure 6-13, the queries are not subject to summarization boundaries; the query for subnet 10.1.2.0/24 is immediately sent to router Charlie. Nevertheless, Charlie has never received any information for any subnet in network 10.0.0.0. It can therefore immediately reply with an infinite metric and stop diffused computation. Router Delta is consequently not affected.

Conclusion

Autosummarization does establish query boundaries between major networks, but the boundary is established one hop beyond the summarization point. All the queries are propagated between the major networks and stopped by the first router in the adjacent major network.

Benefits and Drawbacks of Autosummarization

To summarize the discussion in the previous sections, let's review the benefits and drawbacks of the EIGRP autosummarization feature before proceeding to how you can manually fine-tune the EIGRP summarization with per-interface summarization commands.

Autosummarization is definitely beneficial to networks being migrated from IGRP (or RIP) to EIGRP because it retains all the routing properties the network had before. That guarantees that you'll not experience unexpected routing loops (for example, due to a combination of static and dynamic routes) or changed traffic flows after the migration. Autosummarization also introduces query boundaries in networks that use many different major IP networks. As it turns out, many corporate networks have started using the private IP address network 10.0.0.0, making the whole corporate network one major IP network, so there are no bounds on which to autosummarize.

Conversely, autosummarization hurts all those network designs that deploy discontiguous subnets of major networks, such as the following:

- Using one major IP network for the core network and subnets of another major IP network in various regions
- Using subnets of a major public IP network on the LANs throughout the network and private IP addresses on WAN links

In these cases, it is best to turn off autosummarization and replace it with manual summarization where needed or desired. An alternative design might propose turning off autosummarization only in those points where discontiguous subnets appear. Such a design requires careful evaluation to verify that only proper networks are summarized. This design is also very sensitive to operator configuration errors (for example, entering another network number, as shown in Figure 6-5.)

NOTE   Networks that require autosummarization to be turned off to work correctly will probably be hard to configure, troubleshoot, and operate. Your network designs should not use discontiguous networks unless you are forced to use them due to IP address shortage.

Manual Per-Interface Summarization

Whenever the autosummarization does not fit the network design due to discontiguous networks or because the network IP addressing scheme is not composed of multiple major networks, you can still configure summarization by using the per-interface EIGRP summary commands from Table 6-2.

Table 6-2   *EIGRP Per-Interface IP Address Summarization*

Command	Results
ip summary-address eigrp <as-number> <prefix> <mask>	Configures per-interface IP address summarization for single EIGRP process

NOTE   Configuring or removing an IP summarization range on an interface clears all EIGRP adjacencies over that interface to enable the neighbors reachable over that interface to delete more specific routes from their topology databases. It's probably not the most efficient implementation of that requirement, but that's how it's implemented.

You're therefore advised to use this command only during maintenance windows and to combine several changes to the per-interface IP summarization in a batch that is downloaded to the router via any of the batch configuration mechanisms. (See also "Adjacency Resets—Causes and Consequences" in Chapter 2, "Advanced EIGRP Concepts, Data Structures, and Protocols.")

You can configure the per-interface IP address summarization per-EIGRP process in case several EIGRP processes run over the same interface. No limit exists on the number of summarization ranges you can configure on a given interface as long as the ranges don't overlap.

NOTE   The interactions between autosummarization and per-interface summarization are not well defined. As a generic rule, do not use overlapping summarization ranges on one interface; the case of interface summarization combined with autosummarization can constitute such a scenario. The results of configuring overlapping per-interface summarization and autosummarization are unpredictable.

Contrary to the link-state routing protocols such as OSPF or IS-IS, EIGRP enables the network designer to create a deep summarization hierarchy that reflects the designed network hierarchy. Therefore, you are not limited to a star-shaped network consisting of a backbone plus other regions as you are in OSPF.

NOTE   Although the EIGRP fans often emphasize the modularity and flexibility of per-interface summarization and hierarchy of summarization levels, the OSPF fans are quick to point out that configuring OSPF summarization is easier because it has to be done only on the area level in the routing process, not on every individual interface. As always, the truth is somewhere in the middle. Some networks benefit from the flexibility of EIGRP, and other networks encounter management problems trying to make sure that all the summarization ranges are configured correctly on the core routers with a large number of interfaces.

The per-interface IP address summarization follows similar rules to EIGRP autosummarization.

EIGRP Manual Summarization Rule 1

For each summary range configured over any interface belonging to an EIGRP process, the EIGRP process creates a summary route for the summarization range as soon as at least one more specific route falling within the summary range appears in EIGRP topology table.

EIGRP Manual Summarization Rule 2

The summary route created by Rule 1 points to Null 0 interface and has the minimum metric of all the more specific routes covered by the summary route. The summary route is also inserted into the main IP routing table with an administrative distance of 5 (nonconfigurable).

EIGRP Manual Summarization Rule 3

More specific routes summarized by Rules 1 and 2 are suppressed when updates are sent over the interface where the summarization range is configured. Updates sent over other interfaces are not affected.

NOTE   It's very important to make the lowest metric route folded into the summary very stable; otherwise, the summary address will flap as often as the lowest-cost subnet. (More precisely, its cost changes, but that might also induce a diffusing computation on the router receiving the update.)

Why Do We Need a Summary Route to Null 0?

One often-misunderstood design decision is summarization Rule 2 that dictates that a summary route be installed for every summarization range being advertised to EIGRP neighbors. The purpose of that summary route is to prevent routing loops between routers with different granularity of the IP address space in their routing tables, as illustrated by the example in Figure 6-9.

Figure 6-9 *Summarization Scenario Leading to a Potential Routing Loop*

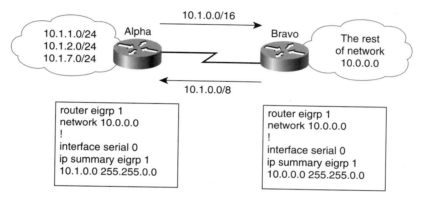

Imagine that the routers Alpha and Bravo would not have summary routes for prefixes 10.1.0.0/16 and 10.0.0.0/8, respectively, pointing to Null 0. The routing table on Alpha would contain routes for subnets 10.1.0.0/24 through 10.1.7.0/24 plus the route to 10.0.0.0/8 pointing toward Bravo. The routing table on Bravo would contain a route to 10.1.0.0/16 pointing toward Alpha plus some other routes in network 10.0.0.0.

A packet for destination 10.1.13.13 received by Alpha would be sent to Bravo because the only route covering that part of the address space would be 10.0.0.0/8 received from Bravo. On receiving that packet, Bravo would route the packet back to Alpha because the most specific route covering 10.1.13.13 on Bravo is the 10.1.0.0/16 route received from Alpha, resulting in a routing loop between Alpha and Bravo.

EIGRP prevents this kind of routing loop with the summary routes. Router Alpha contains a route for prefix 10.1.0.0/8 pointing to Null 0, so the packet for destination 10.1.13.13 received by Alpha is immediately discarded. The same packet received by Bravo is forwarded to Alpha where it is yet again discarded due to the summary route.

EIGRP Query Boundary with Per-Interface Summarization

Per-interface summarization ranges create EIGRP query boundaries in much the same way as autosummarization; the important difference is that you can create these ranges as needed. Like the autosummarization query boundary, the per-interface summarization query boundary is one hop farther than one would expect. For an example, consider the network in Figure 6-10.

Figure 6-10 *Updates in Network with Per-Interface Summarization*

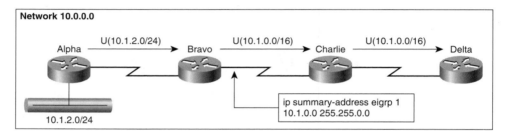

The subnet 10.1.2.0/24 is subsumed by the summarization range on the WAN link between Bravo and Charlie. Therefore, only the summary range 10.1.0.0/16 is announced from Bravo to Charlie and propagated further to Delta. Yet, when the subnet 10.1.2.0/24 disappears, the summarization boundary does not stop the query, as shown in Figure 6-11.

Figure 6-11 *Query Propagation in Network with Per-Interface Summarization*

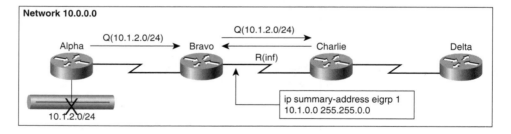

When router Alpha starts a diffusing computation, a query is sent to Bravo that continues the diffusing computation and propagates the query beyond the summarization boundary to Charlie. Router Charlie never receives any information about subnet 10.1.2.0/24, so it stops the diffusing computation and immediately replies with infinite metric. Router Delta is not affected at all.

Case Study—EIGRP Behavior in DUAL-Mart Network after Regional Summarization

For more information on this case study, please visit www.ciscopress.com/eigrp.

The hierarchical DUAL-Mart network, first introduced in Chapter 5 and redrawn in Figure 6-12, can illustrate the benefits of using EIGRP summarization features to improve network scalability. Compare the EIGRP behavior in this case study with the behavior in "Case Study 2—Diffused Computation in Hierarchical Network," of Chapter 5 to see the vast improvement in scalability.

Figure 6-12 *Hierarchical DUAL-Mart Network*

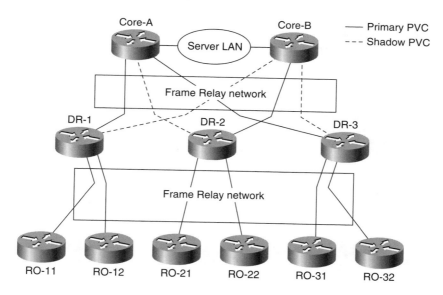

The IP addressing scheme in the DUAL-Mart network is well suited to EIGRP summarization (see Table 6-3).

Table 6-3   *IP Addressing Scheme in DUAL-Mart Network*

Router Name	LAN IP Subnet
Core-A, Core-B	10.0.1.0/24
DR-x (x being the region number)	10.x.0.0/24
RO-xy (x being the region number, y being office number within region)	10.x.y.0/24

In the initial summarization phase, the summarization is done on the DR routers that announce only the regional prefix (10.x.0.0/16) to the remote offices and the core routers. The relevant part of DR-1 configuration is shown in Example 6-6.

Example 6-6   *DR-1 Configuration in Regional Summarization Design*

```
!
hostname DR-1
!
interface Serial0
 encapsulation frame-relay
 description Links toward branch offices
 ip address 10.1.100.100 255.255.255.0
 ip summary-address eigrp 42 10.1.0.0 255.255.0.0
 bandwidth 640
!
interface Serial0.1 multipoint
 description Primary interface toward central site (Core-A)
 ip address 10.100.1.1 255.255.255.0
 ip summary-address eigrp 42 10.1.0.0 255.255.0.0
 bandwidth 512
!
! Insert DLCI # toward Core-A here
!
 frame-relay interface-dlci 213
!
interface Serial0.2 multipoint
 description Backup interface toward central site (Core-B)
 ip address 10.100.4.1 255.255.255.0
 ip summary-address eigrp 42 10.1.0.0 255.255.0.0
 bandwidth 256
 delay 4000
!
! Insert DLCI # toward Core-B here
!
 frame-relay interface-dlci 322
!
!
router eigrp 42
network 10.0.0.0
```

NOTE	The reasoning behind bandwidth setting on Frame Relay subinterfaces leading toward the core routers can be found in "Case Study 2—Diffused Computation in Hierarchical Network," in Chapter 5. The bandwidth on a multipoint subinterface connecting the remote offices to DR router is set to the sum of all CIRs on that interface. (See Part III for more details.)

NOTE	Clearly, the Frame Relay connections between DR-1 and Core-A, Core-B and remote offices have to be separated into three different subnets using subinterfaces. PVCs toward Core-A and Core-B are implemented using multipoint subinterfaces to allow one subinterface on core routers to cover all distribution routers.
	PVCs toward remote offices are configured on the main interface to minimize the router configuration changes. If these PVCs are implemented on a subinterface, a new **frame-relay interface-dlci** command must be entered each time a remote office is added. In the implementation in Example 6-6, new PVCs are automatically added to the main interface requiring no reconfiguration of DR-1.

Compared to the baseline network in "Case Study 2—Diffused Computation in Hierarchical Network" in Chapter 5, the routers in the improved DUAL-Mart network carry a smaller number of routes, as documented in Table 6-4. Depending on the IP addressing scheme used in the network, the number of routes carried in any one router can be decreased by an order of magnitude or more.

Table 6-4 *Routes Carried in Different Types of Routers in DUAL-Mart Network*

Router	Routes Carried in Original Network	Routes Carried in Network with Summarization
RO-xy	All routes in the network	Local subnets and all regional prefixes (/16)
DR-x	All routes in the network	Local subnets, all subnets of remote offices in the region, regional prefixes from other regions
Core-A, Core-B	All routes in the network	Local subnets and all regional prefixes

The EIGRP behavior in the new network will be evaluated in only two failure scenarios:

- The PVC between distribution router and remote office fails
- The primary PVC fails and the traffic is rerouted over the shadow PVC

Shadow PVC failure will not be evaluated because the behavior on shadow PVC loss is identical to that in "Shadow PVC Failure" of Chapter 5. As before, all failures will be evaluated in region 1 only.

Remote Office PVC Failure

DR-1 router notices remote office PVC failure through Frame Relay LMI signaling or EIGRP hello protocol failure. It has no alternate route to the lost subnet; the subnet route becomes active and DR-1 sends queries to all its neighbors. None of them receive any information about the lost subnet (refer to Table 6-4), so all the remaining remote office routers attached to DR-1 and the core routers reply with infinite metric (see Figure 6-13).

Figure 6-13 *EIGRP Convergence Following Remote Office PVC Failure*

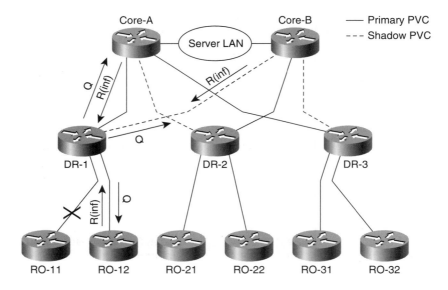

Primary PVC Failure

The DR-1 router and the core router behave exactly as in the case study in "Primary PVC Failure with Traffic Rerouting" in Chapter 5 with one significant difference—the number of routes that become active:

- DR-1 sends information about only increased cost of all regional prefixes to remote office routers. (Previously, the information about all the subnets in the network was sent.)

- All the other routers in the network still start diffused computations at various times during the convergence process, but the diffused computation is started for only one route (the regional prefix) whereas it was started for all the subnets in the region before.

Case Study Analysis and Comparison with OSPF

The DUAL-Mart network with regional summarization behaves almost as though it were implemented with OSPF areas in which the DR routers are Area Border Routers (ABR) between the backbone area and other areas with proper area-summarization manually configured:

- Remote office PVC failure does not spread beyond core routers. (OSPF performs slightly better; the core routers are not involved.)

- Shadow PVC failure does not involve any other router. (OSPF performs slightly worse; all DR routers are involved in shadow PVC failure.)

- Primary PVC failure involves all routers, but they have to recompute only a small number of routers (namely the affected regional prefixes). OSPF performs in almost the same way.

Case Study—EIGRP Behavior in DUAL-Mart Network after Two-Step Summarization

For more information on this case study, please visit www.ciscopress.com/eigrp.

EIGRP behavior in DUAL-Mart network (refer to Figure 6-12) can be further improved when a second layer of summarization is introduced; the core routers announce only the 10.0.0.0/8 prefix to the regional routers and suppress all regional prefixes. The relevant configuration of one of the core routers is shown in Example 6-7.

Example 6-7 *Core Router Configuration in Hierarchical Summarization Design*

```
!
hostname Core-A
!
interface Serial0
 encapsulation frame-relay
!
interface Serial0.1 multipoint
 description Primary links to distribution routers
 ip address 10.100.1.100 255.255.255.0
 ip summary-address eigrp 42 10.0.0.0 255.0.0.0
 bandwidth 512
 ip bandwidth-percent eigrp 42 200
!
! Insert primary DLCI # toward distribution routers
!
```

continues

Example 6-7 *Core Router Configuration in Hierarchical Summarization Design (Continued)*

```
  frame-relay interface-dlci 213
  frame-relay interface-dlci 214
 !
interface Serial0.2 multipoint
  description Backup links to distribution routers
  ip address 10.100.2.1 255.255.255.0
  ip summary-address eigrp 42 10.0.0.0 255.0.0.0
  bandwidth 256
  delay 4000
 !
 ! Insert shadow DLCI # toward distribution routers
 !
  frame-relay interface-dlci 313
  frame-relay interface-dlci 314
 !
 !
router eigrp 42
network 10.0.0.0
```

The second layer of summarization further reduces the routes carried in various routers—
sometimes even by another order of magnitude, as shown in Table 6-5.

Table 6-5 *Routing Tables of Various Routers in the Network with Two Layers of Summarization*

Router	Routes Carried in Network with One Layer of Summarization	Routes Carried in Network with Two Layers of Summarization
RO-xy	Local subnets and all regional prefixes (/16)	Local subnets, local regional prefix (/16), and network prefix (10.0.0.0/8).
DR-x	Local subnets, all subnets of remote offices in the region, regional prefixes from other regions	Local subnets, all subnets of remote offices in the region, network prefix (10.0.0.0/8)
Core-A, Core-B	Local subnets and all regional prefixes	Local subnets and all regional prefixes

Summarization retains the redundancy properties of the DUAL-Mart network; in many
cases, the routers have both a successor and a feasible successor for a given destination. The
successors and feasible successors for various routes are shown in Table 6-6.

Table 6-6   *Successors and Feasible Successors in DUAL-Mart Network with Two Summarization Layers*

Router	Destination	Successor	Feasible Successor
RO-xy	Any	DR-x	None
DR-x	10.x.y.0/24	RO-xy	None
	10.x.0.0/16	Locally generated	---
	10.0.0.0/8	Core-A for x odd Core-B for x even	Core-B for x odd Core-A for x even
Core-A	10.x.0.0/16	DR-x for x odd Core-B for x even	None for x odd DR-x for x even
	10.0.0.0/8	Locally generated	---
Core-B	10.x.0.0/16	Core-A for x odd DR-x for x even	DR-x for x odd None for x even
	10.0.0.0/8	Locally generated	---

The extra summarization performed at the core routers further reduces the impact of PVC failures in a DUAL-Mart network. The remote office PVC failure and the shadow PVC failure are not considered here because the EIGRP diffused computation is already bounded for these scenarios even in the previous case study.

Primary PVC Failure

When the PVC between DR-1 and Core-A fails, the DR-1 immediately selects an alternate route for 10.0.0.0/8 through Core-B. 10.0.0.0/8 is also the only route ever received by DR-1 from Core-A or Core-B, so the amount of processing is minimal. Updates are sent to remote offices informing them that the cost of reaching 10.0.0.0/8 has increased. Remote offices try to start a diffused computation, but it's stopped immediately because they have no other neighbors.

Core-A starts a diffusing computation for 10.1.0.0/16 because it has no feasible successor for that route. That is also the only route that becomes active because it was the only route ever received from DR-1. The number of routes for which the diffusing computations are run in the network is therefore highly limited.

Core-A sends query packets to all its neighbors: Core-B and the other DR routers. The DR routers never receive any information about network 10.1.0.0/16, so they immediately reply with infinite metric. Core-B has a feasible successor for the route; DR-1 reachable over shadow PVC becomes the successor, and Core-B can reply to Core-A with the information about an alternate route. Core-B also tries to inform its other neighbors that the cost of reaching 10.1.0.0/16 has increased, but the update is stopped at the summarization boundary and never leaves Core-B. The network convergence is thus complete (see Figure 6-14 for detailed packet flow).

Figure 6-14 *EIGRP Convergence after Primary PVC Failure in Hierarchically Summarized Network*

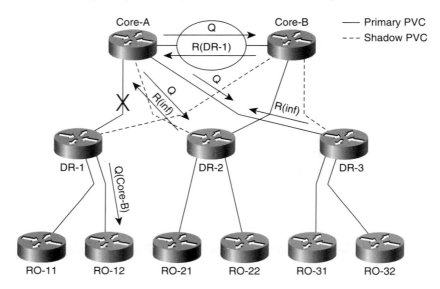

It's important to note that in this case study the DR routers never really got involved in the diffusing computation. The isolation of remote office routers in the other regions was even better; they never received a single query packet. Several layers of summarization give the DUAL-Mart network maximum possible isolation between the regions.

Summary

EIGRP autosummarization and per-interface summarization are powerful scalability tools that can make EIGRP scale to huge networks when implemented properly.

Autosummarization should be used with care, especially in networks that deploy discontiguous subnets. It has no effect in networks that use only one major IP network (for example, newly designed networks using only private IP addresses from IP network 10.0.0.0/8).

Per-interface summarization gives EIGRP great flexibility that cannot always be matched by other routing protocols, particularly in large hierarchical networks. On the other hand, the flexibility in network design places a higher burden on network implementers who have to configure summarization ranges on each interface.

CHAPTER 7

Route Filters

EIGRP route summarization, introduced in Chapter 6, "EIGRP Route Summarization," gives you a versatile hierarchical tool that can make an EIGRP network extremely scalable. Whenever the addressing scheme or the network design deviates from the hierarchical design, summarization can give suboptimal results or even lead to partial connectivity in the network, as you'll see in the first case study. This chapter introduces additional scalability tools—EIGRP route filters and prefix lists —that can provide scalability even in some networks where the summarization cannot be properly deployed due to deviations from a hierarchical design.

Case Study—Partial Connectivity over ISDN Backup

For more information on this case study, please visit www.ciscopress.com/eigrp.

DUAL-Mart, a large department store chain (see "Case Study—Large Enterprise Network Experiencing Meltdown Situations" in Chapter 5, "Scalability Issues in Large Enterprise Networks," for more information on DUAL-Mart), has implemented a stable and redundant EIGRP network with hierarchical multilevel summarization shown in Figure 7-1. (See "Case Study—EIGRP Behavior in DUAL-Mart Network after Two-Step Summarization" in Chapter 6 for details.)

The main design principle throughout the network design was to minimize EIGRP query diameters by deploying summarization wherever possible. A carefully planned IP addressing scheme detailed in Table 7-1 was implemented to support the summarization.

Table 7-1 *IP Addressing Scheme in DUAL-Mart Network*

Router Name	LAN IP Subnet
Core-A, Core-B	10.0.1.0/24
DR-x (x being the region number)	10.x.0.0/24
RO-xy (x being the region number, y being the office number within region)	10.x.y.0/24

Figure 7-1   *DUAL-Mart Network—Logical Topology*

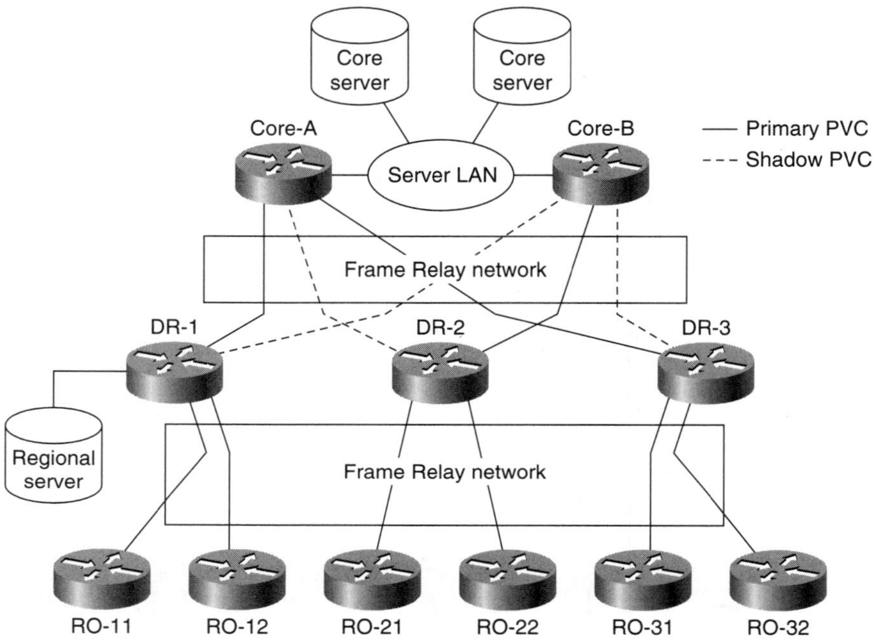

Summarization was deployed on distribution and core routers according to rules in Table 7-2.

Table 7-2   *Summarization Rules in DUAL-Mart Network*

Router	Interface	Summarization Rules
Core routers	Subinterfaces toward distribution routers	Announce only 10.0.0.0/8
Distribution routers	Subinterfaces toward core and remote offices	Summarize subnets within region to 10.x.0.0/16

The end result was close to perfect; every router in the network carried only the minimum set of routes required for proper network operation as summarized in Table 7-3.

Table 7-3   *Routing Tables of Various Routers in the Network with Two Layers of Summarization*

Router	Routes Carried in Network with One Layer of Summarization	Routes Carried in Network with Two Layers of Summarization
RO-xy	Local subnets and all regional prefixes (/16)	Local subnets, local regional prefix (/16), and network prefix (10.0.0.0/8).
DR-x	Local subnets, all subnets of remote offices in the region, regional prefixes from other regions	Local subnets, all subnets of remote offices in the region, network prefix (10.0.0.0/8)
Core-A, Core-B	Local subnets and all regional prefixes	Local subnets and all regional prefixes

As new applications were introduced in the DUAL-Mart network, the network itself became more and more mission-critical. Old applications in the remote offices that relied on occasional file transfer were replaced with interactive applications that required real-time access to central servers. It turned out that a remote office could no longer operate without the network. (Of course, the networking team found that out only after the applications were deployed and remote users started to complain after every Frame Relay glitch.) A high-priority project was started immediately to solve the redundancy issue, and the project team quickly discovered that ISDN dial backup was the only cost-effective way to provide network redundancy to a large number of remote offices. It decided to use ISDN dial backup from the remote offices to the central site where a new ISDN Remote Access Server would be installed.

NOTE   The crucial questions in dial-backup design are as follows:

- Is the dial backup initiated from the central site or from the remote offices? Technically, it's simpler to initiate dial backup from the remote offices, but in some centralized corporations the solution might not be politically correct.

- Is the ISDN dial-backup call terminated at the next layer of hierarchy (from remote-office router to distribution-layer router in DUAL-Mart case) or are all dial-backup calls terminated at the central site?

- Should the ISDN links be unnumbered or should a separate subnet be used for each ISDN network?

These questions have no clear answers. The optimal solution depends on the number and duration of expected outages, ISDN costs, the number of routers in the network, and the network topology. An optimal dial-backup solution must be tailored to specific organization requirements and topology.

After the ISDN dial-backup design was approved, an ISDN Primary Rate Interface (PRI) was installed at the central site, and ISDN Basic Rate Interfaces (BRIs) were installed in the remote offices and at the regional sites. The new network diagram is shown in Figure 7-2. (Only the ISDN connections in Region 1 are drawn.)

Figure 7-2   *DUAL-Mart Network with ISDN Dial-Backup*

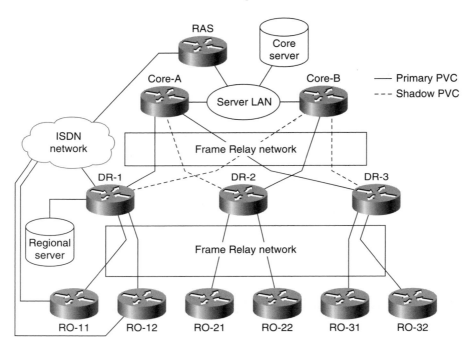

Initial dial-backup tests were just starting when a large-scale Frame Relay failure hit DUAL-Mart. ISDN dial backup was hurriedly deployed in as many remote offices as possible and there was no time to test the whole solution. Very early in the implementation efforts, the engineers discovered that the ISDN addressing scheme hadn't been agreed upon yet, so they made an ad-hoc decision to use an unused portion of IP address space (10.210.0.0/16) for all ISDN interfaces.

Due to its previous investment in ISDN dial backup, DUAL-Mart survived the Frame Relay network failure with no substantial business damage. Analysis of the help-desk logs show, however, that a curious phenomenon occurred during the Frame Relay failure: All remote users that were connected over the ISDN dial backup were able to access all the applications on the central servers, but not the applications running on their regional servers.

Controlled simulations of a single Frame Relay PVC failure have confirmed the user observations; whenever a remote office was connected to the DUAL-Mart network through the ISDN dial backup, the users in that office were unable to access applications running on their regional servers.

Exercise 7-1

Before you continue reading, try to figure out what happened in the DUAL-Mart network. Probably the best approach would be to rebuild the DUAL-Mart network in your lab using configurations of DUAL-Mart routers with two levels of summarization as provided in "Case Study—EIGRP Behavior in DUAL-Mart Network after Regional Summarization" and "Case Study—EIGRP Behavior in DUAL-Mart Network after Two-Step Summarization" in Chapter 6.

DUAL-Mart engineers tried to troubleshoot what appeared to be an IP routing problem by using pings and traceroutes. Their results are summarized in Table 7-4. (Home regional router/server in the table denotes the IP address of the router or server within the region in which the remote office belongs. Other regional router/server denotes IP address of the router or server in another region.)

Table 7-4   *Results of Initial IP Troubleshooting*

Operation	From	To	Result
Ping	Remote office router	Central server	Works
		Regional server	Works
		Regional router	Works
	Remote office PC	Central server	Works
		Home regional server	Fails
		Home regional router	Fails
		Other regional server	Works
		Other regional router	Works
Traceroute	Remote office PC	Regional server	Fails on regional router
	Regional server	Remote office PC	Fails on regional router

Exercise 7-2

Why did the ping from the remote office router to the regional server work whereas the ping from the remote office PC to the same router failed?

Based on the results from Table 7-4, the troubleshooting efforts quickly focused on the regional router (DR-1) and the DUAL-Mart engineers finally found the culprit; summarization on DR-1 caused a summary route for 10.1.0.0/16 pointing to Null 0 to be installed. Because the core routers announce only 10.0.0.0/8 to the regional routers, DR-1 was not aware that the most specific route for one of its remote offices goes through the core router. The summary route to Null 0 was the most specific route for remote office PC on the regional distribution router and caused all the traffic for that remote office to be dropped.

Successful ISDN dial-backup implementation in DUAL-Mart network requires route propagation rules that are slightly modified from those in Table 7-2. The new rules are documented in Table 7-5.

Table 7-5   *Summarization Rules in DUAL-Mart Network*

Router	Interface	Announce the Following Routes
Core routers	Subinterfaces toward distribution routers	10.0.0.0/8 and 10.x.y.0/24 for remote offices on ISDN dial backup
Distribution routers	Subinterfaces toward core and remote offices	10.x.0.0/16

Unfortunately, the new rules cannot be implemented using EIGRP summarization. DUAL-Mart engineers were faced with a seemingly unsolvable problem until they found out about EIGRP route filters.

EIGRP Route Filters

As you remember from Chapter 2, "Advanced EIGRP Concepts, Data Structures, and Protocols," EIGRP behaves like a distance vector protocol when propagating routes through the network. The three basic steps performed by EIGRP during the route propagation phase are as follows:

Step 1   Receive incoming update about a new route and adjust the update with inbound interface metrics.

Step 2   Insert the received information in the EIGRP topology database and select the best route.

Step 3   Announce the best route to all other EIGRP neighbors.

Route filters can be inserted in Steps 1 and 3 to influence which routes a router is willing to accept from its neighbors (Step 1) or which routes the router is willing to propagate to its neighbors (Step 3).

NOTE   Route filters are normally considered to be a security mechanism, not a scalability tool because they are often used to increase the security and reliability of routing information exchanged. This notion is wrong, as you'll see in the next sections, because route filters can be used very successfully to establish query boundaries.

The security implications of EIGRP route filters are further documented in Chapter 15, "Secure EIGRP Operation."

EIGRP offers a rich set of filtering options:

- Inbound or outbound route filters can be applied globally (to all EIGRP neighbors) or on a per-interface basis (to all neighbors reachable over the specified interface).
- Additional route filters can be applied to routes redistributed into EIGRP from other routing protocols.

All these options are also documented in Figure 7-3.

Figure 7-3   *EIGRP Route Filters*

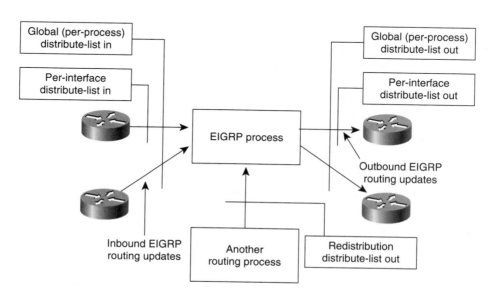

To configure EIGRP route filters, use the commands from Table 7-6. The IP access list (ACL) used in all the commands can be numbered or named simple IP access list.

Table 7-6   *Configuring EIGRP Route Filters*

Router Configuration Command	Results
distribute-list <ACL> in	Applies specified ACL to all updates received from all neighbors.
distribute-list <ACL> in <interface>	Applies specified ACL to all updates received through specified interface.
distribute-list <ACL> out	Specified ACL is applied to all updates sent.
distribute-list <ACL> out <interface>	Specified ACL is applied to all updates sent through specified interface.
distribute-list <ACL> out <routing-process>	Specified ACL is applied to all routes received through redistribution from specified routing process before these routes are stored in EIGRP topology database.

NOTE   The global **distribute-list** and per-interface **distribute-list** are *combined* (contrary to what IOS documentation states). Per-interface lists *do not override* global list—a route has to match both global and per-interface **distribute-list** to be accepted (for inbound lists) or announced (for outbound lists).

NOTE   Every time the global **distribute-list** is changed or the ACL used in the global **distribute-list** is changed, all EIGRP adjacencies of that EIGRP process are reset. Every time the per-interface **distribute-list** is changed or the ACL used in it is changed, all EIGRP adjacencies over that interface are reset.

EIGRP route filters are not applied to all EIGRP packets; query packets are not affected at all. All the other EIGRP packets are affected according to the following rules:

- Route received in an update packet but rejected by **distribute-list in** is ignored (equivalent to receiving the route with infinite metric).

- Route in topology database but rejected by **distribute-list out** is not sent in outgoing update packet.

- The reply packet for a route that would be filtered by either global or per-interface **distribute-list out** is sent with infinite metric.

- The reply packet received for a route that would be filtered by either global or per-interface **distribute-list in** is processed as if it contains infinite metric.

Query Boundaries Established by EIGRP Route Filters

EIGRP route filters always create query boundaries because the router itself (or its neighbors) doesn't have an entry in its topology databases for some subnets filtered by inbound or outbound filters.

Outbound route filters create a query boundary that is one hop beyond the route filter, producing similar effects to route summarization. Consider, for example, the network in Figure 7-4.

Figure 7-4   *Updates in Network with Outbound Route Filters*

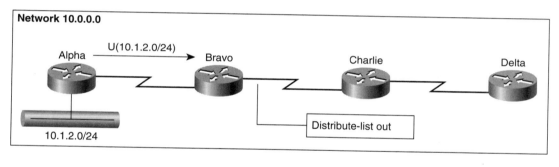

The update for subnet 10.1.2.0/24 is not propagated from Bravo to Charlie due to an outbound route filter. Charlie (and subsequently Delta) thus has no information on subnet 10.1.2.0/24 in its EIGRP topology database. When the subnet 10.1.2.0/24 disappears, the query is propagated from Bravo to Charlie according to rules in "EIGRP Route Filters" in this chapter, but Charlie immediately replies with infinite metric because it has no information about the subnet being queried in its topology database. Router Delta is not affected at all (see Figure 7-5 for graphical representation of packet flow).

Figure 7-5 *Query Propagation in a Network with Outbound Route Filters*

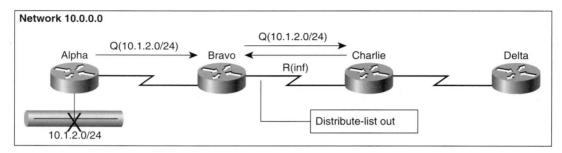

Contrary to outbound route filters, inbound EIGRP route filters establish a query boundary on the router where the filter is deployed. Consider the network in Figure 7-6, which is very similar to the one in Figure 7-4, only the outbound filter on Bravo is replaced with the inbound filter on Charlie.

Figure 7-6 *Updates in a Network with Inbound Route Filters*

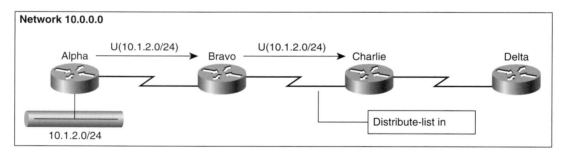

The update for subnet 10.1.2.0/24 is propagated from Alpha through Bravo to Charlie where it's dropped by inbound **distribute-list** and never entered in the EIGRP topology database. When the subnet 10.1.2.0/24 is subsequently lost, Alpha starts a diffusing computation and sends a query to Bravo that propagates it to Charlie. Charlie, however, immediately replies with infinite metric because it has no information about subnet 10.1.2.0/24 in its topology database due to an inbound route filter. The whole process is also illustrated in Figure 7-7.

Figure 7-7   *Query Propagation in a Network with Inbound Route Filters*

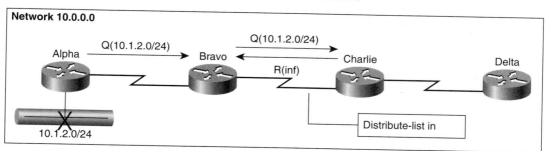

Case Study—DUAL-Mart ISDN Dial-Backup Network Redesign

For more information on this case study, please visit www.ciscopress.com/eigrp.

Equipped with the new information from "EIGRP Route Filters," and "Query Boundaries Established by EIGRP Route Filters," in this chapter, you are now ready to solve the DUAL-Mart case study from "Case Study—Partial Connectivity over ISDN Backup" in this chapter. The DUAL-Mart network designer already identified the necessary routes that must be advertised by individual routers in the DUAL-Mart network to properly support centralized ISDN dial backup. These routes are repeated in Table 7-7.

Table 7-7   *Summarization Rules in DUAL-Mart Network*

Router	Interface	Announce the Following Routes
Core routers	Subinterfaces toward distribution routers	10.0.0.0/8 10.x.y.0/24 for remote offices on ISDN dial backup
Distribution routers	Subinterfaces toward core and remote offices	10.x.0.0/16

Summarization can still be used on distribution routers to generate the 10.x.0.0/16 prefix. It can no longer be used on core routers because any summarization on Frame Relay interfaces from core to distribution routers suppresses the 10.x.y.0/24 routes needed for proper dial-backup connectivity.

This dilemma can be solved in the following configuration steps on the core routers:

Step 1   Remove summarization from Frame Relay interfaces.

Step 2   Add route filters on Frame Relay interfaces. These filters should permit only 10.0.0.0/8 and 10.x.y.0/24 routes and deny all the regional prefixes (10.x.0.0/16).

Step 3   A route to 10.0.0.0/8 must be generated somehow because the summarization process no longer generates it.

Although the first step may be evident, building the right IP access list turns out to be far from easy. Standard IP access lists cannot match subnet masks; you're limited to matching IP network addresses only. Careful evaluation of routes that have to be accepted by the access list lead to the following conclusions (graphically represented in Example 7-1):

- Prefix 10.0.0.0/8 should be permitted.

- The ACL should deny all routes where the third byte is zero and the second byte is anything. (These routes would probably be the regional prefixes.)

- The ACL should deny all routes where the second byte is zero and the third byte is anything. (These routes would probably be the subnets of the core location.)

- The ACL should permit all other routes in network 10.0.0.0 where the fourth byte is zero. (The check on the fourth byte would probably stop prefixes longer than /24.)

NOTE   As you've probably noticed, the explanations for various checks in the target ACL are rather vague. That's because the standard IP access lists cannot match subnet masks. The best you can do with standard IP access lists is to filter on presence or absence of zeroes in specific parts of the IP address and hope that your network does not contain unusual routes like subnet zero.

The corresponding IOS standard IP ACL is also given in Example 7-1.

Example 7-1   *Graphical Representation of IP Route Filter on Core Routers*

```
Core-A#show ip access-lists
Standard IP access list NoRegPrefix
    permit 10.0.0.0
    deny   10.0.0.0, wildcard bits 0.255.0.0
    deny   10.0.0.0, wildcard bits 0.0.255.0
    permit 10.0.0.0, wildcard bits 0.255.255.0
```

The relevant portions of core-router configuration are shown in Example 7-2. The configurations of the distribution layer or remote office routers are not changed.

Example 7-2   *Core Router Configuration in DUAL-Mart Network*

```
hostname Core-A
!
interface Serial0
 encapsulation frame-relay
!
interface Serial0.1 multipoint
 description Primary links to distribution routers
 ip address 10.100.1.100 255.255.255.0
 no ip summary-address eigrp 42 10.0.0.0 255.0.0.0
 bandwidth 512
 frame-relay interface-dlci 213
 frame-relay interface-dlci 214
!
interface Serial0.2 multipoint
 description Backup links to distribution routers
 ip address 10.100.2.1 255.255.255.0
 no ip summary-address eigrp 42 10.0.0.0 255.0.0.0
 bandwidth 256
 delay 4000
 frame-relay interface-dlci 313
!
router eigrp 42
 network 10.0.0.0
 distribute-list NoRegPrefix out Serial0.1
 distribute-list NoRegPrefix out Serial0.2
!
ip route 10.0.0.0 255.0.0.0 Null0
!
ip access-list standard NoRegPrefix
 permit 10.0.0.0
 deny   10.0.0.0 0.255.0.0
 deny   10.0.0.0 0.0.255.0
 permit 10.0.0.0 0.255.255.0
```

Prefix Lists—Improved Route Filters

Case study solution in "Case Study—DUAL-Mart ISDN Dial-Backup Network Redesign" in this chapter illustrated how hard it is to filter IP network prefixes in situations where the real filtering should have been performed on the subnet mask, not on the network number.

The proper tools to use when the network design requires subnet mask filters are **prefix lists**. They can be used in any place where an IP access list can be used for route filter—from **distribute-list** commands to **route-maps**. Their syntax and behavior, as shown in Table 7-8, is very similar to named IP access lists with two major exceptions:

- Lines in prefix lists are numbered, making it easy to insert or delete a specific line.
- The match condition is modeled optimally for route filters as detailed in Table 7-9.

Table 7-8 *IP Prefix List Syntax*

Command	Results
ip prefix-list <name> permit|deny <cond>	Inserts the line at the end of the prefix list. The line is automatically numbered.
no ip prefix-list <name> seq <seq#> …	Deletes the specified line from the prefix list.
ip prefix-list <name> seq <seq#> …	Inserts the specified line at the desired insertion point in the prefix list. Cannot be used to overwrite an existing line; the existing line has to be deleted first.
ip prefix-list <name> description <line>	Assigns description to the prefix list.

Table 7-9 *IP Prefix List Conditions*

Command	Results
ip prefix-list <name> permit|deny <ip prefix>/<prefix-length>	Matches the specified prefix
ip prefix-list <name> permit|deny <ip prefix>/<prefix-length> ge <pfx-len>	Matches all routes that fall within the specified IP address space and have subnet masks longer or equal (in number of prefix bits) than the specified prefix length
ip prefix-list <name> permit|deny <ip prefix>/<prefix-length> le <pfx-len>	Matches all routes that fall within the specified IP address space and have subnet masks shorter than or equal to the specified prefix length
ip prefix-list <name> permit|deny <ip prefix>/<prefix-length> ge <min-len> le <max-len>	Matches all routes that fall within the specified IP address space and have subnet masks lengths between min-len and max-len (inclusive)

NOTE   Prefix lists are implemented in IOS 11.3 and above in all IOS versions that include BGP support. However, they are not officially documented even in the IOS 12.0 release.

To use the prefix list in place of the IP access list to filter EIGRP routing updates, you have to use the slightly modified syntax of the **distribute-list** statement, as documented in Table 7-10.

Table 7-10 *Configuring EIGRP Route Filters*

Router Configuration Command	Results
distribute-list prefix <prefix-list> in	Applies specified prefix list to all updates received from all neighbors.
distribute-list prefix <prefix-list> in <interface>	Applies specified prefix list to all updates received through specified interface.
distribute-list prefix <prefix-list> out	Specified prefix list is applied to all updates sent.
distribute-list prefix <prefix-list> out <interface>	Specified prefix list is applied to all updates sent through specified interface.
distribute-list prefix <prefix-list> out <routing-process>	Specified prefix list is applied to all routes received through redistribution from specified routing process before these routes are stored in EIGRP topology database.

To illustrate the versatility of the prefix lists, compare the route filter on the DUAL-Mart core router as implemented with a prefix list (Example 7-3) with the same filter implemented with an IP access list (Example 7-1).

Example 7-3 *Route Filter Implemented with a Prefix List*

```
ip prefix-list NoRegPrefix description Outbound filter toward regional distribution
  routers
ip prefix-list NoRegPrefix seq 5 permit 10.0.0.0/8
ip prefix-list NoRegPrefix seq 10 permit 10.0.0.0/8 ge 24 le 25
```

Case Study—Network Meltdown after Frame Relay Failure

For more information on this case study, please visit www.ciscopress.com/eigrp.

DUAL-Mart engineers implemented proper routing policies on the core routers and wanted to validate their concept in a series of tests. The initial test went pretty well; correct routes were established, full connectivity was retained after the ISDN dial-backup was activated, and the remote office router properly disconnected the ISDN call when the Frame Relay connectivity was reestablished.

Encouraged by the early results, the engineers continued the testing by simulating a distribution layer node failure. They simply shut down the Frame Relay interface of the DR-1 router. ISDN calls from all the remote offices in region 1 to the central access server were established, and all connectivity checks proved that the routing was working correctly. It seemed that the new network design was optimal until someone discovered that every router in the whole network carries all routes toward the remote offices.

Exercise 7-3

Using the core router configuration from Figure 7-9 and distribution-layer router configuration from Figure 6-18 in Chapter 6, figure out why every router in the DUAL-Mart network carried routes to ISDN-connected remote offices.

Based on their previous experiences with EIGRP and DUAL (see "Remote Office PVC Failure" in Chapter 5), the engineers felt that these new very specific routes could present a potential network meltdown trigger. However, some of the engineers thought that the extra routes carried by all the routers were cosmetically displeasing because the ISDN routes would be superseded by better routes before ISDN connection would be torn down; ISDN call disconnect would therefore not trigger the DUAL event. Unfortunately, they were proved wrong. When the distribution-layer Frame Relay connection was reestablished and ISDN calls from remote offices were disconnected, the DUAL-Mart network experienced a series of Stuck-in-Active events, nearly causing a complete network meltdown.

Exercise 7-4

Using results from Exercise 7-3, figure out why the ISDN route to RO-11 on DR-2 and RO-21 was not superseded by a better route to RO-11 when the Frame Relay interface on DR-1 was enabled. Router names are defined in the network diagram in Figure 7-2.

Exercise 7-5

Continuing from Exercise 7-4, simulate the EIGRP events in the DUAL-Mart network after the ISDN dial-up connection is disconnected by the RO-11. Use results from "Remote Office PVC Failure" in Chapter 5, which discusses diffusing computation following a PVC failure to the remote office router as the basis for your analysis.

Luckily for the DUAL-Mart engineers, the final fix they had to apply in their network was extremely easy. The only additional design rule they had to incorporate was as follows:

• Announce individual remote office routes reachable over ISDN dial-backup to only the distribution layer router to which the remote office is normally connected.

Implementing this design rule placed a large configuration and maintenance burden on the DUAL-Mart engineers because the core routers had to contain a number of different outbound filters (one for each region). By a simple twist (filtering the routers on the inbound interface in the distribution layer routers), the whole design became simple and clear:

- Core routers use a static route to Null 0 interface to guarantee that the route to 10.0.0.0/8 will always be reachable.

- Core routers announce only 10.0.0.0/8 and routes to remote offices reachable over ISDN dial backup to the distribution layer routers.

- Distribution layer routers accept only routes for remote offices in their region from the core routers.

The relevant portions of the distribution-layer router configuration are shown in Example 7-4.

Example 7-4 *Distribution-Layer Router Configuration*

```
router eigrp 42
 network 10.0.0.0
 distribute-list prefix MyRegionOnly in Serial0.1
 distribute-list prefix MyRegionOnly in Serial0.2
 !
ip prefix-list MyRegionOnly seq 5 permit 10.0.0.0/8
ip prefix-list MyRegionOnly seq 10 permit 10.1.0.0/16 ge 24
```

Exercise 7-6

Simulate the EIGRP behavior that follows ISDN link disconnect in DUAL-Mart's network with the modified design rules.

Summary

EIGRP offers a rich set of route filters due to its close proximity to distance-vector protocols. The route filters can be applied either globally or on a per-interface basis and can affect inbound or outbound routing updates.

Route filters can be used as a security mechanism to increase the reliability of routing information exchange; they are also versatile scalability tools because every route filter establishes an EIGRP query boundary. The router establishes a query boundary where the inbound filter is deployed or one hop beyond the router where the outbound filter is deployed.

EIGRP supports both simple route filters based on IP access lists where you can filter routing information based on network number, but not on the subnet mask, as well as prefix lists where the filter can be specified in terms of IP prefix and the subnet mask length. Usage of extended IP access lists to facilitate IP subnet mask route filtering was not discussed because this use of extended IP access lists was made obsolete by the introduction of the prefix lists.

CHAPTER 8

Default Routes

In this chapter, you see how IOS implements default IP routing and the options you have for transporting default routes in EIGRP. The chapter concludes with a case study illustrating how the extensive use of default routes can introduce query boundaries in a network with no hierarchical addressing scheme.

Chapter 6, "EIGRP Route Summarization," and Chapter 7, "Route Filters," gave you powerful EIGRP scalability tools that have a single common drawback; they can usually be applied only in networks with a good, carefully thought-out IP addressing scheme. In networks that historically have had no hierarchical IP address structure, a different approach to network layering can be used:

- Central (core) routers know every possible route in the network.
- Remote (access) routes know only the routes in their neighborhood and a route toward the core of the network (default route).

The same layering approach can be applied recursively resulting in a multilayer hierarchy where the following rules apply:

- Routers in layer 1 (access layer) know only their local routes and the default route toward the next layer.
- Routers in layer N know all routes from layer-N-1 routers and the layer-N routers connected to them as well as the default route toward layer N+1.

When this approach is put to use in an enterprise network connected to the Internet, the structure looks similar to the one in Figure 8-1.

As you can see in Figure 8-1, the multilayer hierarchical structure is also used within the Internet and extends all the way down from the core Internet routers that carry all the known routes in the Internet to the enterprise access router, which carries only its own subnet routes and a default route toward the enterprise distribution layer.

Figure 8-1 *Multilayer Structure in an Enterprise Network Connected to the Internet*

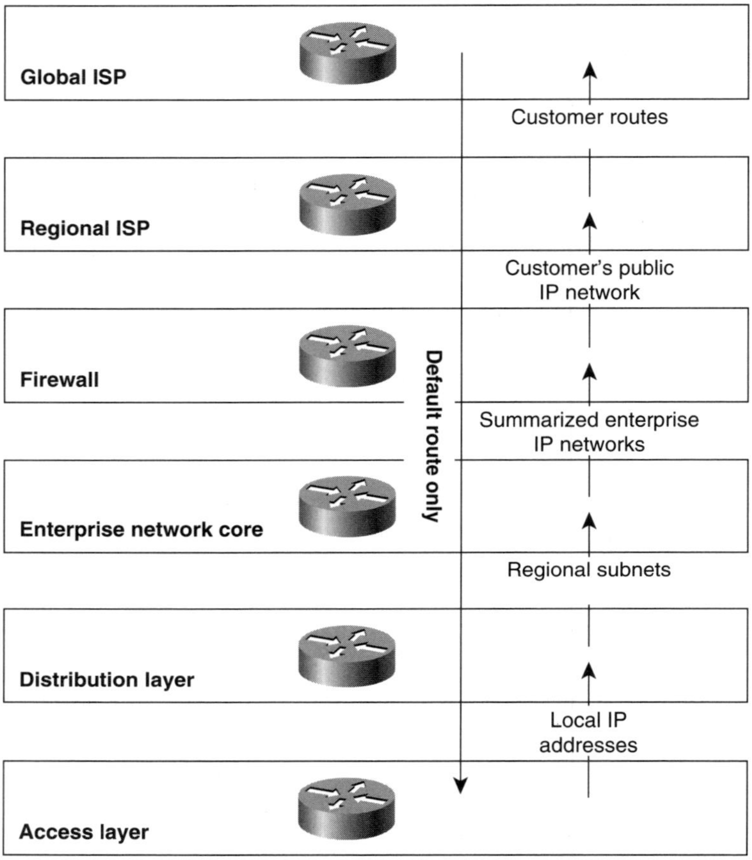

IP Default Routing and IOS Specifics

Every modern IP router follows the *classless* IP routing model that can be described using a simple set of rules:

- For every packet, find the longest matching prefix for the destination address in the routing table.
- Drop packets where you cannot find any matching prefixes.

Using this model, it's easy to understand why the route 0.0.0.0/0 is also called a default route:

- Whenever another route matching the destination address in the routed IP packet exists in the routing table, the other route is used because no route has a shorter prefix than the default route.

- If there is no other matching route, the default route is always used because it matches every destination IP address.

NOTE   Based on these findings, you'd assume that IP default routing is a straightforward mechanism—and you'd be wrong. To complicate matters, IOS contains several features that interfere with this model: *classful versus classless* routing, *default candidates*, and the *gateway of last resort*.

Classful and Truly Classless Routing in IOS

IOS has routed IP packets following the *longest prefix match* rule since IOS version 9.1. The difference between truly classless and classful routing in IOS lies in the way supernet routes (including the default route) are used for subnets of known networks:

- In the classless mode, the IOS strictly follows the classless routing model outlined in "IP Default Routing and IOS Specifics" in this chapter.

- In the classful mode, IOS does not use the supernet routes for unknown subnets of known networks; whenever a single subnet of a major IP network appears in the IP routing table, the supernet routes (including the default route) are not used for other subnets of the same network.

You could also simulate the classful behavior of IOS by assuming that IOS installs a hidden summary route pointing to Null 0 for every major network as soon as the first subnet of that network appears in the routing table. The hidden summary route prevents the supernet routes from being used because it is always the best matching prefix for all unknown subnets in that network.

The classful versus classless behavior is configured using the **ip classless** command as shown in Table 8-1.

Table 8-1   *The **ip classless** Command*

Command	Results
ip classless	Configures true classless routing. Default in IOS 11.3 and above.
no ip classless	Partial classless routing is enabled. Supernet routes are not used for unknown subnets of networks where some subnets are known in the routing table. Default for all IOS versions up to 11.2.

Default Candidates and Gateways of Last Resort

Further deviations from the standard IP classless routing model are the *default candidate routes* and associated gateways of last resort. Several routes in the IP routing table can be marked as the default candidates, meaning that they mark the exit from the local routing environment toward another layer that has more routing information. The default candidates are not used as default routes themselves; IOS evaluates all default candidates and chooses the one with minimum administrative distance and minimum routing metric as the best default candidate. The next hop router of the best default candidate becomes the gateway of last resort.

NOTE   The default route is considered to be just another default candidate in IOS. Whenever a better default candidate is found in the routing table, the default route is ignored (deviating from the classless routing model) and another gateway of last resort is used to forward packets to unknown destinations, as shown in Example 8-1.

Example 8-1   *Sample **show ip route** Printout*

```
DR-1#show ip route
Gateway of last resort is 10.100.4.100 to network 10.0.0.0

  *   10.0.0.0/8 is variably subnetted, 8 subnets, 3 masks
D        10.1.1.0/24 [90/40537600] via 10.1.100.1, Serial0
D*       10.0.0.0/8 [90/11535872] via 10.100.4.100, Serial0.2
D        10.1.0.0/16 is a summary, Null0
C        10.1.0.0/24 is directly connected, Ethernet0
C        10.100.4.0/24 is directly connected, Serial0.2
C        10.100.1.0/24 is directly connected, Serial0.1
C        10.1.100.0/24 is directly connected, Serial0
D        10.210.0.0/16 [90/41024000] via 10.1.100.1, Serial0
D*EX 0.0.0.0/0 [170/166656000] via 10.1.100.1, Serial0
```

The default candidates can be configured locally on the router using the **ip default-network** command or learned via a routing protocol that supports default candidates—currently, the only two routing protocols that support them are IGRP and EIGRP.

The **ip default-network** command works in several different ways, as documented in Table 8-2.

Table 8-2   *The **ip default-network** Command*

Command	Results
ip default-network <major-network> for connected networks	Marks the network as default candidate in the IP routing table. Starts redistributing the network in all IGRP and EIGRP processes. Marks the network in the EIGRP topology database with default candidate flag.
ip default-network <major-network> for nonconnected networks	Marks the network as default candidate in the IP routing table. If the network is already in EIGRP topology database, marks the network with default candidate flag. Takes no further actions to insert the network into EIGRP topology database.
ip default-network <subnet>	Equivalent to **ip route <major-network> <mask> <subnet>**. Inserts the summary route for the major network into which the subnet belongs in the routing table.

Monitoring Default Candidates

The routes that are default candidates are marked with an asterisk in the main routing table (as seen in Example 8-2). They also carry an *exterior flag* that can be observed in the EIGRP topology database by using the **show ip eigrp topology <network> <mask>** command (see Example 8-3).

NOTE   The asterisk in the routing table printout has a double meaning because it is also used for marking the currently used process switched path when a router has multiple equal-cost paths to the same destination.

Example 8-2   *IP Routing Table with Several Default Candidates*

```
RO-11#show ip route
Codes: C - connected, S - static, D - EIGRP,
       EX - EIGRP external, * - candidate default

Gateway of last resort is 10.1.100.100 to network 10.0.0.0

    10.0.0.0/8 is variably subnetted, 7 subnets, 3 masks
```

continues

Example 8-2 *IP Routing Table with Several Default Candidates (Continued)*

```
D*       10.0.0.0/8 [90/42048000] via 10.1.100.100, 00:00:58, Serial0.1
C        10.1.1.0/24 is directly connected, Ethernet0
D        10.1.0.0/16 [90/40537600] via 10.1.100.100, 00:07:56, Serial0.1
D        10.100.4.0/24 [90/41536000] via 10.1.100.100, 00:07:56, Serial0.1
D        10.100.1.0/24 [90/41024000] via 10.1.100.100, 00:07:56, Serial0.1
C        10.1.100.0/24 is directly connected, Serial0.1
C        10.210.0.0/16 is directly connected, Serial2.22
D*EX 0.0.0.0/0 [170/166144000] via 10.210.0.2, 00:00:58, Serial2.22
```

Example 8-3 *EIGRP Topology Database Entry with Default Candidate Marker Set*

```
RO-11#show ip eigrp topology 10.0.0.0
IP-EIGRP topology entry for 10.0.0.0/8
  State is Passive, Query origin flag is 1, 1 Successor(s), FD is 42048000
  Routing Descriptor Blocks:
  10.1.100.100 (Serial0.1), from 10.1.100.100, Send flag is 0x0
      Composite metric is (42048000/11535872), Route is Internal
      Vector metric:
        Minimum bandwidth is 64 Kbit
        Total delay is 80000 microseconds
        Reliability is 255/255
        Load is 1/255
        Minimum MTU is 1500
        Hop count is 2
      Exterior flag is set
```

Default Routes and Default Candidates in EIGRP

EIGRP supports the IP default route (0.0.0.0/0) as well as candidate default routes (*default candidates*). There are, however, several differences between EIGRP and other routing protocols, such as RIP, OSPF, or IS-IS:

- EIGRP is the only classless routing protocol that supports default candidates.

- Although EIGRP can carry the default route (0.0.0.0/0) as a regular IP route, it never generates it in the topology database. Contrary to that, RIP always generates the default route as soon as the router itself has gateway of last resort set. OSPF generates the default route in a stub or NSSA area and IS-IS generates the default route pointing toward the nearest level-2 router on any level-1 router.

- To insert the default route into the EIGRP topology database, you have to manually configure redistribution of the default route. Contrary to that, you can configure the default route announcement in OSPF routing process using the **default-information originate** command.

- Whenever the default route is redistributed into the EIGRP topology database, the default candidate marker is set automatically on the entry in the topology database.

- EIGRP automatically redistributes connected network (or subnets) marked as **ip default-network** into the EIGRP process. No other classless routing protocol performs redistribution behind the scenes; you always have to configure it.

EIGRP enables you to further fine-tune default information. You can selectively erase the default candidate flag from incoming or outgoing routing updates using the commands from Table 8-3.

Table 8-3   *Default Information Propagation Control in EIGRP*

EIGRP Router Configuration Command	Result
default-information in <ACL>	Erases the default candidate marker from all received routes not matched by the IP access list <ACL>
default-information out <ACL>	Erases the default candidate marker from all routes not matched by <ACL> when they are advertised to EIGRP neighbors
no default-information in	Does not accept any default candidate markers
no default-information out	Does not mark any routes as default candidates in outgoing updates. The router itself still uses the default candidate markers on the routes in the EIGRP topology database to select its own gateway of last resort.

EIGRP Default Routes—Design Examples

The variety of EIGRP tools you can use to implement IP default routing in the EIGRP environment makes your life easier, but also more interesting because you have more options from which to choose. In this section, you'll see a few simple designs and their alternate implementations using a variety of EIGRP tools. A more complex design with default route hierarchy is detailed in the case study later in this chapter.

Enterprise Network with a Single Connection to the Internet

In the first example, we'll focus on a simple, yet very common scenario: An enterprise network is connected to the Internet in a single point, similar to the setup shown in Figure 8-2.

WARNING   Your connection to the Internet should always be implemented in a secure way. The least you should do is use the firewall feature set on the router connecting your enterprise network to the Internet. Better yet, you should deploy a full-scale firewall.

Figure 8-2   *Simple Customer Connection to the Internet*

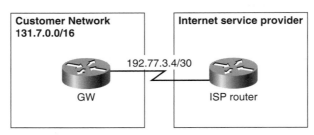

There are two possible ways of configuring the GW router. The first is to declare the external subnet connecting the GW router and the Internet service provider as the default network (see the configuration in Example 8-4). The external subnet is automatically redistributed into EIGRP with the vector metric of the interface connecting the GW router to the ISP. It is also flagged as the default candidate, making all the other routers aware that they should use the next-hop router toward GW as the gateway of last resort.

Example 8-4   *Default Routing toward the Internet Implemented with the **default-network** Command*

```
hostname GW
!
interface serial 0
ip address 192.77.3.6 255.255.255.252
bandwidth 64
!
interface ethernet 0
ip address 131.7.13.5 255.255.255.0
!
router eigrp 42
network 131.7.0.0
!
ip default-network 192.77.3.0
```

The second method is to configure the static default route pointing to the external subnet or to the physical interface itself and manually redistribute the default route into EIGRP (see the configuration in Example 8-5). The redistributed route would normally inherit interface parameters, but you could also overwrite the interface metrics by specifying metrics directly in the **redistribute** command.

Example 8-5 *Default Routing toward the Internet Implemented with the Static Default Route*

```
hostname GW
!
interface serial 0
ip address 192.77.3.6 255.255.255.252
!
interface ethernet 0
ip address 131.7.13.5 255.255.255.0
!
router eigrp 42
network 131.7.0.0
redistribute static metric 64 20000 255 1 1500
!
ip route 0.0.0.0 0.0.0.0 192.77.3.5
```

WARNING   Static routes pointing to an interface were considered to be static in old IOS versions; then the IOS was changed to consider them *connected* (recent IOS versions up to and including IOS 11.2). The latest IOS versions again treat the static routes pointing to an interface as *static* (IOS 11.3 and 12.0). Configurations relying on static routes pointing toward physical interfaces could break when you upgrade your router from IOS 11.2 (or any prior version) to 11.3 or 12.0.

Both alternatives are almost identical, with a few minor differences:

- The EIGRP vector metric of the default route can be better controlled in the second setup because you can control the redistribution of the default route into the EIGRP process. (In the first setup, the redistribution is automatic and you cannot configure or tune it.)

- The second setup works even when the IP subnet on the link between the GW router and the ISP belongs to the customer's address space.

Enterprise Network with Multiple Connections to the Internet

A multihomed customer connection to the Internet does not represent any additional burden on the EIGRP side; two gateway routers (see Figure 8-3) are configured in exactly the same way as the gateway router in "Enterprise Network with a Single Connection to the Internet" earlier in this chapter.

It's important, however, to fine-tune the EIGRP metrics of the default candidates. If they are implemented correctly, all the routers in the network choose the better exit point. The exit point might always be the same if the links to the Internet have different link speeds (for example, primary and backup links to the Internet). If the links to the Internet have approximately the same speed, routers closer to one of the interconnection points use that interconnection point resulting in proper load sharing between the interconnection points.

Figure 8-3 *Multihomed Customer Connection to the Internet*

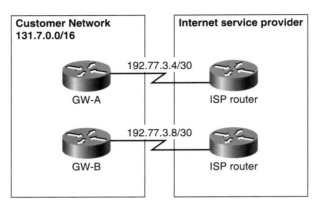

NOTE This design addresses only the requirements of the outgoing traffic (traffic sent from the enterprise network toward the Internet). Assuring proper return traffic flow is a much harder task requiring careful design on the ISP end.

Case Study—GreatCoals Network

For more information on this case study, please visit www.ciscopress.com/eigrp.

GreatCoals mining corporation (see also "Case Study—Connectivity Loss Following Private IP Address Deployment" in Chapter 6 for more information on the company) has evolved into a multinational corporation with operations in the United States and several foreign countries with sales offices throughout the world. Its network grew as the company expanded, but no real network design was ever put in place. It's already introduced some hierarchy in the network, mainly to reduce WAN costs. Typical parts of the current network are schematically represented in Figure 8-4.

Although GreatCoals never did a real network design, it nonetheless followed a set of loose rules:

- The core of the network is implemented with a 7576 fully redundant router. Corporate-wide servers connect directly the LAN interfaces of this router, and all international links terminate on it. All links toward the regional concentration sites also terminate on the same router.

- Sales offices in countries where GreatCoals has only a sales presence link to the central 7576 with low-speed Frame Relay connections, with the typical Committed Information Rate (CIR) being 32 kbps.

Figure 8-4   *GreatCoals Network*

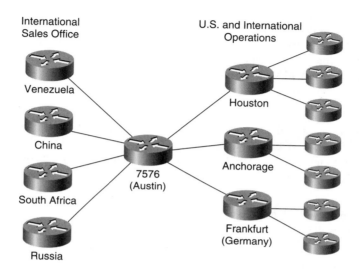

- Central sites in countries where GreatCoals has mining operations link to the central 7576 with high-speed Frame Relay or ATM connections, the typical CIR being over 1 Mbps. All other sites in the country link to the in-country central site, and the international traffic is concentrated there.

- Regional concentration sites in the U.S. serve the same purpose as the foreign in-country central sites. All minor sites in the U.S. connect to the regional concentration sites.

- Major U.S. sites connect directly to the core router with high-speed ATM PVCs.

GreatCoals never had a structured IP addressing scheme. Initially, the company got a class-B address (131.7.0.0/16) that was subnetted using 8-bit subnet masks. Additional public class-C addresses were introduced when the company ran out of address space, and finally, the private IP addresses were used for WAN links and loopback addresses on the routers. In short, the routing tables were a total mess. They used no scalability tools; so all the routers had to carry all the routes of the whole GreatCoals global network. No wonder they started to experience Stuck-in-Active events.

Exercise 8-1

Simulate EIGRP behavior in the GreatCoals network when any WAN connection is lost. Use the results from "Why Did DUAL-Mart Fail?" and "Case Study 2 —Diffused Computation in Hierarchical Networks" in Chapter 5, "Scalability Issues in Large Enterprise Networks," to help you.

When the GreatCoals' engineers tried to improve the scalability of their network, they faced a huge obstacle. Because they had no hierarchical IP addressing scheme, they couldn't use any traditional scalability tools, such as route summarization. The only tool they could use was IP default routing in combination with route filters. They proposed the following design:

- The core router (7576) would have a static default route pointing toward the Internet firewall. This default route would be redistributed into EIGRP.

- The core router would announce only the default route to all the other routers. Route filters would be used to implement the necessary filtering mechanism.

- All the concentration routers would announce only the default route to the remote offices. A floating static route would be installed in the concentration routers to guarantee default route presence even if the WAN link to the core router failed.

- All routers in the network would announce all their routes to their upstream neighbors.

The relevant portions of the core router configuration are shown in Example 8-6. Relevant portions of concentration router configuration are shown in Example 8-7.

Example 8-6 *GreatCoals Network—Core Router Configuration*

```
hostname Core-7576
!
router eigrp 131
 network 131.7.0.0
 network 10.0.0.0
 redistribute static metric 64 20000 255 1 1500
 distribute-list DefaultOnly out
!
! Default route toward the firewall
ip route 0.0.0.0 0.0.0.0 131.7.10.2
!
! Backup default route in case the firewall subnet is gone
ip route 0.0.0.0 0.0.0.0 Null0 250
!
ip access-list standard DefaultOnly
 permit 0.0.0.0
```

Example 8-7 *GreatCoals Network—Concentration Router Configuration*

```
hostname Houston
!
router eigrp 131
 network 131.7.0.0
 network 10.0.0.0
 redistribute static metric 64 20000 255 1 1500
!
! distribute-list applies only to FR links toward remote offices
!
 distribute-list DefaultOnly out Serial 0
!
! Backup default route in case the core default route is gone
ip route 0.0.0.0 0.0.0.0 Null0 250
!
ip access-list standard DefaultOnly
 permit 0.0.0.0
```

Exercise 8-2

When the new network design was implemented, the number of routes in all routers drastically decreased and the number of SIA events was reduced. SIA events still occurred occasionally, though, and the network was still converging slowly. Why? Hint: Focus on low-speed international links. Simulate what happens when a regional WAN connection in Germany fails.

Exercise 8-3

How could you improve the GreatCoals design to solve the low-speed international link bottleneck?

In the end, GreatCoals implemented additional scalability measures proposed by an external consultant. (You could do it yourself after completing Exercises 8-2 and 8-3.) The network worked optimally, until the users got the upper hand again. The international sales offices decided to install their own Internet connections to accelerate the information exchange with local business partners and claimed that they should not receive a default route from the core router because their default route pointed to the Internet.

Exercise 8-4

Assuming that there is good business justification for the requests of international sales offices, is the default route received from the core router really preventing them from connecting to the Internet? Is there any way they could successfully connect to the Internet locally and still use the default route supplied by the core router to reach all corporate networks? Hint: Consider proxy servers or double-NAT.

Summary

Default routes by themselves are not scalability tools; deployment of default routes can never result in reduction of the routing table size. They are, however, an excellent complement to route filters:

- Route filters cannot be used by themselves because their usage would probably result in lost connectivity. Default routes can be deployed to replace the lost information.

- Default routes cannot be used by themselves because they don't reduce the size of the IP routing table. Route filters can be configured to eliminate the routing information made redundant by the default route.

The traditional classless IP routing model supports only a single default route (0.0.0.0/0). IOS implementation gives you the ability to include several default candidates in the network. The next-hop router of the best default candidate becomes the gateway of last resort.

EIGRP support of the default routes (and default candidates) differs slightly from the way all other routing protocols support default routes; the default route is never generated by the routing protocol but has to be configured manually and redistributed into EIGRP. On the other hand, EIGRP gives you better control over default information exchange than any other interior routing protocol.

CHAPTER 9

Integrating EIGRP with Other Enterprise Routing Protocols

In some situations, even the most judicious use of EIGRP scalability tools cannot improve the way a network behaves. Examples of these scenarios (some of them covered in the initial case studies) include the following:

- Logically structured networks with no IP addressing structure or hierarchy
- Large networks with no logical structure (for example, no core/distribution/access layer)
- Networks with an extremely large number of routes (usually as a result of scenario 1)

In all these scenarios, you cannot design a scalable network using only EIGRP. You have to combine the benefits of EIGRP with benefits of other routing protocols to make the network stable and scalable.

EIGRP needs to be integrated with other routing protocols in other situations as well, for example:

- Migration scenarios, where the customer is migrating toward (or away from) EIGRP
- Integration scenarios, where routers or other devices from other vendors that don't support EIGRP have to be integrated in the network

In all these cases, you need to integrate several routing protocols into a seamless whole using an IOS function called *redistribution*. Redistribution enables you to propagate routing information learned via one routing protocol into another routing protocol, filtering and making metric adjustments on the way.

In this chapter, you'll be faced with several case studies that illustrate the various scenarios listed previously. You're encouraged to solve these case studies before reading the solutions at the end of this chapter. The case studies are followed by the in-depth discussions on redistribution in general—how it works, when it's safe to redistribute between various routing protocols, and how you can make redistribution safer. The redistribution theory is augmented by the solutions to the case studies giving you examples from real-life EIGRP networks.

Case Study 1—Large Network with No Addressing Structure

For more information on this case, please visit www.ciscopress.com/eigrp.

DUAL-Mart, one of the large department store chains in the U.S. has gone through a complete reorganization. (See Chapter 5, "Scalability Issues in Large Enterprise Networks," Chapter 6, "EIGRP Route Summarization," and Chapter 7, "Route Filters," for detailed information on how its network evolved over time.) The network design had to follow the business reorganization, resulting in complete reordering of WAN connections:

- Some of the regional offices (hosting distribution-layer routers) were eliminated because it turned out they were not profitable enough.

- A large percentage of the stores were reassigned to a different regional office to make the regions more comparable in size and revenue (and generate equal opportunity for the regional managers—or so the CEO explained).

The reorganization and rewiring of WAN connections (see Figure 9-1) completely destroyed the hierarchical structure of the DUAL-Mart network and the hierarchical mapping of IP addresses into the network structure.

Figure 9-1   *DUAL-Mart Network after Reorganization*

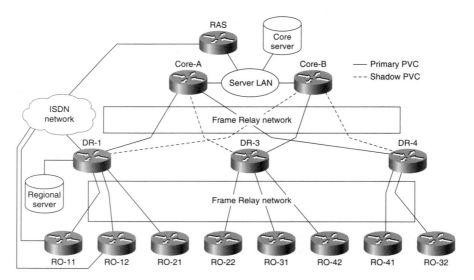

As you can see from Figure 9-1, remote offices belonging to one region (for example, RO-21) were connected to another distribution-layer router, so the distribution layer routers can no longer summarize routes towards the core.

Exercise 9-1

Figure out why the summarization in DUAL-Mart network (as designed in "EIGRP Behavior in Dual-Mart Network after Two-Step Summarization" in Chapter 6 would no longer work. Review the case study in "Dual-Mart: Partial Connectivity over ISDN Backup" in Chapter 7 for initial hints.

Exercise 9-2

How could you maximize the scalability of the DUAL-Mart network even though the distribution-layer router cannot summarize the routes it is advertising into the core any more? Review "Dual-Mart ISDN Dial-Backup Redesign" in Chapter 7 to get ideas from a similar design.

The network designers in the DUAL-Mart network were aware of the solution from Exercise 9-2, but that solution did not solve one of the major instability issues in the network: Whenever a link to a remote office went down, all the other remote offices (and both core routers) were still forced to participate in the diffusing computation. They wanted to make the access part of their network more stable and it looked like the only practical solution to their design requirements was to limit EIGRP to the core of the network and use another routing protocol in the access layer.

Exercise 9-3

Why would a PVC failure to a remote office involve other remote offices in diffusing computation?

Case Study 2—Large Network with No Layering

For more information on this case, please visit www.ciscopress.com/eigrp.

GreatCoals' network has evolved as the organization has grown in the last decade—from small national network to large multilayer global network. Although the IT department tried to insert some layering structure in the network, it was more often than not turned down for budgetary reasons. The end results are obvious; the network has no layered structure (for example, international access routers are connected directly to the main core router) as seen in Figure 9-2. To make matters worse, the network has no hierarchical addressing scheme. On the positive side, the network designers did implement various EIGRP scalability tools (see "Case Study—GreatCoals Network" in Chapter 8, "Default Routes," for more details).

Figure 9-2   *GreatCoals Network*

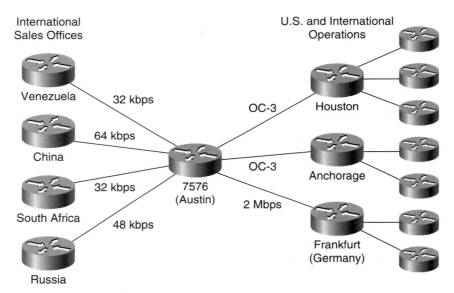

Looking at Figure 9-2, it's obvious that most of the network has the traditional multilayered structure with core (7576), distribution (Houston, Anchorage, Frankfurt) and access layer being clearly defined. The remaining (small) parts of the network (the international sales offices) are not structured; the access-layer routers connect directly into the core router. Although this inconsistency might appear to be only a minor cosmetic issue, it causes significant scalability problems. Every time a route is lost from the GreatCoals' network, each international sales office is involved in the diffusing computation. The GreatCoals' network designers tried every possible tool and concluded that the only solution that would prevent this behavior was to exclude the international sales offices from the EIGRP process.

Case Study 3—Network Migrating from Another Vendor to Cisco

For more information on this case, please visit www.ciscopress.com/eigrp.

MultiCOM is a large national service provider. It decided to use an ATM backbone and a uniform POP design throughout the country. The leased line concentration is done on Cisco 7513 routers, and it chose Ascend for dial-in access due to special features Ascend implemented specifically for it. A sample POP configuration is shown in Figure 9-3.

Figure 9-3 *MultiCOM Sample POP*

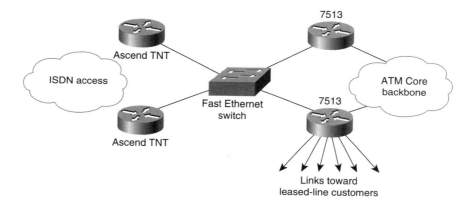

Dial-in access would be given to residential customers (individual PCs) and business customers for dial-backup (in case their leased line goes down). Business customers are also given the ability to dial into another MultiCOM POP in case the POP they normally attach to is lost completely.

MultiCOM decided to implement persistent IP addresses for residential customers; if a PC dials in and requests a specific IP address that was assigned to it a short time ago (based on the username), the request would be granted. Persistent IP addresses work only within a single POP.

NOTE   Having the ability to retain your IP address across dial-in sessions is a really handy feature if you are connected to the Internet via an unreliable dial-up connection. This feature enables you to continue with your FTP transfer even if the connection is lost in the middle of the transfer—assuming your TCP stack does not abort the FTP session immediately. It's really a shame this feature is not supported by all ISPs.

The network designers decided to use EIGRP as the routing protocol in the core, but Ascend routers do not support EIGRP. The only way to integrate the dial-in routers with the core backbone was to run RIPv2 within the POP and propagate the routes learned via RIPv2 into the EIGRP backbone process.

Case Study 4—Service Provider with a Large Number of Routes

For more information on this case, please visit www.ciscopress.com/eigrp.

MultiCOM is very successful, and the number of its leased-line customers has increased from a few tens to several thousand. It never implemented Border Gateway Protocol (BGP) in its core because it never provided transit access to downstream Internet service providers (ISP) and therefore considered BGP to be more trouble than it was worth. BGP is run only where necessary——on the routers connecting MultiCOM to other ISP peers.

As the number of routes in the MultiCOM EIGRP network increased, it experienced more and more instabilities (usually connected with *Stuck-in-Active* events). As a result, several network meltdowns that were extremely hard to fix occurred. It looked like the network grew to a point where it was in an unstable equilibrium; any major core link outage or router failure could bring the whole network down.

MultiCOM engineers tried to increase the SIA timeout, but the situation improved only marginally; the network failed less often, but when it did, it was even harder to recover from the network meltdown situation. At the end, they gave up and brought in an external network designer, who immediately recognized that EIGRP could not carry all the MultiCOM routes any more. The solution the designer proposed was to implement BGP throughout the MultiCOM backbone, migrate customer routes into BGP, and propagate only the BGP next-hop addresses in EIGRP.

NOTE   It's worth noting that there is no fixed upper limit on the number of routes any routing protocol, including EIGRP, can successfully propagate. The upper limit is usually very soft and depends on the network topology, stability, bandwidth available on WAN links, and their utilization.

Redistribution between Routing Processes

All the case studies discussed in this chapter have something in common. All the networks discussed in the case studies require more than one routing protocol to operate properly. Additionally, in all the cases, the information has to be collected in one routing protocol and propagated into the other. To implement routing information propagation in Cisco IOS, you use the *route redistribution* mechanism configured using **redistribute** router configuration command. The **redistribute** command looks quite simple and easy to use (see Example 9-1 for command syntax), but its proper usage raises several design and implementation questions.

Example 9-1   *redistribute Command Syntax*

```
redistribute <source-protocol>
[metric <metric>]
[route-map <route-map>]
[match internal | external ...]
```

Parameters of the **redistribute** command have the meanings defined in Table 9-1:

Table 9-1   *redistribute Command Parameters*

Parameter	Meaning
source-protocol	Protocol from which the routing information is redistributed into the target protocol. Any routing protocol supported by the router can be used (including **static**, **mobile**, or **connected**). If the source-protocol supports AS numbers or process IDs, the AS number or process ID has to be specified.
metric (optional)	The metric of the redistributed route.
route-map (optional)	The route-map used to filter redistributed routes and optionally set attributes of redistributed routes (for example, route tags).
match	Applies only to specific source protocols. For example, when you redistribute from OSPF into EIGRP, you can specify that you only want to redistribute internal OSPF routes.

The design questions usually raised when designing route redistribution include the following:

- Is the information redistributed only in one direction (for example, from the access layer into the core) or in both directions (for example, core network implemented with two routing protocols or two networks being merged)?

- Is the redistribution between any two routing protocols performed only in one point (for example, on a single router) or in many points (for example, several routers to provide redundancy)?

These design questions are hard to answer generically and you'll see some of the benefits and drawbacks of different redistribution designs in the following sections. The implementation questions, however, are easier to answer:

Which information is redistributed from the source into the target routing protocol?

Only the routes from the source routing protocol that the router itself uses for packet forwarding are redistributed into the target routing protocol. In other words, redistribution is done from the routing table, not from the EIGRP topology table or OSPF topology database.

NOTE   All the routes coming from a specific routing protocol and being used for packet forwarding can be displayed with the **show ip route <routing-protocol>** command.

What is the metric of the redistributed information?

EIGRP tries to calculate the proper EIGRP metric to advertise with the redistributed route if possible. EIGRP can calculate the metric for routes imported from other IGRP or EIGRP processes, connected routes redistributed into EIGRP, and for static routes that have a next-hop for which EIGRP metric is computable. For all other redistributed routes, the metric has to be set manually, either using the **metric** option on the **redistribute** command itself or using the **default-metric** router configuration command. Routes for which the EIGRP metric cannot be computed (and no metric is specified manually) are not redistributed into EIGRP.

Are subnets from the source routing protocol redistributed or not?

Redistribution into EIGRP is always classless; all the routes from the source routing protocol that are eligible for redistribution are redistributed regardless of their subnet masks.

Can I filter the information while doing redistribution?

Redistributed information can be filtered using the **route-map** option of the **redistribute** command or it can be filtered with the **distribute-list out** command in the target routing protocol.

NOTE   The **distribute-list out** command usage is extremely counterintuitive. The seemingly *outbound* filter is specified in the *target* routing protocol. The reason for this behavior is that the redistribution is always a pull process; the routing protocol where the **redistribute** command is configured pulls the information from the main IP routing table. Due to this design, it's impossible to specify in one routing protocol what it should export to another routing protocol.

How are the routes received through different routing processes compared to when they try to enter the IP routing table?

The only means of comparing routes received through different routing processes is by comparing the *administrative distances* of the routes. Even if the routing processes are compatible (for example, two EIGRP processes or two OSPF processes), the route metrics are not compared.

NOTE   If two routing processes are carrying the same information with the same administrative distance, the results are unpredictable. Usually, the route appearing last in the topology database (the less stable route) overwrites the previous route that came into the routing table from another routing protocol with the same administrative distance.

NOTE   The results are more predictable if both routing processes are EIGRP processes. The route with the best metric is inserted in the routing table, and it's even possible to load share between routes received through different EIGRP processes if they have the same administrative distance and the same metric.

Various Redistribution Designs and Potential Caveats

When used properly, redistribution can be a powerful tool. In the previous section, you saw how the route redistribution is configured and implemented. In this section, we'll evaluate various redistribution designs—from a simple one-way redistribution at a single point to a complex multipoint two-way redistribution.

One-Point, One-Way Redistribution

One-point, one-way redistribution is always safe from redistribution perspective. However, you must take special care to ensure full connectivity. Consider, for example, the network in Figure 9-4.

Figure 9-4 *RIP to EIGRP Redistribution*

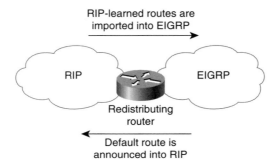

All routes received via RIP are redistributed into EIGRP, giving EIGRP routers full visibility of subnets in the RIP part of the network. RIP-speaking routers, however, do not have any information about subnets in the EIGRP part of the network. To give RIP-speaking routers full connectivity throughout the network, you can use either one of the following two techniques:

- Redistribute EIGRP routes into RIP. This design is discouraged because it's extremely hard to scale to more than one redistribution point. It can also lead to routing loops even in some scenarios where redistribution is only done in one point.

- Announce only the default route into the RIP part of the network. All the traffic originated in the RIP cloud would end up on the redistributing router. That router has full visibility of the network and can decide whether to forward the packets into the EIGRP cloud or drop them because they are addresses to unreachable destinations.

Multipoint One-Way Redistribution

Single-point redistribution is almost never a good design choice because it always results in a single point of failure. Most network designers would rather implement multipoint redistribution, but in many cases, they end up using single-point redistribution due to problems encountered when trying to implement redistribution at several points. The problems you might encounter if you do naïve redistribution at several points might range from suboptimal routing (best case) to constant network instabilities or routing loops (worst case).

The suboptimal routing in multipoint one-way redistribution can result from the difference in administrative distances. Consider, for example, the network in Figure 9-5.

Figure 9-5   *Multipoint Redistribution between RIP and OSPF*

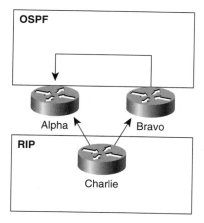

Routers Alpha and Bravo learn a subnet from Charlie. They both redistribute the subnet into OSPF, and the routing information reaches the other router through the OSPF cloud as well. However, the information received through OSPF (for example, information sent to Alpha by Bravo) has better administrative distance than the information received directly from RIP (for example, information received by Alpha from Charlie). Router Alpha thus starts routing packets toward Charlie through Bravo.

NOTE   The situation can get even worse when you redistribute between two OSPF processes because there is inherent delay between information being received and the corresponding route calculation being performed. I've seen several networks endlessly oscillating between two states, running SPF algorithm every few seconds on every router in the network.

Suboptimal routing or routing oscillation can never happen in networks where you only redistribute information *into* EIGRP due to the difference in administrative distances of internal and external routes. Consider, for example, the network in Figure 9-6 where OSPF has been replaced with EIGRP.

Figure 9-6   *Multipoint RIP to EIGRP Redistribution*

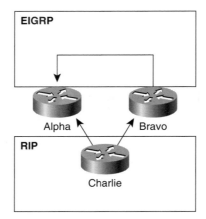

As before, Charlie announces a subnet to both Alpha and Bravo. The default administrative distance of the route is 120 (RIP). When the information gets redistributed into EIGRP, the redistributed route gets the default administrative distance of the external EIGRP route (170) and never supersedes the RIP route when the same route is received through EIGRP.

The only scenario where redistribution into EIGRP might lead to suboptimal routing or even routing instabilities is a multistage EIGRP-to-EIGRP redistribution design, such as the one shown in Figure 9-7.

Figure 9-7   *Multistage EIGRP Redistribution*

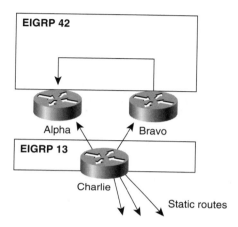

In the network in Figure 9-7, Charlie redistributes static routes into EIGRP process 13. The redistributed routes already have an administrative distance of 170. When these routes get further redistributed into EIGRP process 42, the same routing information appears from two sources (EIGRP 13 and EIGRP 42) with the same administrative distance, resulting in either suboptimal routing or network instability. To alleviate the potential problems, you have to change default EIGRP administrative distances of either EIGRP 13 or EIGRP 42 using the **distance eigrp** command documented in Table 9-2.

Table 9-2   *distance eigrp Command*

Command	Results
distance eigrp <internal> <external>	Sets default distance for internal (default is 90) and external (default is 170) EIGRP routes. Administrative distance of internal routes can be further modified with distance command. Administrative distance of individual external routes cannot be modified.

Multipoint Two-Way Redistribution

Multipoint, two-way redistribution is the hardest to implement and is best avoided in good network designs. Multipoint, two-way redistribution can result in several serious routing symptoms:

- Persistent routing loops, when the metrics between routing processes are not compatible

- Count-to-infinity problems (including long-term network instabilities) when the metrics can be transferred between the routing processes

Fortunately, you only have to follow a very simple principle to resolve the routing instabilities caused by multipoint two-way redistribution. Never announce information originally received from routing process X back into routing process X.

You can implement stable multipoint, two-way redistribution in several ways—all of them relying on filtering mechanisms to achieve stability, from redistributing only internal routes to route filters.

Redistribute Only Internal Routes

The simplest stable implementation of multipoint, two-way redistribution redistributes only internal routes from one routing protocol into the other routing protocol. Consider, for example, the OSPF-to-EIGRP design shown in Figure 9-8.

Figure 9-8 *Stable Two-Way OSPF to EIGRP Redistribution*

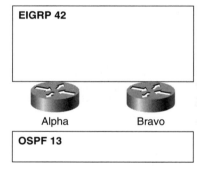

Alpha and Bravo should only redistribute internal OSPF routes into EIGRP and internal EIGRP routes into OSPF. These filters will immediately stop any routing loops because any redistributed information appears as an external route in the target process. The configuration you can use to implement these filters is shown in Example 9-2.

Example 9-2 *Two-Way Redistribution of Internal Routes*

```
hostname Alpha
!
router eigrp 42
redistribute ospf 13 match internal
!
router ospf 13
redistribute eigrp 42 route-map InternalOnly
```

Example 9-2 *Two-Way Redistribution of Internal Routes (Continued)*

```
!
route-map InternalOnly permit 10
match route-type internal
```

Redistribute Routes Using Route Tags

The two-way redistribution design gets slightly more complex when at least one of the routing protocols involved already carries some external routes that have to be redistributed into the other routing protocol. The most efficient filters to use in these designs are *route tags*.

NOTE   Route tags are numbers that can be attached to the route without influencing the route selection. Route tags have no meaning for the routing protocol itself, but can be used in route maps to filter redistributed routes.

To illustrate the use of route tags, consider the network in Figure 9-9 where OSPF already carries external static routes redistributed into OSPF by router Charlie.

Figure 9-9 *Two-Way OSPF to EIGRP Redistribution with External Routes*

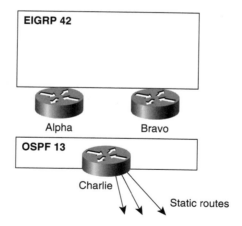

Routers Alpha and Bravo can implement the following filtering approaches:

- Tagging of all routes redistributed from OSPF 13 into EIGRP 42 with a tag of 13

- Tagging of all routes redistributed from EIGRP 42 into OSPF 13 with a tag of 42
- No redistributing of any routes carrying tag 13 from EIGRP 42 into OSPF 13
- No redistributing of any routes carrying tag 42 from OSPF 13 into EIGRP 42

You can implement these rules with the configuration commands in Example 9-3.

Example 9-3 *Two-Way Redistribution with Route Tags*

```
hostname Alpha
!
router eigrp 42
redistribute ospf 13 route-map Ospf13_NoTag42
!
router ospf 13
redistribute eigrp 42 route-map Eigrp42_NoTag13
!
route-map Ospf13_NoTag42 deny 10
match tag 42
!
route-map Ospf13_NoTag42 permit 20
set tag 13
!
route-map Eigrp42_NoTag13 deny 10
match tag 13
!
route-map Eigrp42_NoTag13 permit 20
set tag 42
```

Redistribution Control with Route Filters

Sometimes, you're faced with a network design that requires two-way redistribution, but one of the routing protocols does not support the notion of internal/external routes or route tags (for example, RIP version 1), such as the design in Figure 9-10.

In these scenarios, the only way to safely implement two-way redistribution is to filter redistributed routes based on their IP prefix. These designs are usually hard to maintain (because the list of prefixes to be redistributed can change over time) and are therefore best avoided. You should always consider one-way redistribution with a default route (see "Multipoint One-Way Redistribution" in this chapter) as a preferred approach.

Figure 9-10 *Two-Way RIP to EIGRP Redistribution*

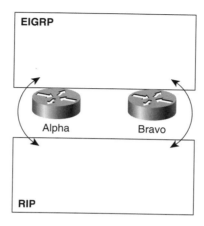

Case Study Solutions

Armed with the theoretical understanding of IP redistribution, let's solve the case studies presented at the beginning of this chapter. Each case study solution begins with a recapitulation of the routing problem and concludes with router configuration examples that solve the specified problem.

Case Study 1 Solution—Integrating RIP with EIGRP

DUAL-Mart network (redrawn in Figure 9-11) has no hierarchical addressing structure; EIGRP summarization is therefore impossible. The best scalability can be achieved with default routes; every layer in the network announces only the default route to the underlying layer. It also receives full routing information from the underlying layer and propagates that routing information to the layer above (see Chapter 8 for a similar design).

Figure 9-11 *DUAL-Mart Network*

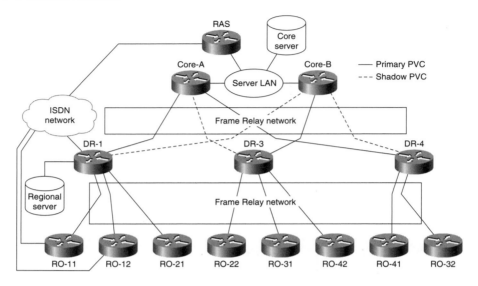

Exercise 9-4

Evaluate how EIGRP would perform in the network in Figure 9-11 when a link to a remote office is lost. Also, evaluate what happens when a link between distribution and core router is lost.

DUAL-Mart engineers found out that a large number of routers are involved in a diffusing computation following a link failure regardless of the number of scalability tools used in their network. Because of this, they decided to reduce the EIGRP diameter to the core and distribution-layer routers.

RIPv2 is introduced in the distribution-layer routers and in the RAS router. These routers announce only the default route via RIPv2 to the remote offices and collect subnet information from the remote offices. The information collected via RIPv2 is then propagated to the EIGRP process. Sample configuration of a distribution-layer router (DR1) is shown in Example 9-4.

Example 9-4 *Configuration of a Distribution-Layer Router*

```
hostname DR1
!
! - RIP version 2 is forced
! - only default route is sent to RIP neighbors
! - do not run RIP on subinterfaces toward core
router rip
network 10.0.0.0
passive-interface Serial0.1
passive-interface Serial0.2
version 2
distribute-list DefaultOnly out
!
! - RIP routes are redistributed into EIGRP
! - redistribution metric BW=64 kbps, delay=20000
! - do not run EIGRP on links toward remote offices
router eigrp 42
network 10.0.0.0
redistribute rip metric 64 2000 1 255 1500
passive-interface Serial0
!
ip access-list standard DefaultOnly
permit 0.0.0.0
!
! - floating static route in case the link to core is lost
ip route 0.0.0.0 0.0.0.0 null 0 250
```

It's interesting to note that no EIGRP scalability tools are deployed on the distribution-layer router. The addressing scheme is random, and thus summarization cannot be used. Route filters cannot be used because the core routers need to know paths to every subnet in the network.

Core router configuration uses EIGRP route filters and default routes to enhance EIGRP scalability as seen in Example 9-5.

Example 9-5 *DUAL-Mart Core Router Configuration*

```
hostname Core-A
!
! - use filters only on links toward distribution-layer routers
! - other core router needs unfiltered information
! - static routes are redistributed to ensure default is announced
router eigrp 42
network 10.0.0.0
redistribute static metric 64 2000 1 255 1500
distribute-list DefaultOnly out serial 0.1
distribute-list DefaultOnly out serial 0.2
!
ip access-list standard DefaultOnly
```

continues

Example 9-5   *DUAL-Mart Core Router Configuration (Continued)*

```
permit 0.0.0.0
!
! - default points to null 0
! - alternatively it could point to the Internet gateway
ip route 0.0.0.0 0.0.0.0 null 0
```

Exercise 9-5

Given the network diagram in Figure 9-11 and router configurations in Example 9-4 and Example 9-5, evaluate how EIGRP performs in the redesigned DUAL-Mart network. Focus particularly on diffusing computation diameter. Compare the behavior of the redesigned network with results from Exercise 9-4.

Case Study 2 Solution—Multiple EIGRP Processes

GreatCoals has built a network that lacks necessary hierarchy in a single point. High-speed links to concentration sites are mixed with low-speed international links on the core router (see Figure 9-12).

Figure 9-12   *GreatCoals Network Structure*

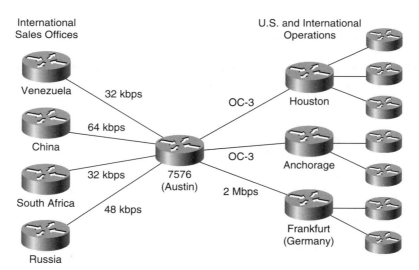

Lack of logical hierarchy, combined with the lack of a hierarchical IP addressing scheme, leads to amazing result; with whatever scalability approach used (refer to Chapter 8) every time a single link fails, all international sales offices are involved in diffused computation.

Exercise 9-6

Verify the validity of the previous statement.

GreatCoals designers decided to split their network into two EIGRP processes: One process runs between only the core router and international offices. The other process runs in the rest of the network. The initial idea was to simply redistribute information between these two EIGRP processes on the core router to retain full connectivity (see Example 9-6 for corresponding router configuration).

Example 9-6   *GreatCoals Core Router Configuration*

```
hostname Core7576
!
! old EIGRP process is run in the major parts of the network
router eigrp 131
network 131.7.0.0
redistribute eigrp 132
!
! another EIGRP process is run on low-speed international links
router eigrp 132
network 10.0.0.0
redistribute eigrp 131
```

To their astonishment, the GreatCoals' engineers found out that the diffusing computation diameter has not decreased; it looked like the diffused computation would jump over the EIGRP process boundaries.

Query Boundaries in Multiple EIGRP Processes

The behavior experienced in GreatCoals' network should come as no big surprise because all information was blindly redistributed between two EIGRP processes. All subnets from one EIGRP process also appeared in the topology table of the other EIGRP process. Subsequently, when the subnet was lost in the first process, the EIGRP diffusing computation ran and the routers concluded that the subnet was unreachable. This information was propagated into the second EIGRP process (via redistribution) where it triggered another diffused computation. Detailed behavior on the Core7576 router is also illustrated with the debugging printouts in Example 9-7.

Example 9-7 *Diffused Computation Started by Redistributed Route Loss*

```
core7576#debug eigrp fsm
Query received in EIGRP process 131
DUAL: dual_rcvquery():131.7.13.0/24 via 131.7.1.5 metric 4294967295/
4294967295, RD is 2297856
DUAL: Find FS for dest 131.7.13.0/24. FD is 2297856, RD is 2297856
DUAL:        131.7.1.5 metric 4294967295/4294967295 not found
Route lost in EIGRP process 131, update sent to EIGRP process 132
DUAL: dual_rcvupdate(): 131.7.13.0/24 via Redistributed metric 4294967295
/4294967295
DUAL: Find FS for dest 131.7.13.0/24. FD is 2297856, RD is 2297856
DUAL:        0.0.0.0 metric 4294967295/4294967295 not found
Route becomes active in the second EIGRP process, query is propagated into the second
process
DUAL: Dest 131.7.13.0/24 entering active state.
DUAL: Set reply-status table. Count is 1.
DUAL: Not doing split horizon
```

The conclusion of GreatCoals' engineers was wrong. Queries do not jump over EIGRP process boundaries. It was the uncontrolled redistribution of routing information between EIGRP processes that caused the spread of diffused computations all over the network.

NOTE   Two-way redistribution between several EIGRP processes is complex and almost never improves the network stability. Whenever you are forced to use several EIGRP processes in the network to limit the query diameter, make sure that you redistribute routes in only one direction.

As it turned out, the design fix for GreatCoals' network was simple enough. Redistribution was removed altogether, and the core router announced a default route into both EIGRP processes. The new core router configuration is shown in Example 9-8.

Example 9-8 *GreatCoals Core Router Configuration*

```
hostname Core7576
!
! old EIGRP process is run in the major parts of the network
router eigrp 131
network 131.7.0.0
redistribute static route-map DefaultOnly
!
! another EIGRP process is run on low-speed international links
router eigrp 132
network 10.0.0.0
redistribute static route-map DefaultOnly
```

Example 9-8 *GreatCoals Core Router Configuration (Continued)*

```
!
ip route 0.0.0.0 0.0.0.0 null 0
!
route-map DefaultOnly permit 10
match ip address DefaultRoute
!
ip access-list standard DefaultRoute
permit 0.0.0.0
```

Case Study 3 Solution—RIPv2 and EIGRP Integration with Filters

MultiCOM, a national Internet service provider, built its POPs with Cisco core routers and Ascend dial-in routers. The network designers decided to use EIGRP over the core ATM backbone and they had to deploy RIPv2 between Ascend and Cisco routers. They decided to allow the customers to retain their IP addresses across several dial-in sessions (persistent IP addresses).

To implement persistent IP addresses, all dial-in host routes must be propagated inside the POP via RIPv2 to ensure that all routers within the POP know to which dial-in router the user is currently connected. These routes do not have to be propagated into EIGRP because they fall within the address range of the POP. Only a summary route for all dial-in routes must be announced.

Business customer routes must be propagated into the EIGRP process because the customer IP addresses are not hierarchically structured.

Initial routing implementation was extremely simple; routes learned via RIPv2 were redistributed into EIGRP and summarized before being sent over the ATM interface, as shown in Example 9-9.

Example 9-9 *MultiCOM POP Router Configuration*

```
hostname SanJose_Rtr1
!
! summarize intra-POP routes on outgoing ATM interface
interface atm 0/0
ip summary-address eigrp 133 133.7.16.0 255.255.240.0
!
! run RIP in network 133.7.0.0 but only on Ethernet
router rip
version 2
network 133.17.0.0
passive-interface default
no passive-interface FastEthernet 1/0
!
! run EIGRP in whole network 133.7.0.0
! redistribute RIP routes into EIGRP
```

continues

Example 9-9 *MultiCOM POP Router Configuration (Continued)*

```
router eigrp 133
network 133.7.0.0
redistribute rip metric 64 2000 1 255 1500
```

NOTE   The **passive-interface default** command is implemented in IOS 12.0 and gives you a nice way of configuring routing processes that are supposed to run over a small number of interfaces. In previous IOS versions, you had to configure all the other interfaces as passive.

The POP routing implementation shown in Example 9-9 exhibited an interesting behavior (as you might suspect after reading "Query Boundaries in Multiple EIGRP Processes" in this chapter). Every time a dial-in user disconnected, all core routers across the ATM backbone got involved in a diffusing computation.

All the host routes learned via RIP got into the EIGRP topology database due to uncontrolled redistribution. Although they were never propagated out of the POP router, the POP router started diffused computation in EIGRP every time the host route disappeared from RIP and subsequently from the EIGRP topology database.

To make the network stable, MultiCOM designers had to make the redistribution slightly more complex:

- Summary route for dial-in IP address range was statically configured on both POP routers and redistributed into EIGRP. More specific routes toward individual dial-in customers were received via RIP but never propagated into the EIGRP topology database.

- Business customer routes were redistributed from RIPv2 into EIGRP based on their subnet masks; any route less specific than /28 was redistributed into EIGRP.

The resulting configuration for one of the routers in the San Jose POP is shown in Example 9-10.

Example 9-10 *Improved MultiCOM POP Router Configuration*

```
hostname SanJose_Rtr1
!
! run RIP in network 133.7.0.0 but only on Ethernet
!
router rip
version 2
network 133.17.0.0
passive-interface default
no passive-interface FastEthernet 1/0
!
! run EIGRP in whole network 133.7.0.0
! redistribute RIP routes for business customers into EIGRP
```

Example 9-10 *Improved MultiCOM POP Router Configuration (Continued)*

```
! redistribute static summaries and business customer routes into EIGRP
!
router eigrp 133
network 133.7.0.0
redistribute rip metric 64 2000 1 255 1500
redistribute static
distribute-list prefix NoDialIn out rip
!
ip route 133.7.16.0 255.255.240.0 null 0
!
ip prefix-list NoDialIn permit 0.0.0.0/0 le 27
```

Case Study 4 Solution—BGP and EIGRP Integration

The last case study is not really an EIGRP redistribution case study, but more of an illustration of how to use BGP in combination with EIGRP to improve network stability.

All internal routing protocols have a limit on the number of routes they can carry—usually the upper limit is a few thousand routes. Although the exact number varies based on implementation details and overall network stability. The upper limit is not usually reached in enterprise networks that have a hierarchical addressing scheme due to routing table reduction achievable through summarization. The upper limit is easily reached in large enterprise networks with random address assignments and in the service provider networks. In these networks, BGP used in combination with an interior routing protocol can overcome that limit.

NOTE   So far, I have seen three scenarios where an enterprise customer would want to implement BGP:

- Security or routing policy reasons (for example, departments not trusting each other)

- Address assignment problems (for example random addresses that cannot be summarized)

- Implementation of new IOS features that require BGP (for example, IP Quality of Service or TAG-VPN)

In the MultiCOM network, migration from the EIGRP-only network toward the EIGRP/ BGP network turned out to be simple. All routes previously redistributed into EIGRP were redistributed into BGP, and EIGRP was run only over the ATM backbone to give all core routers optimum connectivity to all directly connected subnets of all other core routers. Configuration of the San Jose POP router after the redesign is shown in Example 9-11.

Example 9-11 *San Jose POP Router Configuration after Network Redesign*

```
hostname SanJose_Rtr1
!
! run RIP in network 133.7.0.0 but only on Ethernet
!
router rip
version 2
network 133.17.0.0
passive-interface default
no passive-interface FastEthernet 1/0
!
! run EIGRP in whole network 133.7.0.0
! do not redistribute any routes into EIGRP
!
router eigrp 133
network 133.7.0.0
passive-interface default
no passive-interface FastEthernet 1/0
no passive-interface atm 0/0
!
! redistribute RIP and static routes into BGP
!
router bgp 133
redistribute rip
redistribute static
distribute-list prefix NoDialIn out rip
!
ip route 133.7.16.0 255.255.240.0 null 0
!
ip prefix-list NoDialIn permit 0.0.0.0/0 le 27
```

NOTE   BGP configuration in Example 9-11 is not complete. The BGP part of the router configuration is beyond the scope of this book. Interested readers should refer to the Cisco Press title *Internet Routing Architectures* by Basam Halabi that gives in-depth coverage of BGP.

Summary

EIGRP scalability tools, from address summarization to route filters and default routes cannot make all networks scalable. The exceptions usually include networks without layered logical topology and/or with random IP address assignment. In these cases, the network can sometimes be made scalable by using several routing protocols in the same network; for example, RIP in the access part, EIGRP in the core, and BGP to transport a large number of routes.

Whenever a network design involves several concurrently running routing protocols, the routing information must be at least partially exchanged between them to ensure full connectivity in the overall network. Routing information exchange is implemented with *route redistribution*—a powerful, but also potentially dangerous Cisco IOS feature.

Route redistribution is a complex tool that must be carefully designed and implemented. Improper implementation of route redistribution can result in suboptimal routing, routing loops, or overall routing instability.

One-way redistribution of routing information is easier to implement than two-way redistribution and is therefore the preferred design choice. Multipoint two-way redistribution is best avoided, although some tools (for example, route tags) can make it stable and manageable.

One-way redistribution into EIGRP usually works as expected. The default administrative distances of EIGRP routes have proper values to ensure optimum routing. The amount of information inserted into the EIGRP topology database must be carefully evaluated, however, or the whole redistribution design might not yield any increase in network stability. The information inserted into the EIGRP process must be summarized and filtered before it's redistributed, not after it has already appeared in the EIGRP topology database.

CHAPTER 10

Designing Scalable IPX EIGRP Networks

In the last few chapters, you've seen the issues that can arise when IP EIGRP networks grow too large (Chapter 5, "Scalability Issues in Large Enterprise Networks,"), and several tools can make these networks scalable. Summarization was discussed in Chapter 6, "EIGRP Route Summarization," route filters in Chapter 7, "Route Filters," default routes in Chapter 8, "Default Routes," and route redistribution in Chapter 9, "Integrating EIGRP with Other Enterprise Routing Protocols."

All EIGRP implementations use the same core route calculation mechanism: Diffused Update Algorithm (DUAL). Therefore, it is not surprising that the same scalability issues you saw in IP EIGRP also appear in IPX networks built on EIGRP. Unfortunately, due to both protocol limitations and EIGRP implementation, network designers cannot use the same scalability toolkit as in the IP world. The most notable differences are as follows:

- IPX did not support route summarization (it's called *aggregation* in the IPX world) for a long time. The IPX route aggregation was defined in the Netware Link State Protocol (NLSP) specification. IPX EIGRP was designed several years before Novell started to think about scalable internetworks and consequently does not support summary IPX routes.

- IPX did not support the default route when IPX EIGRP was designed; the IPX default route was also defined later in the NLSP specification. IPX EIGRP can still carry the IPX default route, because the IPX default route is just a special IPX network number. However, it lacks the flexibility from the IP world.

A few more limitations are a consequence of the IOS implementation of IPX routing. There are no IPX route maps and you can't influence IPX administrative distances.

Apart from all these limitations, it's still possible to build large and scalable IPX networks, as you'll see in the case studies at the end of this chapter. The case studies use the tools briefly described in the remainder of the chapter:

- IPX Route Filters
- IPX Default Route
- Controlling Route Redistribution between IPX Routing Protocols

IPX Route Filters

For historical reasons, IPX route filters have different syntaxes for different routing protocols. To configure IPX route filters for RIP, you use the commands from Table 10-1 in interface configuration mode.

Table 10-1 *IPX RIP Route Filter Configuration Commands*

Task	Command (in Interface Configuration Mode)
Filter inbound IPX RIP updates on the interface	**ipx input-network-filter <ACL>**
Filter outbound IPX RIP updates on the interface.	**ipx output-network-filter <ACL>**

To configure IPX route filters for IPX EIGRP or NLSP, you have to use the commands from Table 10-2 in IPX router configuration mode.

Table 10-2 *IPX EIGRP Route Filter Configuration Commands*

Task	Command (in IPX Router Configuration Mode)
Filter inbound IPX EIGRP update	**distribute-list <ACL> in**
Filter inbound IPX EIGRP updates received over the specified interface	**distribute-list <ACL> in <interface>**
Filter outbound IPX EIGRP updates	**distribute-list <ACL> out**
Filter outbound IPX EIGRP updates sent over the specified interface	**distribute-list <ACL> out <interface>**
Filter IPX routes redistributed into IPX EIGRP from another routing process	**distribute-list <ACL> out <protocol>**

NOTE   In older versions of IOS, the commands from Table 10-1 were also used to filter IPX EIGRP routing updates. In recent IOS versions, these commands no longer work for IPX EIGRP.

Similar differences in commands exist for SAP filters. Filter the services received through IPX SAP protocol using commands from Table 10-3 in interface configuration mode. Filter the services received through the IPX EIGRP SAP mechanism or NLSP using commands from Table 10-4 in IPX router configuration mode.

Table 10-3   *IPX SAP Filter Configuration Commands*

Task	Command (in Interface Configuration Mode)
Filter inbound IPX SAP updates received through the interface	**ipx input-sap-filter <ACL>**
Filter outbound IPX SAP updates received through the interface	**ipx output-sap-filter <ACL>**

Table 10-4   *IPX EIGRP SAP Filter Configuration Commands*

Task	Command (in IPX Router Configuration Mode)
Filter all SAP services received through IPX EIGRP	**distribute-sap-list <ACL> in**
Filter SAP services received in IPX EIGRP SAP packets inbound over the specified interface	**distribute-sap-list <ACL> in <interface>**
Filter services in all outbound IPX EIGRP SAP updates	**distribute-sap-list <ACL> out**
Filter services announced in IPX EIGRP SAP packets over the specified interface	**distribute-sap-list <ACL> out <interface>**
Filter services announced through IPX EIGRP SAP and learned from another SAP source (for example, IPX SAP or NLSP)	**distribute-sap-list <ACL> out <protocol>**

IPX Default Routes

The IPX default route is defined by Novell to be IPX network FFFFFFFE (or −2 if you prefer signed decimal over unsigned hex). The IPX default route was defined in the NLSP specification when Novell needed a way of integrating NLSP (which supports IPX route summarization) with IPX RIP (which doesn't support summarized routes). Novell designers envisioned the IPX default route to be used in the following scenarios:

- The network core (or even most of the IPX routers) runs NLSP and carries all the individual and summarized routes.

- The remaining routers run RIP and carry the individual routes (which RIP can transport) plus the default route (to give them full connectivity).

- The default route is originated by every NLSP-speaking router into the RIP domain to attract the traffic from RIP-only routers to the nearest NLSP entry point.

NOTE   It's worth noting that some older IPX implementations do not support the default route and thus cannot work in a network that deploys summarized NLSP routes or the IPX default route.

Generating an IPX default route within a network that runs only IPX EIGRP and RIP is much harder than on a network that runs NLSP. The default route must be generated manually (for example, by using a static route) on the core routers and disseminated by IPX EIGRP and RIP to all the other routers. A sample router configuration of a core router is shown in Example 10-1.

Example 10-1 *Generating IPX Default Route on a Core Router*

```
ipx routing
ipx internal-network ACE001
ipx route default ACE001.0000.0000.0002
```

NOTE   Combining NLSP and EIGRP on the same router does not insert the default route in EIGRP as it would in RIP. The default route must still be declared manually as a static route.

You can use the default route to significantly reduce the size of IPX RIP updates. The interface configuration command **ipx advertise-default-route-only** causes only the default route to be advertised in the RIP updates sent over the specified interface, resulting in decreased bandwidth requirement and CPU usage.

Controlling Route Redistribution between IPX Routing Protocols

IPX route redistribution is simpler, but also less flexible than IP route redistribution. The redistribution is configured using the **redistribute** command, as in the IP world. The redistribution between RIP and IPX EIGRP, RIP and NLSP, and static routes and all routing protocols is automatic (although it can be turned off if necessary). All the other redistributions (for example, IPX EIGRP to NLSP) must be configured manually.

You can always filter routes redistributed between IPX routing protocols using the
distribute-list out command as documented previously in Table 10-2.

IPX routing supports a notion of administrative distances, although it's slightly different
from the IP world:

- Static IPX routes always take precedence over routes received through dynamic
  routing protocols.

- Routes received through dynamic routing protocols always take precedence over
  floating static IPX routes.

- If the same route is received through several different routing protocols, the IPX RIP
  part of the metric is compared, and the NLSP or EIGRP metric is ignored. The route
  with the lower tick/hop value is better.

- When several routes with the same IPX RIP metric are received through different
  routing protocols, IPX EIGRP routes are preferred over NLSP and IPX RIP routes.

Case Study—GreatCoals

For more information on this case study, please visit www.ciscopress.com/eigrp.

GreatCoals mining corporation is a multinational corporation with operations in the United
States and several foreign countries and with sales offices throughout the world. Its network
grew as the company expanded, but no real network design was ever put in place. It's
already introduced some hierarchy in the network, mainly to reduce WAN costs. Typical
parts of the current network are schematically represented in Figure 10-1.

Figure 10-1 *Great Coals Network*

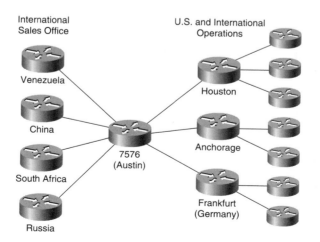

Although GreatCoals never did a real network design, it none-the-less followed a set of loose rules:

- The core of the network is implemented with a 7576 fully redundant router. All international links and all links toward the regional concentration sites terminate on this router.

- Sales offices in countries where GreatCoals has only a sales presence link to the central 7576 with low-speed Frame Relay connections with a typical Committed Information Rate (CIR) being 32 kbps.

- Central sites in countries where GreatCoals has mining operations link to the central 7576 with high-speed Frame Relay or ATM connections with a typical CIR being over 1 Mbps. All other sites in the country link to the in-country central site, and the international traffic is concentrated there as well.

- Regional concentration sites in the United States serve the same purpose as the foreign in-country central sites. All minor sites in the United States connect to the regional concentration sites.

- Major U.S. sites connect directly to the core router with high-speed ATM PVCs.

GreatCoals never had a structured IPX addressing scheme although an IPX numbering plan was used and enforced throughout the company.

NOTE   You'll probably find that all the older IPX networks don't have structured addressing in place. All these networks and their numbering plans were designed well before Novell ever announced the intention to support route aggregation. Proper addressing structure was therefore never an issue when the IPX addressing plan was designed.

The GreatCoals network uses no scalability tools. Therefore, all the routers carry all the IPX routes of the whole GreatCoals global network. It shouldn't come as a surprise that the company started to experience Stuck-in-Active events when the network grew.

Exercise 10-1

Simulate EIGRP behavior in GreatCoals network when any WAN connection is lost. Use results from Chapter 5, "Scalability Issues in Large Enterprise Networks," and Chapter 8, "Default Routes," to help you.

Because IPX EIGRP does not support route aggregation, the only scalability solution that could work in GreatCoals' network is the usage of IPX default routes. This solution was already proven in the IP world (see Chapter 8 for the corresponding IP case study) and network designers decided to mirror the IP solution into the IPX world:

- The core router (7576) has a static IPX default route pointing toward the *null* interface, which effectively instructs the router to drop all traffic for unreachable destinations. This default route is redistributed into EIGRP.

- The core router announces only the default route to all the other routers. Route filters are used to implement the necessary filtering mechanism.

- All the concentration routers announce only the default route to the remote offices. A floating IPX default route is installed in the concentration routers to guarantee default route presence even if the WAN link to the core router fails.

- All routers in the network announce all their routes to their upstream neighbors.

The relevant portions of the core router configuration are shown in Example 10-2. Relevant portions of concentration router configuration are shown in Example 10-3.

Example 10-2 *GreatCoals Network—Core Router Configuration*

```
hostname Core-7576
!
ipx routing
ipx internal-network FFFFFF01
!
ipx router eigrp 131
 network all
 distribute-list DefaultOnly out
!
! Default route to null 0
!
ipx route default FFFFFF01.0000.0000.0002
!
ip access-list standard DefaultOnly
 permit -2
```

Example 10-3 *GreatCoals Network—Concentration Router Configuration*

```
hostname Houston
!
ipx routing
ipx internal-network FFFFECA3
!
ipx router eigrp 131
 network all
 redistribute floating-static
!
! distribute-list applies only to FR links toward remote offices
!
 distribute-list DefaultOnly out Serial 0
!
! Backup default route in case the core default route is gone
ipx route default FFFFECA3.0000.0000.0002 floating-static
```

continues

Example 10-3 *GreatCoals Network—Concentration Router Configuration (Continued)*

```
!
ip access-list standard DefaultOnly
 permit -2
```

Exercise 10-2

When the new network design was implemented, the number of routes in all routers drastically decreased, and the number of SIA events was reduced. SIA events still occurred occasionally, though, and the network was still converging slowly. Why? Simulate what happens when a regional WAN connection in Germany fails.

Exercise 10-3

How could you improve the GreatCoals design to solve the low-speed international link bottleneck?

Case Study—Reducing IPX EIGRP Diameter in GreatCoals Network

For more information on this case study, please visit www.ciscopress.com/eigrp.

The GreatCoals network still experienced SIA events even after the first phase of network redesign because the low-speed international links were terminated on the core router. Whenever there was a route flap anywhere in the network, the core router became involved in the diffusing computation and queried all the international routers over low-speed Frame Relay links.

Exercise 10-4

Why would the core router become involved in a diffusing computation whenever an IPX network was lost?

The only way to eliminate SIA events on the core router is to remove the low-speed links from the core EIGRP process by running a different routing protocol over these links. This can be done in two ways: These links could use IPX RIP or another IPX EIGRP process. The network designers chose to use IPX RIP over these links because it provides better isolation between remote sales offices. IPX RIP carries only the default route from the core router, resulting in very low bandwidth usage.

Exercise 10-5

Why would IPX RIP provide better isolation between the remote sales offices? Hint: Simulate a link failure on the connection to Russia. Is there any routing traffic going over the link to Venezuela if it runs IPX RIP on that link? What happens if IPX EIGRP is run on that link?

The core router configuration implementing reduced IPX EIGRP diameter is shown in Example 10-4.

Example 10-4 *GreatCoals Network—Core Router Configuration with Reduced IPX EIGRP Diameter*

```
hostname Core-7576
!
ipx routing
ipx internal-network FFFFFF01
!
! Advertise only default route over RIP on the low-speed links
!
interface serial 0
 description Frame Relay links to international sales offices
 ipx network AA0004
 ipx advertise-default-route-only AA0004
!
ipx router eigrp 131
!
! IPX EIGRP cannot be run on all networks, just on the core links
!
 network AA0001
 network AA0002
 network AA0003
 distribute-list DefaultOnly out
!
! Default route to null 0
!
ipx route default FFFFFF01.0000.0000.0002
!
ip access-list standard DefaultOnly
 permit -2
```

Case Study—Combining IPX RIP and IPX EIGRP in an Access Network

For more information on this case study, please visit www.ciscopress.com/eigrp.

The arguments used in the previous case study are valid from the routing protocol perspective. IPX RIP carrying only a default route gives the remote offices more isolation than another IPX EIGRP process. The network designers, however, were too IP oriented and tried to transplant good IP designs into the IPX world. As it turns out, the IPX EIGRP performs more than route dissemination; it also provides very efficient SAP transport mechanism. When IPX EIGRP was replaced with IPX RIP on the low-speed serial links, they instantly became overloaded with periodic SAP traffic. It looked like the network design faced a deadlock due to conflicting constraints:

- IPX EIGRP cannot be used over low-speed WAN links because the isolation between the remote sales offices would be lost.

- IPX EIGRP has to be used over the same links to reduce SAP bandwidth usage.

Fortunately, the IPX EIGRP implementation allows exactly this design. IPX EIGRP could be used only for SAP transport and not as a routing protocol (see Chapter 3, "IPX EIGRP," for details). In this design, IPX EIGRP is configured on all interfaces, but does not carry any routes over the low-speed international links. The improved configuration of the core router is shown in Example 10-5.

Example 10-5 *GreatCoals Network—Core Router Configuration with IPX EIGRP/IPX RIP Combination on Low-Speed WAN Links*

```
hostname Core-7576
!
ipx routing
ipx internal-network FFFFFF01
!
! Advertise only default route over RIP on the low-speed links
!
interface serial 0
 description Frame Relay links to international sales offices
 ipx network AA0004
 ipx advertise-default-route-only AA0004
 ipx sap-incremental eigrp 131 rsup-only
!
ipx router eigrp 131
!
! IPX EIGRP cannot be run on all networks, just on the core links
!
 network all
 distribute-list DefaultOnly out
!
! Default route toward the firewall
```

Example 10-5 *GreatCoals Network—Core Router Configuration with IPX EIGRP/IPX RIP Combination on Low-Speed WAN Links (Continued)*

```
ipx route default FFFFFF01.0000.0000.0002
!
ip access-list standard DefaultOnly
 permit -2
```

Summary

IPX EIGRP is subject to the same scalability issues as IP EIGRP due to a common design and algorithm. The breadth of scalability tools is somewhat more limited. IPX EIGRP does not support route aggregation and offers only limited support for default routes.

However, several good generic designs give excellent scalability in large IPX networks:

- Use IPX EIGRP only in the core network and IPX RIP to transport the routing information in the access layer. This design has to be combined with default routes and route filters to reduce bandwidth usage on the low-speed access links.

- Use default route hierarchy and route filters with IPX EIGRP. This design is slightly less scalable than the previous one due to the larger diffused computation diameter.

- Use IPX EIGRP and IPX route filters in networks where the any-to-any connectivity is not required. This design is particularly well suited for networks where the users have to access only the central resources. The design can be further improved if you replace IPX EIGRP with IPX RIP on the network periphery.

CHAPTER 11

Designing Scalable AppleTalk EIGRP Networks

AppleTalk was not designed to be a scalable protocol, and the AppleTalk EIGRP implementation follows that philosophy very closely. No explicit scalability features exist in AppleTalk EIGRP implementation. AppleTalk EIGRP does not support route summarization or default routes (because the AppleTalk protocol does not support them) and the route filtering and redistribution control capabilities are extremely limited. AppleTalk route filters and a few additional tools (such as multiple routing protocols in the network core) will be discussed briefly in this chapter.

AppleTalk EIGRP Route Filters

AppleTalk does not support routing protocol-specific filters, such as IP or IPX. Additionally, routing filters can only be applied on a per-interface basis; there is no ability to configure global routing filters. Configure the per-interface filters with the commands documented in Table 11-1.

Table 11-1 *AppleTalk Route Filter Commands*

Task	Command (In Interface Configuration Mode)
Configure inbound per-interface AppleTalk routing filter	**appletalk distribute-list <ACL> in**
Configure outbound per-interface AppleTalk routing filter	**appletalk distribute-list <ACL> out**

The route redistribution control in AppleTalk is also extremely rudimentary. You can configure only whether you want route redistribution between EIGRP and RTMP by using commands from Table 11-2. You cannot use redistribution filters or route maps.

Table 11-2 *AppleTalk Route Redistribution Commands*

Task	Command (in Global Configuration Mode)
Enable redistribution between RTMP and EIGRP (default)	**appletalk route-redistribution**
Disable route redistribution between RTMP and EIGRP	**no appletalk route-redistribution**

NOTE Although AppleTalk route filters reduce the overall routing table size and thus increase the scalability of the EIGRP network, they also inevitably cause partial connectivity in the network. The route filters are therefore only applicable to situations where any-to-any connectivity is not requested or desired, for example, in an organization where every remote office accesses only the central resources and there is no peer-to-peer traffic.

Other AppleTalk EIGRP Scalability Options

With the limited availability of AppleTalk EIGRP scalability tools, you would expect a large number of Stuck-in-Active (SIA) events in a large enterprise network due to the large number of routes being constantly exchanged. As you might remember from Chapter 9, "Integrating EIGRP with Other Enterprise Routing Protocols," there are only two mechanisms you can deploy in situations where the EIGRP network has grown too big and you cannot use any of the existing scalability tools:

- Reduce the diameter of the EIGRP network by introducing another routing protocol.
- Increase the SIA timeout by using the command from Table 11-3.

Table 11-3 *Increase AppleTalk Stuck-in-Active Timeout*

Task	Command (in Global Configuration Mode)
Increase AppleTalk SIA timeout	**appletalk eigrp active-time <seconds>**

NOTE Increasing SIA timeout is only a stopgap measure. It does not solve the problem; it only hides it. If you have to increase the SIA timeout beyond the default value of three minutes, it means that your network is converging very slowly anyway.

By increasing the active timer, you also further delay network convergence in case of an SIA condition. The active timer bounds the maximum time the router that originated the query waits before aborting part of the diffusing computation and converging on what is left of the network.

If you want to reduce the EIGRP network diameter, you can generically use one of the following approaches:

- Use EIGRP in the network core and use another routing protocol in the access layer. The solution does not apply well to AppleTalk because the other access layer protocol is usually RTMP, which incurs large and constant overhead on low-speed access links. Using EIGRP in the access layer at least reduces the bandwidth usage due to the routing protocol exchanges.

- Use EIGRP in the access layer and use another routing protocol in the core, which works well with AppleTalk. Bandwidth requirements in the access layer are kept to a minimum and either RTMP or AURP can be used in the core.

Case Study—Frisco Systems, Inc.

For more information on this case study, please visit www.ciscopress.com/eigrp.

Frisco Systems is a large international corporation with offices throughout the United States and in several European countries. The network is designed very cleanly. Two corporate headquarters sites connect via ATM and Frame Relay links with distribution sites covering regions in the United States and individual countries in Europe. All the remote offices connect to these distribution sites, as shown in Figure 11-1. (Only a few remote offices on the U.S. West Coast are shown for clarity reasons.)

Figure 11-1 *Frisco Systems Network*

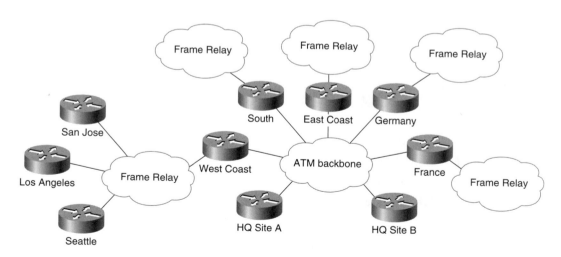

Frisco Systems uses AppleTalk internally, and it has experienced several network meltdowns due to Stuck-in-Active events in the last few months. It's increased SIA timeout on all routers as a temporary measure, but it is aware that this is not a permanent solution. It is looking toward redesigning its AppleTalk routing architecture. The overall corporate culture is very open and encourages information sharing and teamwork; limiting user connectivity by implementing AppleTalk route filters is therefore not possible.

Exercise 11-1

Propose a new AppleTalk routing design that reduces the EIGRP diameter without increasing the load on low-speed access-layer links.

Case Study Solution

The case study requirements are strict and force the solution to be structured along the following lines:

- EIGRP has to be kept in the access layer due to the bandwidth requirements.

- EIGRP has to be switched off in the network core and replaced with another routing protocol due to the EIGRP diameter reduction requirement. AppleTalk EIGRP implementation does not support more than one AppleTalk EIGRP process per router, so the core routing protocol cannot be another EIGRP instance.

- The only remaining AppleTalk routing protocol suitable for the core is AURP.

With these facts in mind, you can redesign the Frisco Systems network with the following configuration changes:

- Establish AURP tunnels between distribution sites and headquarter locations.

- Disable AppleTalk on core WAN links. This action also implicitly splits the large EIGRP network into a number of smaller networks.

- Run AURP over the core tunnels and redistribute routing information between AURP and EIGRP. This concludes the AppleTalk routing redesign.

A sample configuration of a distribution-layer router is shown in Example 11-1.

Example 11-1 *Distribution Layer Router—Partial Configuration*

```
hostname DR-WestCoast
!
appletalk routing eigrp 123
appletalk route-redistribution
!
interface atm 0
 description ATM uplink toward HQ
 ip address 172.16.2.123 255.255.255.0
```

Example 11-1 *Distribution Layer Router—Partial Configuration (Continued)*

```
!
interface serial 0
 description Frame Relay links to the remote offices
 appletalk cable-range 4123-4123
 appletalk protocol eigrp
 no appletalk protocol rtmp
!
interface tunnel 1
 description Tunnel toward HQ site A
 tunnel source atm 0
 tunnel destination 172.16.2.1
 tunnel mode aurp
 appletalk protocol aurp
!
interface tunnel 2
 description Tunnel toward HQ site B
 tunnel source atm 0
 tunnel destination 172.16.2.2
 tunnel mode aurp
 appletalk protocol aurp
```

Summary

AppleTalk protocol itself and the AppleTalk EIGRP implementation do not provide any real scalability tools. The only tools you can use to enable further network growth are route filters (resulting in partial connectivity for the end users), and deployment of multiple routing protocols in the network or AppleTalk inter-enterprise routing.

PART III

Running EIGRP over Switched WAN and Dial-Up Networks

CHAPTER 12

Switched WAN Networks and Their Impact on EIGRP

Every network designer faces two major design obstacles when designing IP routing in a large network:

- Designing a scalable solution tuned to the specifics of the selected routing protocol.
- Designing a network that works well over switched WAN networks (X.25, Frame Relay, or ATM).

Switched WAN networks pose additional challenges on top of the usual set of problems found in large-scale network design due to their specific technology. All of these networks present a multi-access subnet to a router but offer no additional features, such as multicasting, usually found on the LAN networks.

The scalability issues of EIGRP were discussed in several chapters in Part II, "Designing Enterprise EIGRP Networks," of this book. Part III, "Running EIGRP over Switched WAN and Dial-Up Networks," focuses on switched WAN issues, starting from generic issues common to all routing protocols in this chapter. EIGRP-specific issues are covered in Chapter 13, "Running EIGRP over WAN Networks," and dial-up related issues in Chapter 14, "EIGRP and Dial-Up Networks."

A case study is presented in the beginning of this chapter to illustrate some of the problems usually found in growing multiprotocol networks built on switched WAN networks. This chapter also discusses several issues specific to switched WAN technologies, from emulated multicasting to special means of resolving Layer 3 to Layer 2 mapping and logical interfaces available over these media types.

Case Study 1—A Large Number of EIGRP Neighbors over a Frame Relay Link

For more information on this case study, please visit www.ciscopress/com/eigrp.

MetroGas is a large petrochemical conglomerate, covering everything from drilling operations to gas stations throughout the country. The company decided to connect all of its gas stations to the central site through a Frame Relay network with ISDN used as a dial-backup solution. Frame Relay was selected as the main transmission technology for the following reasons:

- The overall deployment costs were lower.

- The central routers needed only one high-speed port as opposed to a large number of low-speed ports in a leased line implementation.

- The Frame Relay service provider performed access concentration. MetroGas would need no concentration routers.

The access speed of the remote gas stations is 64 kbps, and the access speed at the central router is 2 Mbps. Each gas station is connected with the central router with one Permanent Virtual Circuit (PVC) with a Committed Information Rate (CIR) of 16 kbps. The Frame Relay topology of the MetroGas network is displayed in Figure 12-1.

Figure 12-1 *MetroGas Network—Logical Topology*

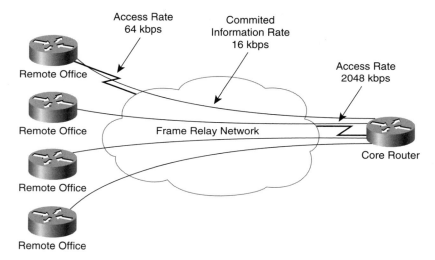

MetroGas's network designers decided to use EIGRP throughout the network to reliably detect Frame Relay outages at the IP layer and to be able to implement load balancing between the Frame Relay PVC and an ISDN dial-up connection. The designers were aware of the scalability issues associated with large-scale EIGRP networks, so they implemented several safeguards, including a hierarchical IP addressing scheme, route filtering, default routes, and so on.

A pilot network linking several gas stations throughout the country with the central site was implemented as the first stage of network deployment. The configuration of access routers (see Example 12-1) and the central router (see Example 12-2) turned out to be extremely straightforward.

Example 12-1 *Access Router Configuration*

```
hostname Access_Wichita
!
interface ethernet 0
 ip address 10.17.2.1 255.255.255.0
!
interface serial 0
 encapsulation frame-relay
 bandwidth 64
 ip address 10.251.17.2 255.255.240.0
!
router eigrp 101
 network 10.0.0.0
```

Example 12-2 *Central Router Configuration*

```
hostname Core_A
!
interface FastEthernet 0/0
 ip address 10.1.1.1 255.255.255.0
!
interface serial 1/0
 encapsulation frame-relay
 bandwidth 2048
 ip address 10.251.16.1 255.255.240.0
 ip summary-address eigrp 101 10.0.0.0 255.0.0.0
!
router eigrp 101
 network 10.0.0.0
!
ip default-network 10.0.0.0
```

The pilot was running for a few months and proved easy to install and maintain, so the networking team got the green light to connect the next 200 gas stations. However, as the number of gas stations exceeded a certain limit (it turned out to be somewhere between 35 and 40), they were not able to connect any more stations. EIGRP adjacencies just could not be established. To make matters worse, a new gas station connected to the network might cause a gas station from the pilot network that was running fine for months to become unreachable.

The troubleshooting efforts quickly centered on the Frame Relay network, and the troubleshooting team discovered an interesting phenomenon: Even with no load on the

Frame Relay interface, the number of interface output drops were constantly increasing as shown in Example 12-3.

Example 12-3 *show interface Printout on the Central Router*

```
Core_A#show interface serial 1/0
Serial1/0 is up, line protocol is up
  Internet address is 10.251.16.1, subnet mask is 255.255.240.0
  MTU 1500 bytes, BW 1544 Kbit, DLY 20000 usec, rely 254/255, load 1/255
  Encapsulation FRAME-RELAY, loopback not set, keepalive set (10 sec)
  LMI enq sent  2, LMI stat recvd 0, LMI upd recvd 0, DTE LMI up
  LMI enq recvd 266, LMI stat sent  264, LMI upd sent  0
  LMI DLCI 1023  LMI type is CISCO  frame relay DTE
  Last input 0:00:04, output 0:00:02, output hang never
  Last clearing of "show interface" counters 0:10:15
  Output queue 0/40, 2468 drops; input queue 0/75, 0 drops
  Five minute input rate 375 bits/sec, 2 packets/sec
  Five minute output rate 3172 bits/sec, 9 packets/sec
     1253 packets input, 55736 bytes, 0 no buffer
     Received 0 broadcasts, 0 runts, 0 giants
     0 input errors, 0 CRC, 0 frame, 0 overrun, 0 ignored, 0 abort
     0 input packets with dribble condition detected
     5627 packets output, 264723 bytes, 0 underruns
     0 output errors, 0 collisions, 2 interface resets, 0 restarts
     3 carrier transitions
```

The troubleshooters tried to alleviate the problem by increasing the interface output queue in several ways. They started by increasing the output queue length with the **hold-queue out** command and then turned on priority queuing and extended the queue lengths with the **priority-list queue-limit** command. However, every configuration change allowed them to add only a few new neighbors. As soon as more neighbors were added, the symptoms returned.

A call to the Cisco Technical Assistance Center (TAC) proved to be more fruitful. The TAC engineer quickly identified the problem as output queue overload due to a large number of EIGRP neighbors reachable over a single Frame Relay interface. He suggested using the **frame-relay broadcast-queue** command, and all of the remote locations became reachable in a few seconds—until the MetroGas team added a large number of additional gas stations over the same Frame Relay connection.

Broadcast Emulation on Switched WAN (Pseudobroadcasting)

The MetroGas engineers faced one of the major obstacles to large-scale Frame Relay deployment: the software emulation of LAN broadcasts over nonbroadcast WAN media done in Cisco IOS (*pseudobroadcasting*). Multi-access WAN technologies, such as X.25, Frame Relay, ATM, or ISDN, do not support the broadcasting mechanisms usually found in the LAN environment. On the other hand, several different applications, including IP routing protocols, use multicast or broadcast capabilities of the LAN environment to find the peer hosts or routers. For example, EIGRP uses multicast hello packets to find other routers connected to the same subnet. To enable these applications to work unmodified over the multi-access WAN subnets, IOS emulates the multicast capabilities of the LAN environment over a multi-access WAN interface.

NOTE   A few multi-access WAN networks do support multicasting; for example, some U.S. Frame Relay networks have implemented *multicast DLCI* capability or private ATM networks that support point-to-multipoint Switched Virtual Circuits (SVC). These implementations have several limitations (for example, you cannot use subinterfaces with multicast DLCI) and are therefore not usable in all environments.

Whenever a multicast packet is routed over a multi-access WAN interface that has no inherent multicasting capability, IOS creates a separate copy of the multicast packet for every neighbor reachable over that interface. Although this is usually the desired behavior, in some situations (for example, on slow-speed X.25 networks) you wouldn't like the multicast packets to be sent to every neighbor. To give the network engineer tighter control over multicast propagation, IOS consults the neighbor maps (see "Layer 2 to Layer 3 Mapping" later in this chapter for more details) when creating multiple copies of the multicast packet. The multicast packet is sent to only those neighbors that have a **broadcast** option specified in the neighbor map. In environments where the neighbor maps are created dynamically (for example, in most Frame Relay networks), all the dynamic neighbor maps allow the multicast propagation.

All the copies of a single multicast packet are created at one time and sent to the interface output queue in a burst. No shaping or rate limiting is performed on these packets. The results of these traffic bursts are usually output queue overloads, and associated output drops whenever a large number of neighbors are reachable over the same interface.

NOTE   The output queue overload is never experienced on X.25 interfaces, where each Virtual Circuit (VC) has its own independent output queue. It's also not experienced on dialer interfaces, which are logical interfaces with no associated output queues, and BRI and PRI interfaces where each D channel has its own output queue.

To get rid of the output drops, you can use one of the two possible solutions: Reduce the number of neighbors reachable over the interface (see section "Subinterfaces" later in this chapter for more details) or extend the output queue. You can extend the output queue with various commands depending on the queuing method used on the serial interface as outlined in Table 12-1.

Table 12-1   *Extending Interface Output Queue*

Queuing Method	Command to Extend the Output Queue
FIFO	**hold-queue <number> out**
Priority queuing	**priority-list <list-number> queue-limit <high> <medium> <normal> <low>**
Custom queuing	**queue-list <list-number> queue <queue-number> limit <packet-limit>**
Weighted fair queuing	**fair-queue <conversation-limit> <dynamic-queues> <reservable-queues>**

The second side effect of emulated multicasting over slower-speed links is a significant amount of jitter introduced by large multicast traffic bursts. To reduce the amount of jitter and solve the output congestion in Frame Relay networks, the **frame-relay broadcast-queue** command was introduced in IOS 10.3. The command has three parameters for fine-tuning the behavior of emulated broadcasts as detailed in Table 12-2.

Table 12-2   *Frame Relay Broadcast-Queue Parameters*

Parameter	Meaning
Size	Number of packets to hold in the broadcast queue. The default is 64 packets.
Byte rate	Maximum number of bytes to be transmitted per second. The default is 256,000 bytes per second.
Packet rate	Maximum number of packets to be transmitted per second. The default is 36 packets per second.

To design the Frame Relay broadcast queue, you should consider the following parameters:

- The only multicast packets generated by EIGRP over Frame Relay are the hello packets that are sent every **hello-interval** seconds and are approximately 40 bytes long unless the Frame Relay network supports Frame Relay level multicasting configured with the **frame-relay multicast-dlci** command.

- The maximum overall byte rate should not exceed one quarter of the local interface speed (or access rate) to prevent local congestion. The per-neighbor byte rate (overall byte rate divided by the number of neighbors) should not exceed one quarter of the slowest remote access rate or one quarter of the smallest CIR to prevent remote congestion.

- The number of packets sent per second (packet-rate) should not exceed the output queue size minus some safety margin. A good value in uncongested networks would be three quarters of the output queue.
- The overall broadcast queue size must be large enough to prevent multicast packet drops.

With these rules in mind, it's easy to design the broadcast queue for the MetroGas central router that can accommodate 200 neighbors over one Frame Relay interface.

NOTE   Having 200 neighbors over one Frame Relay interface is not a good design practice. You should limit the number of neighbors off one interface to between 30 and 50. However, in some circumstances, you might be forced to go beyond the usually recommended limit.

The only multicast traffic sent over the Frame Relay interface are EIGRP hello packets, which are sent every five seconds. The overall amount of multicast traffic is 8000 bytes in five seconds or 1600 bytes per second (12,800 bps). The per-neighbor multicast traffic is 40 bytes in five seconds or 64 bps.

The byte-rate of the broadcast queue is limited to 512 kbps (one quarter of 2 Mbps) by the access rate of the central router, and the per-neighbor byte-rate is limited to 4 kbps (one quarter of the 16 kbps CIR). With 200 neighbors, the minimum of the two values is 512 kbps.

NOTE   You should adjust the parameters of the Frame Relay broadcast queue whenever there is a significant change in the number of neighbors. For example, if you designed the MetroGas broadcast queue for 200 neighbors, but only 50 neighbors were connected in the initial phase, the per-neighbor byte rate would be too high, resulting in Frame Relay PVC overload.

The packet rate of the broadcast queue should be at least 50 packets/second to send 200 packets in less than five seconds. (Otherwise, the hello packets accumulate in the broadcast queue.) The output queue length would therefore have to be extended to approximately 70 packets.

The overall size of the broadcast queue should be around 250 packets. This size easily accommodates the EIGRP hello packets and with some safety margin.

The final configuration of the Frame Relay interface of the MetroGas central router is shown in Example 12-4.

Example 12-4 *Configuration of the Frame Relay Interface on the Central MetroGas Router*

```
interface serial 1/0
 encapsulation frame-relay
 bandwidth 2048
 hold-queue 70 out
 frame-relay broadcast-queue 250 64000 50
```

Layer 2 to Layer 3 Mapping in WAN Environment

Whenever a Layer 3 device (router or end host) has to send a packet to another Layer 3 device over a multi-access network, it needs to uniquely identify the destination device the packet is sent to on the data link layer. MAC addresses are used on LAN subnets to identify the destination devices, and various forms of virtual channel identifiers are used on switched WAN networks for the same purposes. The identifiers for Permanent Virtual Circuits (PVC) range from the X.25 virtual circuit (VC) number and Frame Relay Data Link Connection Identifier (DLCI) to the Virtual Path/Virtual circuit identifier (VPI/VCI) of ATM. The identifiers for Switched Virtual Circuits (SVC) are the X.121 address for X.25 or Frame Relay, E.164 addresses for Frame Relay and public ATM networks, and NSAP addresses for private ATM networks.

NOTE   The router uses SVC identifiers to open a virtual circuit to the destination device. The PVC identifier is assigned to the virtual circuit as soon as it is opened. The PVC identifiers are then used to forward the data traffic toward the destination device.

The second prerequisite for successful data traffic propagation over a multi-access subnet is the ability to map logical next-hop addresses (IP addresses, for example) into the physical addresses of the destination devices. Address Resolution Protocol (ARP) is used for dynamic discovery of Layer 3 to Layer 2 mapping in the LAN environment, but ARP cannot be used over multi-access WAN subnets for two reasons:

- ARP relies on a broadcast mechanism that is not readily available on WAN interfaces. The emulated broadcast capability provided by IOS doesn't help because it requires the neighbors to be known to operate properly.

- LAN environments do not provide on-demand virtual circuits like some WAN environments. Discovering neighbors over on-demand circuits with broadcast mechanisms, such as ARP, is clearly impossible.

Using neighbor maps is the generic mechanism for mapping logical addresses into physical device addresses on all WAN media. The neighbor maps associate logical addresses with

Permanent Virtual Circuit (PVC) or Switched Virtual Circuit (SVC) identifiers as outlined in Table 12-3. Only the basic configuration options are shown; detailed descriptions of all configuration options can be found in the IOS documentation.

Table 12-3   *IOS Neighbor Map Configuration Commands*

WAN Media	IOS Neighbor Map Configuration Command
X.25 PVC	**interface serial 0** **x25 pvc** <vc > **ip** <IP-addr> <X.121-addr> [**broadcast**]
X.25 SVC	**interface serial 0** **x25 map ip** <IP-addr> <X.121-addr> [**broadcast**]
Frame Relay PVC	**interface serial 0** **frame-relay map ip** <IP-addr> <DLCI> [**broadcast**]
Frame Relay SVC	**map-list** <map-name> **source-addr E164|X121** <src-addr> **dest-addr** E164 | X121 <dst-addr> **ip** <ip-addr> [**class** <QoS-class>] ! **interface serial 0** **frame-relay svc** **map-group** <map-name>
ATM PVC	**interface atm 0** **pvc** [<name>] <vpi>/<vci> **protocol ip** <ip-address> [**broadcast**]
ATM SVC	**interface atm 0** **svc** [<name>] <destination-NSAP> **protocol ip** <ip-address> [**broadcast**]
ISDN dial-up connection	**interface dialer 0 | bri 0 | serial 0:15** **dialer map ip** <ip> <E.164> [**user** <username>][**broadcast**]

NOTE   ATM neighbor configuration has changed in IOS 11.3T and IOS 12.0. For the old command syntax, please refer to the IOS documentation.

Manual configuration of neighbor maps is a tedious process, especially in large-scale environments with a large number of neighbors. Two mechanisms can ease the configuration process: automatic PVC discovery in Frame Relay, and inverse ARP in both Frame Relay and the ATM environment. No such mechanisms exist for X.25 or designs that use switched virtual circuits. In these cases, you must perform all configuration manually.

Frame Relay networks are particularly easy to configure because all the autodiscovery mechanisms are enabled by default. In the ATM world, the inverse ARP mechanism must be configured manually on a per-PVC basis; only the generation of corresponding neighbor maps is automatic.

Troubleshooting Neighbor Map Problems

Neighbor map misconfiguration is a major source of WAN-related problems. The troubleshooting process should proceed along the following lines:

- Verify that the neighbor maps are correct by pinging the neighboring routers. If you are able to ping the remote router, both routers have correct entries in their neighbor maps.

WARNING   In the case of two parallel links between two routers, the links can be crossed and the ping can still work correctly, but EIGRP doesn't start due to IP subnet mismatch.

- Verify that the neighboring routers can exchange hello packets. The neighbor maps must specify broadcast propagation. A missing **broadcast** option on the neighbor map is usually indicated by the EIGRP neighbor being visible from one end of the WAN link but not from the other. Pinging IP address 224.0.0.10 also generates replies from all EIGRP neighbors.

The easiest way to check the neighbor maps is by using IOS show commands associated with specific WAN technology: **show x25 map** (see Example 12-5) for X.25 networks, **show frame-relay map** (see Example 12-6) for Frame Relay networks, and **show atm map** (see Example 12-7) for ATM networks.

Example 12-5 *show x25 map Output*

```
Router#show x25 map

Serial0: X.121 386611762 <--> ip 172.1.4.2
    PERMANENT, BROADCAST, 2 VCS: 64 65*
```

Example 12-6 *show frame-relay map Output*

```
Router#show frame-relay map
Serial0 (up): ip 172.1.4.2 dlci 101(0x65,0x1850), dynamic,
              broadcast,, status defined, active
Serial0.2 (up): point-to-point dlci, dlci 112(0x70,0x1C00), broadcast
              status defined, active
Serial0.4 (up): point-to-point dlci, dlci 114(0x72,0x1C20), broadcast
              status defined, active
```

Example 12-7 *show atm map* Output

```
Router#show atm map

Map list atm_pri: PERMANENT
ip 1.2.3.4 maps to NSAP CD.CDEF.01.234567.890A.BCDE.F012.3456.7890.1234.12,
  broadcast,
aal5mux, multipoint connection up, VC 6
ip 1.2.3.5 maps to NSAP DE.CDEF.01.234567.890A.BCDE.F012.3456.7890.1234.12,
  broadcast,
aal5mux, connection up, VC 15, multipoint connection up, VC 6
```

A few troubleshooting scenarios are presented in the following paragraphs, together with the corresponding EIGRP debugging outputs. For simplicity reasons, all the scenarios were performed in a small Frame Relay network linking two routers with single PVC, as shown in Figure 12-2. Static Frame Relay maps were used to introduce various configuration errors.

NOTE   In most designs, dynamic Frame Relay maps should be used on Frame Relay networks to avoid potential configuration problems. Only the networks requiring an increased level of security would use static maps to prevent potential data leakage following a Frame Relay PVC misconfiguration.

Figure 12-2 *Frame Relay Network Used in Troubleshooting Scenarios*

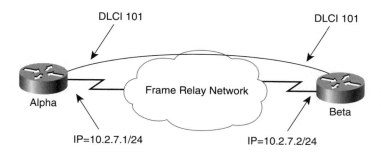

Scenario 1—Missing Broadcast Keyword on a Neighbor Map

In this scenario, one of the routers is missing the **broadcast** keyword in the neighbor map (see Example 12-8 for router configurations).

Example 12-8 *Scenario 1—Router Configurations*

```
alpha#show running-config
. . .
interface Serial0
 ip address 10.2.7.1 255.255.255.0
 no ip directed-broadcast
 encapsulation frame-relay
 no ip mroute-cache
 frame-relay map ip 10.2.7.2 101
. . .
router eigrp 1
 network 10.0.0.0

beta#show running-config
. . .
interface Serial0
 ip address 10.2.7.2 255.255.255.0
 no ip directed-broadcast
 encapsulation frame-relay
 no ip mroute-cache
 frame-relay map ip 10.2.7.1 101 broadcast
. . .
router eigrp 1
 network 10.0.0.0
```

Router Alpha is receiving EIGRP hello packets from router Beta, but is not sending any hello packets back. Router Beta thus cannot detect the presence of router Alpha and rejects all the attempts to initial EIGRP adjacency with router Alpha. The debugging outputs on router Alpha indicate that it tries to establish adjacency with router Beta but eventually drops the adjacency due to excessive retransmissions (see Example 12-9). Router Beta doesn't even try to establish adjacency with router Alpha. Router Alpha is also not seen in the list of EIGRP neighbors on router Beta (see Example 12-10).

Example 12-9 *Scenario 1—Debugging Printouts on Router Alpha*

```
Alpha#show debug
EIGRP:
  EIGRP Packets debugging is on
    (UPDATE, REQUEST, QUERY, REPLY, HELLO, IPXSAP, PROBE, ACK)
  EIGRP Neighbors debugging is on
Alpha#
00:05:03: EIGRP: Received HELLO on Serial0 nbr 10.2.7.2
00:05:03:   AS 1, Flags 0x0, Seq 0/0 idbQ 0/0
00:05:03: EIGRP: New peer 10.2.7.2
00:05:03: EIGRP: Enqueueing UPDATE on Serial0 nbr 10.2.7.2 iidbQ un/rely 0/1
00:05:03: EIGRP:  Requeued unicast on Serial0
```

Example 12-9 *Scenario 1—Debugging Printouts on Router Alpha (Continued)*

```
00:05:03: EIGRP: Forcing multicast xmit on Serial0
00:05:03: EIGRP: Sending UPDATE on Serial0 nbr 10.2.7.2
00:05:03:   AS 1, Flags 0x1, Seq 2/0 idbQ 0/0 iidbQ un/rely 0/0
00:05:05: EIGRP: Sending UPDATE on Serial0 nbr 10.2.7.2, retry 1, RTO 3000
00:05:05:   AS 1, Flags 0x1, Seq 2/0 idbQ 0/0 iidbQ un/rely 0/0
00:05:07: EIGRP: Received HELLO on Serial0 nbr 10.2.7.2
00:05:07:   AS 1, Flags 0x0, Seq 0/0 idbQ 0/0 iidbQ un/rely 0/0
00:05:08: EIGRP: Sending UPDATE on Serial0 nbr 10.2.7.2, retry 2, RTO 4500
00:05:08:   AS 1, Flags 0x1, Seq 2/0 idbQ 0/0 iidbQ un/rely 0/0
00:05:12: EIGRP: Received HELLO on Serial0 nbr 10.2.7.2
00:05:12:   AS 1, Flags 0x0, Seq 0/0 idbQ 0/0 iidbQ un/rely 0/0
00:05:12: EIGRP: Sending UPDATE on Serial0 nbr 10.2.7.2, retry 3, RTO 5000
00:05:12:   AS 1, Flags 0x1, Seq 2/0 idbQ 0/0 iidbQ un/rely 0/0
...
00:06:17: EIGRP: Received HELLO on Serial0 nbr 10.2.7.2
00:06:17:   AS 1, Flags 0x0, Seq 0/0 idbQ 0/0 iidbQ un/rely 0/0
00:06:17: EIGRP: Sending UPDATE on Serial0 nbr 10.2.7.2, retry 16, RTO 5000
00:06:17:   AS 1, Flags 0x1, Seq 2/0 idbQ 0/0 iidbQ un/rely 0/0
00:06:21: EIGRP: Received HELLO on Serial0 nbr 10.2.7.2
00:06:21:   AS 1, Flags 0x0, Seq 0/0 idbQ 0/0 iidbQ un/rely 0/0
00:06:22: EIGRP: Retransmission retry limit exceeded
00:06:22: EIGRP: Holdtime expired
00:06:22: EIGRP: Neighbor 10.2.7.2 went down on Serial0

the retry limit has been exceeded, neighbor is declared dead, but it is
immediately "rediscovered" and the whole cycle starts again

00:06:26: EIGRP: Received HELLO on Serial0 nbr 10.2.7.2
00:06:26:   AS 1, Flags 0x0, Seq 0/0 idbQ 0/0
00:06:26: EIGRP: New peer 10.2.7.2
00:06:26: EIGRP: Enqueuing UPDATE on Serial0 nbr 10.2.7.2 iidbQ un/rely 0/1
00:06:26: EIGRP:  Requeued unicast on Serial0
00:06:26: EIGRP: Forcing multicast xmit on Serial0
00:06:26: EIGRP: Sending UPDATE on Serial0 nbr 10.2.7.2
00:06:26:   AS 1, Flags 0x1, Seq 3/0 idbQ 0/0 iidbQ un/rely 0/0
00:06:28: EIGRP: Sending UPDATE on Serial0 nbr 10.2.7.2, retry 1, RTO 3000
00:06:28:   AS 1, Flags 0x1, Seq 3/0 idbQ 0/0 iidbQ un/rely 0/0
```

Example 12-10 *Scenario 1—EIGRP Show Printouts on Router Beta*

```
Beta#show ip eigrp neighbors
IP-EIGRP neighbors for process 1
Beta#show frame map
Serial0 (up): ip 10.2.7.1 dlci 101(0x65,0x1850), static,
              broadcast,
              CISCO, status defined, active
```

Scenario 2—Wrong IP Address in the Neighbor Map

In the second scenario, both routers have the **broadcast** option configured in the Frame Relay map, but the remote IP address in the neighbor map is misconfigured on router Alpha (see Example 12-11).

Example 12-11 *Scenario 2—Router Configurations*

```
alpha#show running-config
. . .
interface Serial0
 ip address 10.2.7.1 255.255.255.0
 no ip directed-broadcast
 encapsulation frame-relay
 no ip mroute-cache
 frame-relay map ip 10.2.7.3 101 broadcast
. . .
router eigrp 1
 network 10.0.0.0
```

Both routers can send EIGRP hello packets to the remote router, but the communication cannot proceed beyond the hello packet exchange because the IP packets for router Beta are dropped on router Alpha due to a misconfigured IP address. EIGRP debugging does not indicate the exact source of the problem, but the IP packet debugging clearly shows that the packet is dropped due to an encapsulation failure (see Example 12-12).

Example 12-12 *Scenario 2—Debugging Printouts on Router Alpha*

```
Alpha#show debug
EIGRP:
  EIGRP Packets debugging is on
    (UPDATE, REQUEST, QUERY, REPLY, IPXSAP, PROBE, ACK)
  EIGRP Neighbors debugging is on
Alpha#
00:11:46: EIGRP: New peer 10.2.7.2
00:11:46: EIGRP: Enqueuing UPDATE on Serial0 nbr 10.2.7.2 iidbQ un/rely 0/1
00:11:46: EIGRP:  Requeued unicast on Serial0
00:11:46: EIGRP: Forcing multicast xmit on Serial0
00:11:46: EIGRP: Sending UPDATE on Serial0 nbr 10.2.7.2
00:11:46:    AS 1, Flags 0x1, Seq 7/0 idbQ 0/0 iidbQ un/rely 0/0
00:11:47: EIGRP: Received UPDATE on Serial0 nbr 10.2.7.2
00:11:47:    AS 1, Flags 0x1, Seq 2/0 idbQ 0/0 iidbQ un/rely 0/0
00:11:48: EIGRP: Sending UPDATE on Serial0 nbr 10.2.7.2, retry 1, RTO 3000
00:11:48:    AS 1, Flags 0x1, Seq 7/2 idbQ 0/0 iidbQ un/rely 0/0
00:11:51: EIGRP: Sending UPDATE on Serial0 nbr 10.2.7.2, retry 2, RTO 4500
00:11:51:    AS 1, Flags 0x1, Seq 7/2 idbQ 0/0 iidbQ un/rely 0/0
00:11:52: EIGRP: Received UPDATE on Serial0 nbr 10.2.7.2
00:11:52:    AS 1, Flags 0x1, Seq 2/0 idbQ 0/0 iidbQ un/rely 0/0
00:11:56: EIGRP: Sending UPDATE on Serial0 nbr 10.2.7.2, retry 3, RTO 5000
00:11:56:    AS 1, Flags 0x1, Seq 7/2 idbQ 0/0 iidbQ un/rely 0/0
00:11:57: EIGRP: Received UPDATE on Serial0 nbr 10.2.7.2
00:11:57:    AS 1, Flags 0x1, Seq 2/0 idbQ 0/0 iidbQ un/rely 0/0
00:12:01: EIGRP: Sending UPDATE on Serial0 nbr 10.2.7.2, retry 4, RTO 5000
```

Example 12-12 *Scenario 2—Debugging Printouts on Router Alpha (Continued)*

```
00:12:01:    AS 1, Flags 0x1, Seq 7/2 idbQ 0/0 iidbQ un/rely 0/0
00:12:02: EIGRP: Received UPDATE on Serial0 nbr 10.2.7.2
00:12:02:    AS 1, Flags 0x1, Seq 2/0 idbQ 0/0 iidbQ un/rely 0/0

initial UPDATE packets are constantly retransmitted, but the EIGRP debugging
gives you no clues why that's happening

Alpha#undebug all
All possible debugging has been turned off
Alpha#
Alpha#debug ip packet
IP packet debugging is on
Alpha#
00:12:22: IP: s=10.2.7.2 (Serial0), d=10.2.7.1 (Serial0), len 40, rcvd 3
00:12:23: IP: s=10.2.7.2 (Serial0), d=224.0.0.10, len 60, rcvd 2
00:12:26: IP: s=10.2.7.1 (local), d=10.2.7.2 (Serial0), len 40, sending
00:12:26: IP: s=10.2.7.1 (local), d=10.2.7.2 (Serial0), len 40, encapsulation
failed
00:12:27: IP: s=10.2.7.2 (Serial0), d=10.2.7.1 (Serial0), len 40, rcvd 3
00:12:27: IP: s=10.2.7.2 (Serial0), d=224.0.0.10, len 60, rcvd 2
00:12:31: IP: s=10.2.7.1 (local), d=10.2.7.2 (Serial0), len 40, sending
00:12:31: IP: s=10.2.7.1 (local), d=10.2.7.2 (Serial0), len 40, encapsulation
failed
00:12:32: IP: s=10.2.7.2 (Serial0), d=10.2.7.1 (Serial0), len 40, rcvd 3
00:12:32: IP: s=10.2.7.2 (Serial0), d=224.0.0.10, len 60, rcvd 2
```

Contrary to the previous scenario, both routers can see their EIGRP neighbor, but the communication never proceeds beyond the sending of the initial Update packet (see Example 12-13).

Example 12-13 *Scenario 2—EIGRP **show** Commands on Router Beta*

```
Beta#show ip eigrp neighbors detail
IP-EIGRP neighbors for process 1
H   Address                 Interface   Hold Uptime   SRTT    RTO  Q  Seq
                                        (sec)         (ms)         Cnt Num
0   10.2.7.1                Se0          124 00:00:55    0    5000  1  0
    Last startup serial 2
    Version 12.0/1.0, Retrans: 12, Retries: 12, Waiting for Init, Waiting for Init Ack
       UPDATE seq 3 ser 2-2 Sent 55292 Init Sequenced
```

Scenario 3—Wrong DLCI Number in the Neighbor Map

In the third scenario, the IP address in the neighbor map is correct, but the DLCI number is misconfigured, as seen in Example 12-14.

Example 12-14 *Scenario 3—Router Configurations*

```
alpha#show running-config
. . .
interface Serial0
```

continues

Example 12-14 *Scenario 3—Router Configurations (Continued)*

```
ip address 10.2.7.1 255.255.255.0
no ip directed-broadcast
encapsulation frame-relay
no ip mroute-cache
frame-relay map ip 10.2.7.2 102 broadcast
. . .
router eigrp 1
 network 10.0.0.0
```

This scenario is indistinguishable from Scenario 2 both on the EIGRP level—the debugging printouts are identical to those in Example 12-12 and the show command printouts are identical to those in Example 12-13—and on the IP level—IP debugging does not indicate any more than the encapsulation has failed. The only way to diagnose the misconfigured parameter (IP address versus DLCI number) is to use the **show frame map** (see Example 12-15) and **show frame pvc** (see Example 12-16) commands. If you misconfigure the IP address, the destination IP address does not appear in the **show frame map** printout. If you misconfigure the DLCI number, the DLCI displayed in the **show frame map** printout has PVC status **DELETED** in the show frame pvc printout.

Example 12-15 *Scenario 3—show **frame-relay map** Printout*

```
Alpha#show frame-relay map
Serial0 (up): ip 10.2.7.2 dlci 102(0x66,0x1860), static,
              broadcast,
              CISCO, status deleted
```

Example 12-16 *Scenario 3—show **frame-relay pvc** Printout*

```
Alpha#show frame-relay pvc

PVC Statistics for interface Serial0 (Frame Relay DTE)

              Active     Inactive     Deleted     Static
  Local         0           0            1           0
  Switched      0           0            0           0
  Unused        1           1            0           0

DLCI = 101, DLCI USAGE = UNUSED, PVC STATUS = ACTIVE, INTERFACE = Serial0

    input pkts 14          output pkts 1          in bytes 862
    out bytes 30           dropped pkts 0         in FECN pkts 0
    in BECN pkts 0         out FECN pkts 0        out BECN pkts 0
    in DE pkts 0           out DE pkts 0
    out bcast pkts 1        out bcast bytes 30              Num Pkts Switched 0
    pvc create time 00:00:59, last time pvc status changed 00:00:59

DLCI = 102, DLCI USAGE = LOCAL, PVC STATUS = DELETED, INTERFACE = Serial0

    input pkts 0           output pkts 1          in bytes 0
    out bytes 64           dropped pkts 0         in FECN pkts 0
```

Example 12-16 *Scenario 3—***show frame-relay pvc** *Printout (Continued)*

```
in BECN pkts 0          out FECN pkts 0          out BECN pkts 0
in DE pkts 0            out DE pkts 0
out bcast pkts 1        out bcast bytes 64
pvc create time 00:01:48, last time pvc status changed 00:01:02
```

Subinterfaces

All routers reachable through a single physical interface over a switched WAN network are usually handled in the same manner. For example, all the gas stations connected to the central MetroGas router were handled identically. However, several design scenarios where the routers reachable over a single physical interface have to be handled in entirely different ways do exist. For example, the core and access routers in DUAL-Mart network were in different subnets and running different routing protocols (see "Case Study 1 Solution—Integrating RIP and EIGRP" in Chapter 9, "Integrating EIGRP with Other Enterprise Routing Protocols," for more details).

The designs where you have to handle neighbors reachable over the same physical interface in different ways can be easily implemented using subinterfaces. Subinterfaces are logical interfaces encompassing one (point-to-point *subinterfaces*) virtual channel or several (multipoint subinterfaces) virtual channels. The subinterface behaves exactly like the physical interfaces from a routing, accounting, and filtering perspective. The subinterfaces differ from the physical interfaces only in the following details:

- Subinterfaces don't have their own output queues and interface buffers.

- You cannot specify queuing on subinterfaces. You can specify per-DLCI queuing on Frame Relay networks, but the queuing parameters are unique to each DLCI, not to each subinterface.

- Some interface SNMP variables are not available for subinterfaces (for example, input and output errors). In older IOS releases, no SNMP counters were available for subinterfaces.

Point-to-Point and Multipoint Subinterfaces

IOS supports two types of subinterfaces: point-to-point subinterfaces that behave exactly like a point-to-point link (PPP or HDLC interface), and multipoint subinterfaces that behave exactly like multi-access WAN interfaces. You can assign only one virtual circuit (PVC or SVC) to a point-to-point subinterface, and you can assign any number of virtual circuits to a multipoint subinterface. (The limits are the same as the interface limits imposed by IOS.)

Use point-to-point subinterfaces in situations where the connection to each neighbor requires a unique set of parameters or where the split-horizon rules of the routing protocol require them. (See Chapter 13 for more details on split horizon and EIGRP.) Some protocols and technologies (for example, IPXWAN) only run over point-to-point links. Deploying these protocols over switched WAN networks, such as Frame Relay, requires point-to-point subinterface definition for every remote router reachable over the WAN network.

In most other cases, you should use multipoint subinterfaces because they give you better scalability:

- You don't need to define a new interface for each new neighbor.
- Several neighbors can share common configuration parameters, such as routing protocol parameters, packet filters, or accounting options.
- Overall router configuration is smaller and easier to manage.

NOTE   Using point-to-point subinterfaces in networks where the core router has several neighbors can also lead to Interface Descriptor Block (IDB) limit problems; most routers can support only up to 300 physical and logical interfaces when running Cisco IOS prior to version 12.0. The IDB limit is platform-dependent in IOS 11.1CA and IOS 12.0 and has been raised for the high-end routers like 7x00 series routers or AS5800 access servers.

Creating, Configuring, and Removing Subinterfaces

Subinterfaces are created dynamically as soon as you enter the interface command specifying a new subinterface. The subinterface type has to be entered when the subinterface is first referenced; it can be omitted afterwards, but cannot be changed. Individual PVCs or SVCs have to be assigned to subinterfaces using the commands listed in Table 12-4. The table also contains the commands used to create a new subinterface or remove an existing subinterface

---

NOTE   The entire subinterface configuration is lost when you remove a subinterface, and it cannot be recovered. The subinterface is never completely removed prior to router reload; it is only marked as deleted and does not appear in the router configuration anymore. You cannot redefine the subinterface type by removing the subinterface and re-creating the same subinterface with a different type: The router refuses your attempt to re-create a subinterface in deleted state.

Table 12-4   *Subinterface-Related IOS Configuration Commands*

Task	IOS Configuration Commands
Create a new subinterface	**interface serial** \<x\>.\<subint\> **point-to-point | multipoint**
Assign an X.25 PVC or SVC to a subinterface	Enter the **x25 map** or **x25 pvc** statement in the subinterface configuration mode
Assign a Frame Relay PVC to a subinterface	Specify the PVC in the subinterface configuration mode using **frame-relay map** command (for static Frame Relay maps) or **frame-relay interface-dlci** command (for dynamic Frame Relay maps)
Assign a Frame Relay SVC to a subinterface	Assign the Frame Relay map-list describing the SVC to the subinterface using **map-group** command in subinterface configuration mode
Assign an ATM SVC or PVC to a subinterface	Use the **pvc** or **svc** command in subinterface configuration mode
Remove a subinterface	**no interface serial** \<x\>.\<subint\>

Using Subinterfaces to Reduce Interface Output Load Due to EIGRP Hello Packets

You should use subinterfaces in your network design for several reasons, ranging from the need to treat different neighbors in different ways to the cases where the neighbors have to be assigned to different subnets to maintain the uniform subnet mask across the network. Anyway, very few network designs use subinterfaces to reduce the multicast bursts associated with EIGRP hello packets.

Each subinterface behaves exactly like a regular physical interface from the routing perspective and can have its own EIGRP parameters, such as **hello-interval** and **hold-time**. Assigning different hello intervals (and associated hold timers) to groups of neighbors can spread the multicast bursts significantly, more so if the hello intervals are relatively prime to each other.

Consider, for example, a core router with 50 neighbors reachable over a 256 kbps X.25 connection. The default hello interval for lower-speed multi-access networks is 60 seconds, which is usually too long, so the network designer has reduced the hello interval to 15 seconds. The broadcast queue cannot be used over X.25 interfaces, so a burst of 50 packets is generated every 15 seconds.

In an alternative design, the 50 neighbors are divided over five subinterfaces with hello intervals of 13,14,15,17, and 19 seconds. The hello intervals were chosen to be prime to each other. (The only common divisor they have is one.) Therefore, a burst of 50 packets is generated only once in 881790 seconds. Smaller bursts are generated more often, as illustrated in Table 12-5. The results in the table were generated using combinatorial theory, which is beyond the scope of this book.

Table 12-5 *Average Burst Repetition Rate Versus the Burst Size*

Burst Size in Packets	Approximate Average Burst Repetition Rate (in Seconds)
20	24
30	365
40	11,300
50	88,1790

Summary

Switched WAN networks present you with several challenges—from output queue overloads caused by emulated multicasts to intricate problems caused by misconfigured neighbor maps. All of these challenges can be overcome or avoided using several tools available in the Cisco IOS, as summarized in Table 12-6.

Table 12-6 *Useful Switched WAN-Specific IOS Tools*

Challenge	Solution	Applicable WAN Technology
Output drops due to emulated multicasts	Extend the output queue length	All
	Divide the neighbors across several subinterfaces	All
	Configure broadcast queue	Frame Relay
Neighbor maps are hard to maintain	Use automatic PVC discovery	Frame Relay
	Build dynamic maps using inverse ARP	Frame Relay and ATM
Neighbors reachable over one interface have to handled in different ways	Use subinterfaces	All

CHAPTER 13

Running EIGRP over WAN Networks

Chapter 12, "Switched WAN Networks and Their Impact on EIGRP," presented the generic challenges you face when designing a network that includes switched WAN technology, such as X.25, Frame Relay, or ATM, and the impact such technology has on EIGRP operation over switched WANs. This chapter extends the scope of the previous chapter by discussing EIGRP-specific issues and their impact on network design.

Various case studies of the MetroGas network that you encountered in Chapter 12 are used throughout this chapter to illustrate EIGRP-related issues arising in networks that implement either the network core or the access layer with switched WAN technology. The case studies cover slow convergence over WAN media, EIGRP pacing, and EIGRP split horizon.

The chapter concludes with hints that should help you successfully implement EIGRP over most switched WAN technologies.

Case Study—Improving Neighbor Loss Detection

For more information on this case study, please visit www.ciscopress.com/eigrp.

MetroGas is a large petrochemical conglomerate, covering everything from drilling operations to gas stations throughout the country. (For more information on MetroGas, please refer to Case Study 1 in Chapter 12.) The MetroGas management team decided to deploy a new client-server application on all the gas stations to get better insight into their day-to-day operations. The members of the networking department had to provide the infrastructure to support the new application, so they started a project that led to a country-wide network connecting all the gas stations to the headquarters' site where the central server is located. The designers decided to connect all the gas stations to the central site through a Frame Relay network with ISDN as a dial-backup solution. ISDN dial backup is extremely important because the client-server application cannot easily recover from a loss of communication.

The access speed of the remote gas stations is 64 kbps, and the access speed of the central router is 512 kbps. Each gas station is connected to the central router by one Permanent Virtual Circuit (PVC) with a Committed Information Rate (CIR) of 16 kbps.

ISDN dial backup is implemented with ISDN BRI interfaces on the access routers and a separate router with a PRI interface on the central site.

The overall topology of the MetroGas network is displayed in Figure 13-1.

Figure 13-1 *MetroGas Network—Logical Topology*

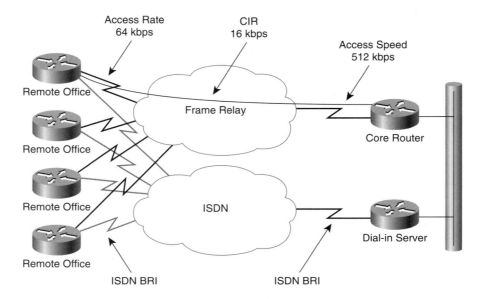

MetroGas' network designers decided to use EIGRP throughout the network to reliably detect Frame Relay outages at the IP layer and to be able to implement load balancing between the Frame Relay PVC and an ISDN dial-up connection. The designers were aware of scalability issues associated with large-scale EIGRP networks, so they implemented several safeguards, including a hierarchical IP addressing scheme, that would allow later deployment of route summarization, route filtering, and default routes.

The initial configuration of access routers (see Example 13-1) and the central router (see Example 13-2) turned out to be extremely straightforward. The designers configured the IP addresses on all the interfaces, turned on EIGRP, and got a running network.

Example 13-1 *Access Router Configuration*

```
hostname Access_Wichita
!
interface ethernet 0
 ip address 10.17.2.1 255.255.255.0
!
interface serial 0
 encapsulation frame-relay
 ip address 10.251.17.2 255.255.240.0
!
router eigrp 101
 network 10.0.0.0
```

Example 13-2 *Central Router Configuration*

```
hostname Core_A
!
interface FastEthernet 0/0
 ip address 10.1.1.1 255.255.255.0
!
interface serial 1/0
 encapsulation frame-relay
 ip address 10.251.16.1 255.255.240.0
!
router eigrp 101
 network 10.0.0.0
!
ip default-network 10.0.0.0
```

The initial ISDN dial-backup implementation relied on the *backup interface* feature of the IOS; ISDN backup should be activated as soon as the link to the Frame Relay network is lost (see Example 13-3).

Example 13-3 *Initial Dial-Backup Implementation on the Access Router*

```
hostname Access_Wichita
!
interface ethernet 0
 ip address 10.17.2.1 255.255.255.0
!
interface serial 0
 encapsulation frame-relay
 backup interface bri 0
 backup delay 10 60
 ip address 10.251.17.2 255.255.240.0
!
interface bri 0
 ip address 10.252.17.2 255.255.240.0
 dialer string 5551212
 dialer-group 1
!
dialer-list 1 protocol ip permit
!
router eigrp 101
 network 10.0.0.0
```

The initial ISDN dial-backup tests looked promising; the modem was disconnected at a remote site, and the ISDN link was immediately established. EIGRP started to run over the ISDN link, and the remote router received a complete routing table over the ISDN line. The only remaining problem was that the client-server application could not establish communications with the central server for several minutes. The users were only able to connect to the central server after the ISDN backup was active for approximately two to three minutes.

The MetroGas engineers tried to troubleshoot the problem with the usual set of tools; they ran *pings* and *traceroutes* between various points of the network (see Figure 13-2) and received the results outlined in Table 13-1.

Figure 13-2 *Dial-Backup Troubleshooting Test Points*

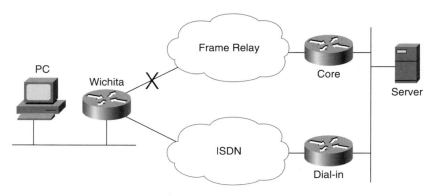

Table 13-1 *Dial-Backup Troubleshooting Results*

Test	Result
Ping from PC to Server	Fails.
Ping from Server to PC	Fails.
Ping from Wichita to Server	Succeeds.
Ping from Server to Wichita	Succeeds.
Traceroute from PC to Server	Last reachable hop is Wichita.
Traceroute from Server to PC	Last reachable hop is Core.
Traceroute from Wichita to Server	Succeeds.
Traceroute from Server to Wichita (Ethernet port)	Last reachable hop is Core.

These troubleshooting results quickly pinpointed the problem. IP connectivity between Wichita and the core site over ISDN worked fine (as proven by the traceroute from Wichita to the Server), but the traffic from the core site to Wichita's Ethernet gets stuck at the Core router. A quick look into the routing table on the Core route verified the problem. The EIGRP route toward 10.17.2.0/24 (Wichita's LAN subnet) still pointed toward the Frame Relay interface even though the Frame Relay port in Wichita was down. The EIGRP process detects the Wichita Frame Relay link failure only after the EIGRP hold timer expires—by default, three minutes.

The MetroGas network engineers decided to improve the network convergence by increasing the speed of EIGRP neighbor loss detection. They decreased the hello timers on access routers from their default value (60 seconds) to 5 seconds and decreased the hold time to 15 seconds (see Example 13-4). The core router could thus detect the remote Frame Relay link failure in 15 seconds and the ISDN backup would be fully functional after that time.

Example 13-4 *Final Dial-Backup Implementation on the Access Router*

```
hostname Access_Wichita
!
interface ethernet 0
 ip address 10.17.2.1 255.255.255.0
!
interface serial 0
 encapsulation frame-relay
 backup interface bri 0
 backup delay 10 60
 ip address 10.251.17.2 255.255.240.0
 ip hello-interval eigrp 101 5
 ip hold-time eigrp 101 15
!
interface bri 0
 ip address 10.252.17.2 255.255.240.0
 dialer string 5551212
 dialer-group 1
!
dialer-list 1 protocol ip permit
!
router eigrp 101
 network 10.0.0.0
```

Overhead Placed on the WAN Links by the EIGRP Hello Packets

The MetroGas network designers improved the EIGRP convergence by decreasing the EIGRP hello interval, but they also increased the overhead placed on the Frame Relay links by the hello packets. The effects of an increased WAN link load must be carefully evaluated whenever the EIGRP hello interval is decreased. The generic formulas used to calculate the EIGRP hello overhead are shown in Equation 13-1.

Equation 13-1

$$HelloPacketSize_{bits} < 400$$

$$HelloOverhead_{bps} = \frac{HelloPacketSize_{bits} \times NumberOfNeigbors}{HelloInterval}$$

$$HelloOverhead_{percentage} = \frac{HelloOverhead_{bps} \times 100}{LinkSpeed_{bps}}$$

The EIGRP hello packet size is approximately 40 bytes and the 400 bits value is used as a conservative estimate that should cover layer-2 encapsulation overhead.

As shown in Equation 13-2, the overhead should always be calculated on both ends of the link—in the MetroGas case, on both the access router and the core router. Assuming that the core router has 50 EIGRP neighbors and the access link speeds are 64 kbps for the access router and 512 kbps for the core router, the EIGRP hello overhead is as follows.

Equation 13-2

$$RemoteHelloOverhead_{bps} = \frac{400 \times 1}{5} = 80 bps$$

$$RemoteHelloOverhead_{percentage} = \frac{80 \times 100}{64000} = 0.12\%$$

$$CoreHelloOverhead_{bps} = \frac{400 \times 50}{5} = 4000 bps$$

$$RemoteHelloOverhead_{percentage} = \frac{4000 \times 100}{512000} = 0.78\%$$

The EIGRP hello overhead in MetroGas network is thus totally negligible even when the hello interval is decreased to five seconds.

Case Study—WAN Link Overload Due to EIGRP Traffic

The number of gas stations connected to the MetroGas network was steadily increasing, but the network designers did not feel that they needed to upgrade the Core router's Frame Relay access speed. The application traffic was sporadic and well distributed, so the Frame Relay link to the Core router was never congested. The network manager was therefore surprised when the network management station reported large traffic peaks on the Frame Relay link. Further analysis indicated that EIGRP placed more and more load on the Frame Relay link as the number of neighbors increased and that it completely saturated the link from time to time. Further investigation also uncovered several retransmissions between the EIGRP neighbors and occasional output packet drops on the Core router.

The network engineers turned to CCO for help and found a document under technical tips named, "*Configuration Notes for the Enhanced Implementation of EIGRP.*" The document explained a feature called *EIGRP pacing* and the importance of setting the correct bandwidth on Frame Relay interfaces. They immediately configured the proper bandwidth on the Frame Relay interfaces of all routers (see Example 13-5 for a Core router configuration and Example 13-6 for a sample access router configuration) and the load placed on the WAN link by the EIGRP never again exceeded 50 percent of the link speed.

Example 13-5 *Core Router Frame Relay Link Configuration*

```
hostname Core_A
!
interface serial 1/0
 encapsulation frame-relay
 bandwidth 512
 ip address 10.251.16.1 255.255.240.0
 ip hello-interval eigrp 101 5
 ip hold-time eigrp 101 15
```

Example 13-6 *Access Router Frame Relay Link Configuration*

```
hostname Access_Wichita
!
interface serial 0
 encapsulation frame-relay
 bandwidth 64
 backup interface bri 0
 backup delay 10 60
 ip address 10.251.17.2 255.255.240.0
 ip hello-interval eigrp 101 5
 ip hold-time eigrp 101 15
```

NOTE   Access speed was used as the interface bandwidth in these configurations, leading to a network that was more stable than the previous one, but still not correctly designed. The rules for setting correct EIGRP bandwidth on the Frame Relay interfaces are outlined in the following sections.

Load Control on WAN Links—EIGRP Pacing

As you saw in the previous case study, EIGRP can easily overload the WAN links with routing updates in scenarios where several neighbors are connected to a router through a single, low-speed WAN interface. Alternatively, the central router with a high-speed link can overload the link between the switched WAN network and the access router with routing updates, causing link congestion and packet drops on that link. EIGRP pacing was introduced in IOS maintenance releases 10.3(11), 11.0(8), and 11.1(3) to prevent these phenomena and to guarantee that EIGRP never uses more than an operator-specified percentage of the WAN link bandwidth.

NOTE	Correct operation of EIGRP pacing is extremely important in scenarios where a router has several neighbors reachable through the same physical interface or where the link speed mismatch between the endpoints of a WAN connection is large. In other scenarios, the EIGRP transport mechanism prevents congestion because it uses a window size of one.

EIGRP pacing prevents WAN link overload by emitting the EIGRP packets onto the WAN link in predefined time intervals. When designing the network, you specify the overall bandwidth available to EIGRP by using the **bandwidth** configuration command on the interface to indicate physical or logical interface bandwidth and the **ip bandwidth-percent eigrp** configuration command to indicate the interface bandwidth percentage available to EIGRP.

Different intervals are used for reliable packets (update, query, and reply packets) which can be as large as the Maximum Transfer Unit (MTU) size of the interface and for unreliable packets (hello and Ack packets) that have fixed length. Both pacing intervals are displayed in the **show ip eigrp interface** printout as shown in Example 13-7.

Example 13-7 *show ip eigrp interface Printout*

```
router#show ip eigrp interface
IP-EIGRP interfaces for process 1

                        Xmit Queue   Mean   Pacing Time   Multicast
Interface    Peers   Un/Reliable   SRTT   Un/Reliable   Flow Timer
Se0            3        0/0         288      10/380         2832
Se1            0        0/0           0       0/10            0
Et1            0        0/0           0       0/10            0
Et0            0        0/0           0       0/10            0
```

The pacing intervals are computed from the interface bandwidth. The bandwidth percentage allocated to EIGRP through the **ip bandwidth-percent eigrp** command (the default is 50 percent) and the interface IP MTU size are shown in Equation 13-3.

Equation 13-3

$$ReliablePacingInterval_{msec} \approx \frac{8 \times 100 \times MTU_{bytes}}{Bandwidth_{kbps} \times BandwidthPercentage_{percent}}$$

$$UnreliablePacingInterval_{msec} \approx \frac{8 \times 100 \times UnreliablePacketSize_{bytes}}{Bandwidth_{kbps} \times BandwidthPercentage_{percent}}$$

The minimum value for reliable pacing interval is 10 msec and there is no minimum value for unreliable pacing interval. (Unreliable packets are not paced on high-speed interfaces.)

The pacing intervals are computed independently for each physical and logical interface, including subinterfaces. Actual EIGRP pacing also works independently on each interface. It's therefore very important to set the proper bandwidth on subinterfaces, or the combined EIGRP traffic sent over a physical interface might overload the WAN link even though the traffic on each subinterface created over the physical interface is properly paced.

The bandwidth available to EIGRP over an interface is shared between all the EIGRP neighbors reachable through that interface. A round-robin algorithm is used to ensure fairness. Every time EIGRP is allowed to send another packet to the interface, a packet is emitted from a different per-neighbor output queue. You can estimate the length of an individual per-neighbor output queue from the Q Cnt field displayed with the **show ip eigrp neighbor** command as shown in Example 13-8.

Example 13-8 *show ip eigrp neighbor Printout*

```
Router#show ip eigrp neighbor
IP-EIGRP neighbors for process 1
H  Address      Interface    Hold Uptime    SRTT    RTO  Q  Seq
                             (sec)          (ms)         Cnt Num
2  10.4.0.4     Et0            14 00:00:05      7    200  0  274
0  10.4.0.2     Et0            11 00:00:08      0   4500  3  357
4  10.5.0.4     Se0           169 02:07:20   1076   5000  1   70
```

NOTE	The Q Cnt field does not count the EIGRP packets to be sent out, but the number of topology table entries that need to be sent to the EIGRP neighbor. The actual number of packets used to send those changes depends on several parameters including the interface MTU and the output filters.

EIGRP Pacing Design

The main parameter of EIGRP pacing design is the overhead (bandwidth percentage) that you are willing to accept throughout your WAN network. The load placed by EIGRP on any individual virtual circuit (VC) or any individual physical interface should not exceed the specified percentage of Committed Information Rate (CIR) or specified percentage of physical interface bandwidth.

After you select the bandwidth percentage, your design can proceed in one of two main directions:

1 You set the **ip bandwidth-percent eigrp** parameter to your desired bandwidth percentage on all the routers in your network and change the interface bandwidth to influence the desired EIGRP bandwidth usage.

2 You compute the actual bandwidth available to EIGRP over any logical (subinterface) or physical interface, set the interface bandwidth to the actual bandwidth and influence the EIGRP bandwidth usage by setting the **ip bandwidth-percent eigrp** parameter to the proper value.

The generic EIGRP pacing design presented in this section is based on actual EIGRP bandwidth usage. When the actual EIGRP bandwidth usage is computed, it's easy to compute the desired interface bandwidth (if the bandwidth percentage is fixed) or bandwidth percentage (if the interface bandwidth is set to a fixed value). The case studies following the generic design discussion focus on examples where you can use various shortcuts and simplify the design calculations.

Generic EIGRP pacing design proceeds as follows:

1 Compute the VC-based bandwidth available to EIGRP for each logical interface on each router in your network. As EIGRP performs round-robin, load-sharing between neighbors reachable over a logical interface, the VC-based bandwidth is determined by the slowest VC on the interface and the number of neighbors:

$$VCBasedEIGRPbandwidth = \\ SlowestVCspeed \times EIGRPBandwidthPercentage \times NumberOfNeighbors$$

2 Compute the physical bandwidth available to EIGRP for each physical interface:

$$PhysicalEIGRPbandwidth = \\ PhysicalInterfaceSpeed \times EIGRPBandwidthPercentage$$

3 Whenever the sum of the VC-based EIGRP bandwidths of all logical interfaces created over a physical interface stays below the physical EIGRP bandwidth, the design is completed. Use the VC-based EIGRP bandwidths to compute either **bandwidth** or **ip bandwidth-percent eigrp** parameter for each physical and logical interface in your network.

4 If the sum of the VC-based EIGRP bandwidths exceeds the bandwidth available for EIGRP over the physical interface, reduce the VC-based EIGRP bandwidth (for example, proportionally for all affected subinterfaces on the router with the largest overbooking). The VC-based EIGRP bandwidth of all routers connected to the other ends of affected VCs must also be adjusted to reduce the EIGRP load received by the affected router.

NOTE　　　EIGRP bandwidths on a virtual circuit must be symmetrical. The design rules compute the EIGRP bandwidth available to outgoing traffic, but the same limitations have to apply to incoming traffic, otherwise the incoming EIGRP traffic could overload your WAN link.

---

5 Repeat Step 3 and Step 4 as necessary.

The design process outlined here is slightly more complex in scenarios where the VC-based bandwidth is not known in advance (for example, in Frame Relay networks where the CIR is set to 0 or in X.25 networks). To follow the design process in these networks, start with Step 2; continue with Step 4, and then repeat Steps 3 and 4 until the bandwidths available for EIGRP are computed for all routers.

EIGRP Pacing Design Examples

Design 1—Hub-and-spoke Frame Relay network with a specified CIR: The easiest design example is a hub-and-spoke network implemented with virtual circuits with known CIR. Assume the network has one central router (hub) and ten remote routers (spokes). The access speed of the central router is 256 kbps, and the access speeds of the remote routers are all 64 kbps. The routers link together through PVCs with a CIR of 16 kbps, as shown in Figure 13-3. EIGRP is allowed to use up to 50 percent of the bandwidth of a VC or physical interface.

Figure 13-3 *Design 1—Hub-and-Spoke Network*

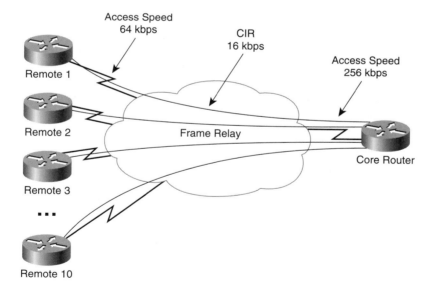

Based on the network topology, the initial design steps yield the EIGRP bandwidths outlined in Table 13-2.

Table 13-2 *Design 1—EIGRP Bandwidths*

Parameter	Bandwidth
VC-based bandwidth on remote router	8 kbps
VC-based bandwidth on central router	10×8 kbps = 80 kbps
EIGRP bandwidth on remote router Frame Relay interface	32 kbps
EIGRP bandwidth on central router Frame Relay interface	128 kbps

The VC-based bandwidth on all interfaces is less than the limit imposed by the access speed, so the pacing design is complete. The interface bandwidths and EIGRP bandwidth percentages could be set to parameters specified in Table 13-3.

Table 13-3 *Design 1—Final Interface Parameters*

Router	Bandwidth	EIGRP Bandwidth Percentage
Central router	256	80/256*100=31
Remote router	64	8/64*100=12

NOTE You can implement EIGRP pacing design by modifying either the bandwidth configured on the (sub)interface or specifying the desired bandwidth and modifying the EIGRP bandwidth percentage. Whichever option you choose, the final bandwidth available to EIGRP must match the bandwidth computed during the design process.

NOTE EIGRP pacing design is a continuous process; if the number of remote routers increases, you also must increase EIGRP bandwidth percentage on the central router. Some network designers try to avoid the constant adjustments by specifying the physical interface bandwidth and hoping that the EIGRP transport protocol limitations (window size of one) will prevent severe link congestion.

Design 2—An overbooked Frame Relay link on the central router: The second design scenario is completely equivalent to the first one, only the CIR of all virtual circuits has been raised to 32 kbps, as shown in Figure 13-4.

Figure 13-4 *Design 2—Frame Relay Topology*

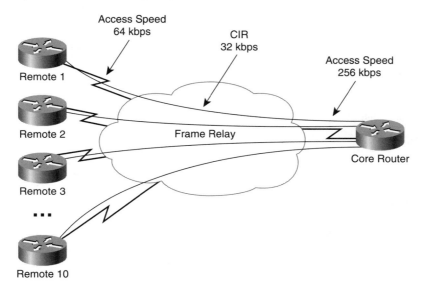

The initial EIGRP bandwidths are detailed in Table 13-4 and it's evident that the Frame Relay link of the central router is the limiting factor.

Table 13-4 *Design 2—Initial EIGRP Bandwidths*

Parameter	Bandwidth
VC-based bandwidth on remote router	16 kbps
VC-based bandwidth on central router	10×16 kbps = 160 kbps
EIGRP bandwidth on remote router Frame Relay interface	32 kbps
EIGRP bandwidth on central router Frame Relay interface	128 kbps

You could accept the fact that the EIGRP load on the central router exceeds the desired 50 percent resource utilization, leading to the interface parameters outlined in Table 13-5.

Table 13-5 *Design 2—Interface Parameters with a Highly Loaded Central Router Frame Relay Link*

Router	Bandwidth	EIGRP Bandwidth Percentage
Central router	256	160/256*100=62
Remote router	64	16/64*100=25

You could also sacrifice the network convergence speed for lower link utilization on the central router and adjust the EIGRP bandwidths; the new bandwidth available to each VC in the network becomes 13 kbps, resulting in the interface parameters shown in Table 13-6.

Table 13-6 *Design 2—Interface Parameters Retaining the Maximum Allowed Load Placed on Frame Relay Links by EIGRP*

Router	Bandwidth	EIGRP Bandwidth Percentage
Central router	256	50
Remote router	64	13/64*100=20

NOTE This design scenario raises an interesting question: How important is proper EIGRP pacing design? In this particular design, one could argue that the EIGRP traffic generated by a remote router is lower than the traffic generated by the central router and that one need not worry about the overbooking in the direction from the remote routers to the central router. In reality, I have seen many EIGRP networks that ran just fine as long as the proper interface bandwidth was specified on each physical interface. However, proper EIGRP pacing design ensures that your network runs optimally regardless of the link speeds, number of EIGRP neighbors, or link congestion. It also prevents hard-to-troubleshoot problems that might arise otherwise.

Design 3—A Frame Relay network with best-effort virtual circuits (CIR = 0): The third scenario is identical to the previous two, only the virtual circuits in the Frame Relay network were replaced with best effort PVCs (CIR = 0) as illustrated in Figure 13-5.

Figure 13-5 *Design 3—Frame Relay Topology*

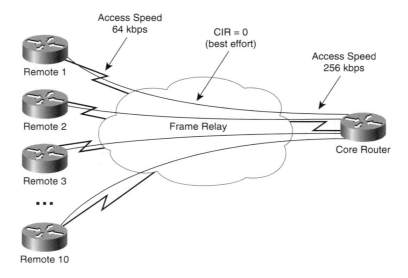

Because the maximum bandwidth available through any single VC is not known, the design is based only on physical interface limitations (access speeds) and the per-VC bandwidth is deduced from the interface bandwidth and the number of neighbors. The initial bandwidth calculations yield the results in Table 13-7.

Table 13-7 *Design 3—Initial EIGRP Bandwidths*

Parameter	Bandwidth
EIGRP bandwidth on remote router Frame Relay interface	32 kbps
Bandwidth available for each VC on remote router	32 kbps
EIGRP bandwidth on central router Frame Relay interface	128 kbps
Bandwidth available for each VC on the central router	128/10=13 kbps

The Frame Relay interface of the central router is the bottleneck that regulates the minimum per-VC EIGRP bandwidth. The per-VC bandwidth on the remote routers has to match the value on the central router, resulting in the interface parameters in Table 13-8.

Table 13-8 *Design 3—Interface Parameters*

Router	Bandwidth	EIGRP Bandwidth Percentage
Central router	256	50
Remote router	64	13/64*100=20

Design 4—A fully meshed core network with PVCs with various speeds: In this design scenario, the core of a network consists of four core routers implemented with a fully meshed Frame Relay network. The access speeds and the CIRs of the PVCs between the routers are specified in Table 13-9.

Table 13-9 *Design 4—Access Speeds and CIRs in the Core Network*

Router	Access Speed	CIR to R1	CIR to R2	CIR to R3	CIR to R4
R1	256 kbps	---	64 kbps	64 kbps	128 kbps
R2	128 kbps	64 kbps	---	32 kbps	16 kbps
R3	512 kbps	64 kbps	32 kbps	---	320 kbps
R4	512 kbps	128 kbps	16 kbps	320 kbps	---

It's easy to verify from Table 13-9 that none of the Frame Relay interfaces are overbooked; the sum of the CIRs on each interface is always lower than the access speed. The bandwidth available to EIGRP is thus dictated by the CIRs and not by the access speeds.

In the simplest possible design, where all the neighboring routers are reachable through the main Frame Relay serial interface, the network convergence is severely impacted by the low-speed PVCs. For example, the maximum overall bandwidth available to EIGRP on R4 is 48 kbps (three times 16 kbps, the CIR of the slowest PVC) or less than 10 percent of the available interface bandwidth.

The best design should optimize the EIGRP convergence for each PVC. You can easily achieve this goal by creating a separate point-to-point subinterface for every PVC in the core network and specifying the CIR of the PVC as the subinterface bandwidth. The design is slightly more complex to implement, but results in optimum EIGRP performance.

Design 5—A core network with best-effort PVCs: The last design example is similar to the previous one, the only difference is that the PVCs in the core network are replaced with best-effort PVCs with CIR = 0. The maximum bandwidth available to EIGRP is thus limited by the access speed of the Frame Relay interfaces.

NOTE   If you subscribe to a Frame Relay service with a CIR of 0, the service provider makes no guarantees that your data will be delivered. It can lead to interesting problems if the provider is not oversubscribed when you sign up for the service and then starts getting congested later.

Similar to the previous example, point-to-point subinterfaces are used for maximum flexibility and the bandwidth specified on each point-to-point subinterface reflects the estimated bandwidth available to the PVC bound to the subinterface.

The bandwidths available to individual PVCs are computed in a number of iterative steps, starting with the router with the slowest access speed and continuing with the increasingly faster routers:

1   The access speed of R2 is 128 kbps, giving the approximate per-PVC bandwidth of 42 kbps.

2   The access speed of R1 is 256 kbps and 42 kbps are already assigned to the PVC between R1 and R2. The per-PVC bandwidth of the remaining two PVCs is thus (256–42)/2=107 kbps.

3   The access speed of R3 is 512 kbps and 149 kbps are already assigned to the PVCs toward R1 and R2. The remaining bandwidth (363 kbps) is assigned to PVC toward R4.

4 The sum of the PVC bandwidths on R4 is equal to the access speed (42+107+363 = 512); the bandwidth allocation is complete. The results are summarized in Table 13-10.

Table 13-10 *Estimated Bandwidth Available to Best-Effort PVCs*

Router	Access Speed	Bandwidth toward R1	Bandwidth toward R2	Bandwidth toward R3	Bandwidth toward R4
R1	256 kbps	---	42 kbps	107 kbps	107 kbps
R2	128 kbps	42 kbps	---	42 kbps	42 kbps
R3	512 kbps	107 kbps	42 kbps	---	363 kbps
R4	512 kbps	107 kbps	42 kbps	363 kbps	---

You can use the bandwidths from Table 13-10 to set the subinterface bandwidths on the four core routers. The default value of **ip bandwidth-percent eigrp** (50 percent) ensures that the EIGRP traffic never exceeds one half of the estimated PVC bandwidth.

Case Study—Partial Connectivity over Frame Relay

For more information on this case study, please visit www.ciscopress.com/eigrp.

MetroGas' network performed very well after the network engineers fine-tuned the EIGRP pacing parameters. The next set of problems started, however, when the application development team wanted to deploy a new application that required any-to-any connectivity between the gas stations. It turned out that the core routers know all the routes to all the gas stations, but that the gas stations know only the routes to the subnets at the central site.

The problem was quickly linked to the *split horizon* that is used by all distance-vector routing protocols including EIGRP. The split-horizon rule prohibits a router from advertising a route through the interface the router itself is using to reach that destination. Because all the remote routers in the MetroGas network were connected to the central router through the same Frame Relay interface, the routes to individual, remote subnets were not announced to other remote routers, effectively disabling connectivity between them.

Two approaches were identified that would give the MetroGas network full connectivity between any pair of nodes:

- Disable split horizon over the Frame Relay network.

- Announce the default route (or a generic enough summary) from the central router to the gas stations, in a manner similar to the configuration in Example 13-9.

Example 13-9 *Core Router Configuration That Results in Any-to-Any Connectivity in the MetroGas Network*

```
hostname Core_A
!
interface serial 1/0
 encapsulation frame-relay
 bandwidth 512
 ip address 10.251.16.1 255.255.240.0
 ip hello-interval eigrp 101 5
 ip hold-time eigrp 101 15
 ip summary-address eigrp 101 10.0.0.0 255.0.0.0
!
router eigrp 101
 network 10.0.0.0
!
ip default-network 10.0.0.0
```

NOTE   Whenever possible, you should resort to default routes or route summarization and not to disabling split horizon. Disabling split horizon increases the EIGRP topology database on the remote routers and the traffic generated by EIGRP.

EIGRP Split Horizon

You control the EIGRP split-horizon behavior with the **ip split-horizon eigrp** command, as outlined in Table 13-11. Split horizon is turned on by default, even on the switched WAN interfaces. Please note that EIGRP's split-horizon behavior is not controlled or influenced by the **ip split-horizon** command.

Table 13-11 *Configuring EIGRP Split Horizon*

Task	Interface Configuration Command
Disable split horizon on an interface	**no ip split-horizon eigrp** \<as-number\>
Re-enable split horizon	**ip split-horizon eigrp** \<as-number\>

WARNING   Changing the EIGRP split-horizon setting on an interface resets all the adjacencies with EIGRP neighbors reachable over that interface.

NOTE   Split horizon should only be disabled on the hub site in a hub-and-spoke network. Disabling split horizon on the spokes radically increases EIGRP memory consumption on the hub router as well as the amount of traffic generated by EIGRP on the spoke routers.

Running EIGRP over Various Switched WAN Technologies

The previous sections of this chapter covered EIGRP issues that are specific to all switched technologies. This section gives you additional tips on the successful implementation of EIGRP over specific switched WAN technologies.

Running EIGRP over X.25

X.25 technology is usually associated with low-speed links giving even lower throughput. Most X.25 public networks are also charged by usage, making judicious use of bandwidth a prime issue. EIGRP design for the X.25 network should therefore use as many scalability tools as possible to minimize the EIGRP traffic transmitted over X.25. You should also be very careful with the placement of query boundaries because the EIGRP queries are always propagated one hop beyond the query boundary. (Please refer to Chapters 5 through 9 of this book for more details.) If the query boundary is established at the edge of the X.25 network, all the queries coming from the rest of the EIGRP domain are still propagated into the X.25 network. Sometimes the only possible solution left to the network designer is to deploy another routing protocol in the X.25 part of the network.

Additional tips for reducing EIGRP traffic over the X.25 network include the following:

- Increase the hello interval and hold time unless the convergence speed is of prime importance.
- Use default routes wherever possible to reduce the number of routes announced over the X.25 network.
- Do not disable the EIGRP split horizon because to do so only increases the traffic; use default routes instead.

Last but not least, do not forget that X.25 configuration in Cisco IOS needs **x25 map** statements to identify the neighbors and that these maps must be configured with the **broadcast** option for EIGRP to work.

Running EIGRP over Frame Relay

EIGRP implementations over Frame Relay usually suffer from the following symptoms:

- Slow convergence due to very long hello intervals and hold timers, unless you use point-to-point interfaces where the default values for hello interval and hold timer are 5 and 15 seconds
- Retransmissions and output drops due to misconfigured interface bandwidths or badly designed EIGRP pacing
- Heavy EIGRP traffic due to nonscalable network design, lack of query boundaries, or misplacement of the query boundaries

Most of these Frame Relay symptoms can be easily avoided by following a few simple steps:

- Make sure that the interface bandwidth represents the derived bandwidth based on CIRs or the real access speed of the interface in combination with **eigrp bandwidth-percentage**.

- Make sure that the subinterface bandwidth represents the CIR of the assigned PVC.

- Reduce the hello interval and hold timer in environments where the convergence speed is of prime importance.

- In large networks or in environments with many neighbors or large differences in access speeds on central and remote sites, do a thorough EIGRP pacing design.

- Use the **frame-relay broadcast-queue** documented in Chapter 12 to avoid link congestion and packet drops related to EIGRP hello packets.

Running EIGRP over ATM

EIGRP implementations over ATM are usually straightforward; the speed of a typical ATM link is usually high enough to make any EIGRP WAN-related issues irrelevant. However, a few caveats do exist, even in the ATM environment:

- Similar to X.25, ATM uses map statements to specify mapping between ATM PVCs or ATM NSAPs and the IP addresses of the remote routers. These map statements have to include a **broadcast** option for EIGRP to work correctly.

- EIGRP does not work well if the ATM cloud is implemented with Classical IP over ATM (RFC 1577) encapsulation. Due to the way IP multicast packets are propagated within the ATM network configured as Classical IP over ATM, EIGRP adjacencies are established only between the ARP server and other routers, resulting in all the IP traffic being routed through the ARP server

Summary

Several mechanisms influence EIGRP operation on switched WAN networks:

- Hello intervals and hold timers that have large default values on low-speed switched WAN interfaces can severely impact the convergence time of the network unless you use point-to-point subinterfaces.

- EIGRP routing traffic can congest the WAN links if the interface bandwidths are misconfigured or if EIGRP pacing is not designed properly. Associated packet drops and retransmissions can lead to prolonged communication failures between EIGRP neighbors, finally resulting in Stuck-in-Active routes.

- EIGRP pacing can also cause extremely slow network convergence, sometimes resulting in Stuck-in-Active routes.

NOTE	One of the easiest ways to simulate Stuck-in-Active events in the lab is to reduce the bandwidth of an interface to a very small value (for example, 1). All the output traffic through that interface (including all the query packets) is stuck for a very long time due to extremely long EIGRP pacing timers resulting in Stuck-in-Active timeout (usually somewhere else in your network).

- EIGRP split horizon might lead to partially connected networks when the network is implemented over partially meshed WAN topology.

With all these issues in mind, the need for careful WAN network design becomes even more evident. Traditional WAN network design usually focuses on expected traffic flows in the network and associated VC capacities. Additionally, EIGRP WAN network design should address convergence issues and EIGRP pacing and include a careful evaluation of query boundaries and associated traffic generated during diffused computation.

CHAPTER 14

EIGRP and Dial-Up Networks

IOS implements dial-up functionality in a variety of ways, from traditional dialer interfaces to dialer profiles and virtual access interfaces. The configuration details of these implementation methods are beyond the scope of this book and the reader is kindly referred to IOS documentation.

NOTE   The Cisco IOS dial-up functionality and configuration is covered in "Dial Solutions Configuration Guide" and "Dial Solutions Command Reference" parts of Cisco IOS documentation. This documentation is available on CCO (www.cisco.com/univercd/home/home.htm) or through Cisco Press.

To understand EIGRP's behavior in combination with various dial-up implementation mechanisms, it's important to understand the properties of all three dial-up implementations from the routing protocol's perspective:

- Dialer interfaces, including BRI and PRI interfaces, behave like a multi-access, nonbroadcast interface (similar to X.25). Several dial-up neighbors can be reached through the same dialer interface. The routing protocol also gets no indication that the neighbor has disconnected and has to rely on some other means (such as the hello protocol in EIGRP) to discover neighbor loss. This implementation mode is also called *legacy DDR*.

- Dialer profiles behave like point-to-point interfaces. Only a single dial-up neighbor can be reached through a dialer profile. As with the dialer interface, the routing protocol gets no indication that the neighbor has disconnected.

- Virtual access interfaces also behave like point-to-point interfaces. The interface is removed when the call is disconnected, giving an indication to the routing protocol that the neighbor is no longer reachable. Virtual access interfaces cannot be used for dial-out purposes prior to 12.0(3)T, which implements the *Large Scale Dial-Out* feature set.

The properties of the dial-up implementations are summarized in the Table 14-1.

Table 14-1 *Functional Summary of IOS Dial-Up Implementations*

Dial-Up Implementation Type	Number of Concurrent Neighbors	Interface Type From Routing Protocol Perspective	Interface Goes Down on Call Disconnect	Dial-Out Capability
Dialer interface	Many	Multi-access	No	Yes
Dialer profile	One	Point-to-point	No	Yes
Virtual access	One	Point-to-point	Yes	No

Throughout this chapter, a number of case studies illustrate the issues you face when designing EIGRP networks in dial-up environments. Three typical dial-up cases are discussed:

- A dial-in scenario, where the remote sites (spokes) dial into the central site (hub) to access servers located there.

- A dial-out scenario, where the central site has to reach remote sites to access data stored there. (A typical application might be network management or remote backup.)

- A dial-backup scenario, where the dial-up connection is used as a backup for the primary link, usually a leased line or switched WAN interface.

Case Study—A Simple Dial-Up Network

For more information on this case study, please visit www.ciscopress.com/eigrp.

MetroGas corporation (please refer to Chapter 13, "Running EIGRP over WAN Networks," for more details) has successfully rolled out a corporate network linking gas stations over a Frame Relay infrastructure. The company found, however, that the solution was not cost-effective for small remote gas stations where the cost of a fixed Frame Relay link was simply too high. Engineers decided to implement dial-up ISDN access for those gas stations, and they decided (for consistency reasons) to retain EIGRP as the routing protocol in the dial-up part of the network. They also decided to use unnumbered ISDN links to ease the configuration and save address space.

NOTE   In the MetroGas network, designers need to ask themselves whether they need to run a dynamic routing protocol with the remote routers. It's surprising how many times the answer to that question is *no*, but often users still insist on running a dynamic routing protocol over dial-up connections.

The pilot network (see Figure 14-1) was very small; the central site housed an access server (AS 5300) connected to the ISDN network via an ISDN PRI interface. A Cisco 1603 router at a remote gas station was connected to the same ISDN network via an ISDN BRI interface.

Figure 14-1 *MetroGas ISDN Dial-Up Pilot*

The initial central access server router configuration was extremely simple. EIGRP was configured on the PRI interface, local usernames were configured on the router to verify the identity of the remote routers, and dynamic dialer maps took care of the rest. The relevant parts of central access server configuration are shown in Example 14-1.

Example 14-1 *Central Access Server Configuration*

```
hostname AccessServer
!
isdn switchtype primary-net5
!
username remote_SanJose password xyz123
!
controller e1 0
!
interface loopback 0
 ip address 10.253.0.1 255.255.255.255
!
interface serial 0:23
 ip unnumbered loopback 0
 encapsulation ppp
 ppp authentication chap
 dialer-group 1
 dialer idle-timeout 600
!
dialer-list 1 protocol ip permit
!
router eigrp 101
 network 10.0.0.0
```

Configuration of the remote routers was even simpler; designers had to add a static default route and a string to dial (see Example 14-2).

Example 14-2 *Remote Dial-Up Router Configuration*

```
hostname remote_SanJose
!
isdn switchtype primary-net3
!
username AccessServer password xyz123
!
interface ethernet 0
 ip address 10.17.5.1 255.255.255.0
!
interface bri 0
 ip unnumbered ethernet 0
 encapsulation ppp
 ppp authentication chap
 dialer-group 1
 dialer idle-timeout 600
 dialer string 408-555-1234
!
dialer-list 1 protocol ip list 101
!
access-list 101 deny eigrp any any
access-list 101 permit ip any any
!
ip route 0.0.0.0 0.0.0.0 bri 0
!
router eigrp 101
 network 10.0.0.0
```

The pilot network worked well, so the network designers decided to roll the solution out to a larger number of gas stations. As they did so and the number of gas stations connected to the access server increased, the whole network unexpectedly melted down in a succession of Stuck-in-Active (SIA) events (see also section "Stuck-in-Active Routes" in Chapter 1, "EIGRP Concepts and Technology," for further details). As is usually the case, the SIA events occurred all over the network, but careful analysis finally pointed to the PRI interface on the access server as the culprit.

EIGRP Bandwidth Issues in Dial-Up Networks

The network meltdown in MetroGas network was caused by the EIGRP pacing on the PRI interface. The default bandwidth of a PRI interface is 64 kbps, reflecting the actual speed toward a remote router. By default, EIGRP uses half the interface bandwidth (32 kbps on PRI interface) for EIGRP updates and the bandwidth allocated to EIGRP is divided evenly across all EIGRP neighbors reachable over a multi-access interface. With 20 remote routers connected to the access server through the PRI interface, per-neighbor bandwidth drops to

1.6 kilobits/second or a mere 200 bytes/second. Any network instability that results in queries being sent over the PRI interface inevitably congests the interface from an EIGRP perspective, leading to long delays, and finally, Stuck-in-Active routes when the router initiating diffusing computation times out.

This problem has several solutions, none of which are completely satisfactory:

- Increasing the interface bandwidth solves the EIGRP pacing problem, but can lead to routing problems. (A route over the ISDN connection might be preferred over a route going over a higher-speed leased line.)

- Increasing the EIGRP bandwidth percentage also solves the EIGRP pacing problem, but can lead to ISDN connections being filled up with EIGRP traffic when few dial-up routers are connected. EIGRP never congests the physical interface due to EIGRP transport protocol limitation (window size is one), but the EIGRP traffic is likely to represent a majority of the traffic sent over the ISDN connection.

- Using dialer profiles solves the pacing problem because the interfaces over which EIGRP runs become point-to-point interfaces. However, this can lead to configuration problems in environments where several remote routers are connected to a central access server. The current IOS versions also limit the total number of interfaces in most routers (including dialer profiles) to approximately 300.

- Using virtual access interfaces solves the pacing problem in the same way as using dialer profiles. However, the virtual access interfaces cannot be used for dial-out.

The solution you prefer to implement in your network depends on a number of parameters, ranging from the number of remote routers and number of changes expected (for example, remote site adds or changes) to dial-up requirements you have (for example, is dial-out required?). Nonetheless, the best solution might be not to use EIGRP over the dial-up network and replace it with another protocol like RIPv2 (see also, "Case Study Solution—Integrating RIP with EIGRP," in Chapter 9, "Integrating EIGRP with Other Enterprise Routing Protocols," for a similar design).

NOTE   Other solutions, such as per-user static routes available in combination with AAA authorization, make routing protocols unnecessary in pure dial-in scenarios.

EIGRP Query Boundaries in a Dial-Up Environment

Similar to low-speed WAN links, EIGRP query boundaries become extremely important if you want to deploy EIGRP over dial-up connections in a large network. Although you can increase the bandwidth available to EIGRP traffic over a dialer interface with the tricks explained in the previous section, the reality remains that a single dial-up connection can carry anywhere from 9.6 kbps to 64 kbps of data. Excessive amounts of EIGRP traffic on a dial-up connection can therefore negatively impact the application traffic throughput and application end-to-end response times.

The query boundaries are relatively easy to establish in networks that use dedicated access servers for dial-up connections. For example, in the MetroGas network, the query boundary is easily established on the central access server by announcing only the default route to it from the core router (see Figure 14-2). Most of the queries received from the core network are stopped at the central access server because it wouldn't have the route being queried about in its EIGRP topology database.

Figure 14-2   *Query Boundary Establishment in the MetroGas Central Site*

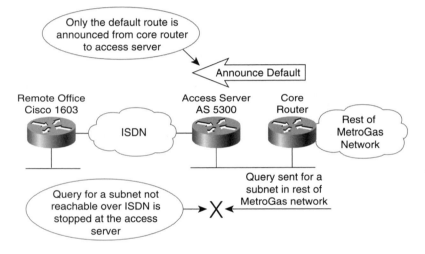

NOTE   Due to EIGRP design, you can never perfectly isolate remote routes from the irrelevant queries. Whenever one of the dial-up routers disconnects and the central access server loses the routes previously announced by that router, it always queries all the other dial-up routers.

Case Study—Route Flaps in a Dial-Up Environment

For more information on this case study, please visit www.ciscopress.com/eigrp.

MetroGas' engineers finally decided to fix the EIGRP pacing problems by using virtual access interfaces on the central access server, resulting in the router configuration shown in Example 14-3. (The commands added to support virtual access interfaces are highlighted.)

The configuration was tested in a lab network and successfully migrated to the MetroGas production network. It looked like the ISDN nightmares were finally over.

Example 14-3 *Central Access Server Configuration with Virtual Access Interfaces*

```
hostname AccessServer
!
isdn switchtype primary-net5
!
username remote_SanJose password xyz123
!
controller e1 0
!
virtual-profile virtual-template 1
!
interface virtual-template 1
 ip unnumbered loopback 0
 encapsulation ppp
 ppp authentication chap
!
interface loopback 0
 ip address 10.253.0.1 255.255.255.255
!
interface serial 0:23
 ip unnumbered loopback 0
 encapsulation ppp
 ppp authentication chap
 dialer-group 1
 dialer idle-timeout 600
!
dialer-list 1 protocol ip permit
!
router eigrp 101
 network 10.0.0.0
```

A few months later, the MetroGas management started complaining about huge ISDN costs. Upon investigation, it turned out that the remote router configurations were suboptimal from the start; someone had inserted **dialer idle-timeout 600** in the ISDN interface configuration. The result was quite expensive. Although the number of transactions performed by small gas stations was low and each transaction took only seconds to complete, the ISDN connection stayed active for 10 minutes after each transaction ended. The fix was obvious; the idle timeout was lowered to five seconds, immediately decreasing the ISDN bills.

NOTE

You can track ISDN costs with a good monitoring and accounting package. In the absence of a good tracking system, the **show isdn history** command (shown in Example 14-4) can also give you some insight into the ISDN costs incurred.

Example 14-4 *Sample show isdn history Printout*

```
Router# show isdn history
--------------------------------------------------------------------
                          ISDN CALL HISTORY
--------------------------------------------------------------------
History Table MaxLength = 320 entries
History Retain Timer = 60 Minutes
--------------------------------------------------------------------
Call  Calling    Called   Duration   Remote      Time until    Recorded Charges
Type  Number     Number   Seconds    Name        Disconnect    Units/Currency
--------------------------------------------------------------------
in    4085551224          240        SanJose_1                 5     u(D)
in    4151234567          Active(90) SantaClara_3 240          13    u(D)
--------------------------------------------------------------------
```

Lowering the **dialer idle-timeout** parameter reduced the ISDN bills, but it also introduced more frequent route flaps into the MetroGas network. The network engineers did not notice the increased EIGRP activity until Stuck-in-Active events started to appear all over the network with no single easily identifiable bottleneck. It turned out that the amount of flapping introduced by the dial-up connections swamped all the low-speed links in the MetroGas network.

NOTE

One of the worst experiences I had with EIGRP in a dial-up scenario involved a network where the route flaps were being introduced from a stack of access routers having all together over 30 PRI ports. The CPU utilization due to the EIGRP process on the low-end routers was constantly exceeding 70 percent and the routers were already starting to drop packets due to overload. SIA events also happened every few minutes. Extensive use of route filters and summarization brought the CPU utilization due to EIGRP down to a few percent on all routers.

The MetroGas engineers had to introduce summarization between the central access server and the core network to reduce the number of queries going into the rest of the MetroGas network. They had not succeeded, however, in reducing the EIGRP traffic introduced on the dial-up connections. Whenever a single remote router disconnected, all the other remote routers got involved in the diffusing computation.

NOTE	I've seen many large networks that did not deploy any EIGRP scalability features and had no EIGRP pacing design, but seemed to work well because the WAN infrastructure the network was using was extremely stable, resulting in almost no route flaps. Nevertheless, when dial-up connections are introduced into such a network, the increased number of route flaps resulting from dial-up routers connecting and disconnecting from the access server quickly brings the network to its knees.

Finally, the MetroGas engineers had to admit defeat. EIGRP simply was not performing well over the dial-up links in their large-scale, dial-in environment. They had to resort to another routing protocol (RIP v2) in the dial-up part of the network, resulting in the access server configuration shown in Example 14-5.

Example 14-5 *MetroGas Access Server Configuration*

```
hostname AccessServer
!
isdn switchtype primary-net5
!
username remote_SanJose password xyz123
!
controller e1 0
!
interface loopback 0
 ip address 10.253.0.1 255.255.255.255
!
interface serial 0:23
 ip unnumbered loopback 0
 encapsulation ppp
 ppp authentication chap
 dialer-group 1
 dialer idle-timeout 600
!
dialer-list 1 protocol ip permit
!
router rip
 version 2
 network 10.0.0.0
 default-information originate
!
router eigrp 101
 network 10.0.0.0
 redistribute rip metric 64 20000 255 255 1500
```

Thinking they finally had a firm grip on the dial-up network and had stopped it from influencing the EIGRP core network, the MetroGas engineers were surprised to learn that the EIGRP process still used a significant amount of CPU time on the access server and the core router. Further investigation showed that the routes to the remote subnets were no longer inserted into the EIGRP process, but the host routes that are automatically created when a remote router dials into the central server were still automatically redistributed into the EIGRP process. These routes were also flapping with the appearance and disappearance of remote dial-in routers, causing high CPU load on the access server itself and the EIGRP neighbors that had to process the queries. MetroGas engineers tried to stop that behavior, but found that there was no way to stop EIGRP from inserting connected subnets of a network where EIGRP is running into the EIGRP topology database. Ultimately, they had to move the whole ISDN dial-up network to another major network—a move that involved renumbering all the remote dial-up routers.

NOTE   The easiest way to stop the host route generation is with the **no peer neighbor-route** interface level command. This solution works well on numbered dialer interfaces and dialer profiles. On virtual access interfaces and unnumbered dialer interfaces or dialer profiles, the host route to remote dial-up peer is necessary for proper routing.

You could also get rid of the host routes that are automatically generated by the router by using a numbered dialer interface and proper IP addressing plan. The host routes are only generated if the remote IP address does not fall within the subnet configured on the dialer interface.

MetroGas engineers might also have used another trick—they could have moved only the loopback interface of the access server into another network, retained the addressing scheme on the remote routers, and run RIP v2 with no automatic summarization.

Case Study—Dial-Out Requirements

For more information on this case study, please visit www.ciscopress.com/eigrp.

MetroGas engineers were soon asked to provide additional services over their dial-up network; electronic sensors were installed in underground gas tanks at the gas stations, and the logistics department wanted to be able to read those sensors from the central location to optimize the dispatch of their delivery trucks. These requirements added a completely new dimension to the MetroGas dial-up network. Previously, the remote routers dialed into the central site whenever the operator started a transaction. To accommodate the new requirements, the central router had dial-out to the remote gas stations whenever the logistics application wanted to read the sensor values.

EIGRP Use in Dial-Out Requirements

Dial-out environments differ from dial-in environments in the routing setup. The central (hub) router that dials out to the remote (spoke) routers must have the routes toward all the remote subnets in its routing table at all times. These routes are then propagated to the rest of the network, leading to packets being attracted to the hub router, which delivers the packets to the spoke routers after establishing dial-up connection with them.

Leaving scalability issues aside (IOS versions prior to 12.0(3)T only enabled one router to act as a dial-out hub router for a certain spoke router), populating the routing table in the hub router remains the main issue of dial-up design and configuration. The routing table can be populated in three different ways:

- Using static routes
- Using dynamic routing protocol
- Using static routes downloaded from a central server (*large-scale dial-out*)

When using a dynamic routing protocol to populate the routing table of the hub router, the major requirement for the routing protocol is that it shouldn't keep the dial-up connection constantly active. The ideal routing protocol establishes a connection, exchanges routes, and closes the connection immediately afterwards. The route exchange process has to be repeated infrequently to cover potential changes in the addressing structure.

Only a few routing protocols satisfy these requirements:

- IGRP, RIP v2, or On-Demand Routing (ODR) with snapshot routing. Because IGRP does not support variable-length subnet masks (VLSM), RIP v2 or ODR are the preferred choices.
- OSPF with demand-circuit functionality (available in IOS 11.2).

EIGRP does not support snapshot routing or any other mechanism that permits infrequent route exchange without constant traffic generated by the hello mechanism, and is thus unsuitable as the routing protocol in a dial-out environment.

Case Study—EIGRP Use in a Dial-Backup Scenario

For more information on this case study, please visit www.ciscopress.com/eigrp.

With the ISDN dial-up network running smoothly, MetroGas engineers wanted to reuse their new knowledge in another problem area; the Frame Relay links to some locations proved to be unreliable and they wanted to use ISDN as the backup technology. Yet again, they started with a simple pilot. A remote router connected to Frame Relay was also connected to the ISDN network and the central access server was reconfigured to support the dial-backup functionality as well (see Figure 14-3). A separate PRI port was allocated on the central server to support dial-backup application to prevent remote gas stations from using up all the available ISDN channels.

Figure 14-3 *Dial-Backup in the MetroGas Network*

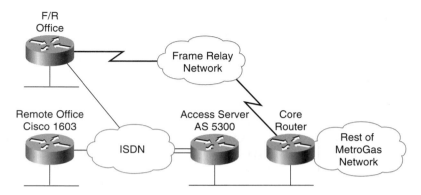

The central access server was already configured to use legacy DDR due to dial-out requirements, so the dial-backup functionality had to be implemented over a multi-access dialer interface although the engineers felt that dialer profiles might give them more flexibility.

The **backup interface** feature was used on the Frame Relay subinterface of the remote router to detect Frame Relay DLCI loss and trigger ISDN backup (see Example 14-6 for router configuration).

Example 14-6 *Dial-Backup Configuration on a Remote Frame Relay Router*

```
hostname Access_Wichita
!
interface ethernet 0
 ip address 10.17.2.1 255.255.255.0
!
interface serial 0
 encapsulation frame-relay
!
interface serial 0.1 multipoint
 bandwidth 64
 backup interface bri 0
 backup delay 5 60
 ip address 10.251.17.2 255.255.240.0
 frame-relay interface-dlci 157
!
interface bri 0
 ip unnumbered ethernet 0
 dialer string 5551212
 dialer-group 1
!
dialer-list 1 protocol ip permit
!
router eigrp 101
 network 10.0.0.0
```

This time, the MetroGas engineers had problems even in the pilot network. The dial backup was established as expected, but when the Frame Relay link was restored and ISDN dial-up line disconnected, traffic to and from the remote site stopped flowing for several minutes.

EIGRP Neighbor Loss Detection Issues

The MetroGas team experienced another common problem in dial-backup scenarios; the remote router disconnected the ISDN connection, but the central access server was not aware that the link had been disconnected, so it still tried to send data over the nonexistent ISDN link. The central access server removed the ISDN route only when it discovered that the EIGRP neighbor was no longer reachable over ISDN.

NOTE	The problem described here arises only if the bandwidth and delay of the ISDN link are comparable to the bandwidth and delay of the primary link. Due to EIGRP vector metric calculation rules, it might also occur for specific destinations if those destinations are reachable through links with bandwidth lower than ISDN bandwidth.

You can use four different solutions in this scenario:

- If the bandwidth of the primary link is higher than the bandwidth of the backup link, all the routers prefer the routes reachable through the primary link. Interface delay should be increased on the dial-up link to make sure that the proper route is always selected (see Exercise 5-1 in Chapter 5, "Scalability Issues in Large Enterprise Networks," for a similar example).

- You can run another routing protocol over the dial-up connection. The administrative distance of EIGRP should be set so that it is lower than the administrative distance of the other routing protocol (which is usually the case anyway). Under these circumstances, the EIGRP route received through the primary link is always considered better than the route received over the dial-up connection.

- The EIGRP hello interval and hold timer can be decreased to very small values on the dialer interface to quickly discover dial-up disconnect.

- Use a dial-up implementation method where the interface is brought down or removed when the dial-up link is disconnected. The change in the interface status triggers immediate neighbor loss in the routing protocol. Virtual-access interfaces for ISDN connections or async interfaces for analog dial-up connections offer this functionality.

In the MetroGas case, the engineers found it easiest to implement virtual-access interfaces because they could use them in combination with the legacy DDR they were using for two-way dial-up connections to the other gas stations.

Summary

The case studies throughout the chapter illustrated the limitations of EIGRP when it's used in dial-up scenarios:

- EIGRP's packet pacing implementation might cause Stuck-in-Active events when EIGRP is run over legacy DDR interfaces. Several solutions, including virtual access interfaces or dialer profiles, can be used to resolve this issue.

- Dial-up environments generate many route flaps that might be several orders of magnitude larger than the number of flaps experienced in networks based on leased lines or switched WAN technology. EIGRP design requires careful placement of query boundaries to prevent router and network overload due to EIGRP diffusing computations.

- EIGRP is not suited for two-way dial-up– or dial-out–only applications.

- Slow neighbor loss detection might cause temporary outages in dial-backup design. Several techniques are available to circumvent this problem.

Due to these issues, you should use EIGRP over dial-up connections only when necessary, primarily in dial-backup scenarios. It is easier to implement routing in dial-in or dial-out scenarios with other routing protocols (for example, RIP v2) or other mechanisms available in Cisco IOS dial-up implementation (per-user static routes or EasyIP). Even when you use other routing mechanisms, the redistribution of dial-up routes into the core EIGRP process must be tightly controlled and managed to prevent network-wide problems due to diffusing computations following each dial-up disconnect.

CHAPTER 15

Secure EIGRP Operation

Security and reliability are extremely important components of every mission-critical network. Host security is a well-understood topic, as is the need for deploying a firewall when you connect several networks with various levels of trust (for example, corporate network to the Internet). However, no universal understanding for the need of all encompassing network security, from secure device management to secure information exchange, exists. More and more users are becoming aware of the need to secure their network devices, and the actions taken to increase the device security range from secure management (secure SNMP) to packet filters and sophisticated logon schemes. These measures usually do not extend to securing routing protocols, which are still exposed to various attacks that can lead to a successful intrusion or denial of service.

Two case studies used in this chapter illustrate the threats present in every network with insecure routing protocols. The rest of the chapter presents various security measures that can improve the security of EIGRP information exchange and thus increase the reliability of your network.

Case Study—Collecting Usernames and Passwords through a Fake Server

For more information on this case study, please visit www.ciscopress.com/eigrp.

One of the widely used and fairly successful forms of attack is based on presenting unsuspecting end-users with a familiar user interface. The end-users believe that they are authenticating themselves to their usual servers and the intruder can collect their usernames and passwords. The information collected in this way can later be used to access the real servers where the intruder posed as the victim of this spoofing attack. The following forms of this attack have been successfully used:

- A hacker installed a program that imitated the login sequence and collected usernames and passwords of users trying to log into a mainframe computer.

- A hacker imitated a server (for example, corporate WWW server or e-mail server) to which the users logged in and collected their credentials, which were later used to read users' e-mail or access the documents to which the hacker couldn't have accessed otherwise.

NOTE   Interestingly, the same concept is also used in other environments. For example, there have been reports of criminals using fake ATM machines or point-of-sale terminals to collect credit card information and Personal Identification Numbers (PIN).

The major obstacle to this form of Trojan horse attack was the installation of the fake program on the target mainframe computer or redirection of user traffic toward the fake host. The second task is, unfortunately, extremely simple in networks running insecure routing protocols.

Imagine a corporate network (as shown in Figure 15-1) where all the servers connect to a common LAN with IP subnet 10.1.1.0/24. The e-mail server has the IP address of 10.1.1.13. The whole corporate network runs EIGRP and uses no scalability tools, such as route summarization or filtering.

NOTE   Although scalability tools prevent some spoofing attacks, usually they are not sufficient to increase the security of the routing protocol.

Figure 15-1 *Corporate Network with Insecure Routing Protocol*

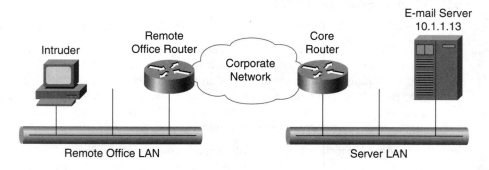

The intruder (who might be a disgruntled employee) gained access to one of the remote office LANs and would like to collect usernames and passwords that would give him or her access to various mailboxes on the corporate e-mail server. Because of insecure network design, an intruder can easily install an additional EIGRP router in the network that announces the route to 10.1.1.13/32, as shown in Figure 15-2. The new route is the most specific route for that part of the address space and all the routers forward all the packets for IP address 10.1.1.13 toward the intruder's router. Installing a PC with a POP3 server on it and connecting that PC to the newly installed router completes the trap. All users in the corporate network log on the fake POP3 server and reveal their usernames and passwords.

Figure 15-2 *Fake POP3 Server Trap Installed in a Remote Office*

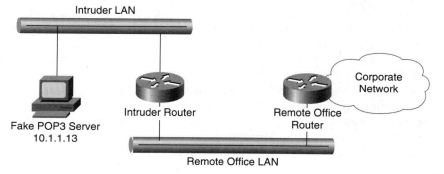

Several security loopholes in the corporate network allowed the intruder to install a fake POP3 server and attract the traffic to it:

* Remote office routers listened to EIGRP updates on their LAN interfaces.
* None of the routers performed any route filtering.
* Remote office routers were willing to form new adjacency and exchange routing information with an untrusted device.

You can easily remove all these loopholes with careful deployment of various EIGRP features:

* Configure LAN interfaces on remote office routers as passive interfaces to prevent the remote office routers from forming adjacencies with other routers on the remote LAN.
* Install route filters in distribution-layer routers to ensure that the remote office routers do not insert fake routes into the core network.
* Use EIGRP MD5 authentication throughout the network to ensure that only the trusted network devices form EIGRP adjacencies.

Case Study—Denial-of-Service Attack on a Core Network

For more information on this case study, please visit www.ciscopress.com/eigrp.

The Trojan horse attack in the previous case study used vulnerabilities in EIGRP router configuration to insert bogus routes in the network and reroute traffic to a fake server. A similar technique could be used in a denial-of-service attack to redirect traffic sent toward the corporate servers and thus prevent the end-users from gaining access to these servers.

Another class of denial-of-service attacks uses vulnerabilities in the routing protocols to disrupt IP routing or disable certain transmission paths in the network. Unfortunately, an intruder located anywhere in the corporate network can very successfully launch such attacks. If an intruder sends EIGRP update packets with a fake source IP address and an INIT flag set to 1 to any EIGRP router in the network (Beta, for example), the remote office router routes the packet based on destination IP address toward core router Beta (see Figure 15-3). Even core router Alpha blindly forwards the packet with its own IP address as the source address toward router Beta. Upon receiving the fake packet, router Beta immediately drops adjacency with router Alpha from which the packet supposedly came, resulting in IP routing disruption. A constant stream of fake packets might disable any link in the network permanently because the EIGRP adjacencies between the routers connected to such a link are constantly dropped.

Figure 15-3 *Intruder Sending Fake EIGRP Packets in the Network*

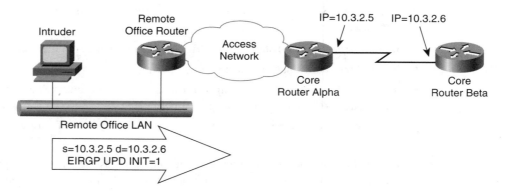

In most well-designed networks, it is exceedingly simple for an intruder to guess the source and destination IP addresses to use in the fake EIGRP packets; the **traceroute** command usually gives him or her enough information. Consider, for example, the **traceroute** output in Example 15-1.

Example 15-1 *Sample **traceroute** Output*

```
C:\WINDOWS>tracert www.cisco.com

Tracing route to www.cisco.com [192.31.7.130]
over a maximum of 30 hops:

 . . . lines deleted . . .
  4    762 ms    761 ms    806 ms   Hssi9-1-0.GW1.FFT1.ALTER.NET [146.188.33.161]
  5    742 ms    779 ms    779 ms   321.ATM1-0-0.CR1.FFT1.Alter.Net [146.188.3.125]
  6    854 ms    839 ms    860 ms   212.ATM5-0.BR1.NYC5.Alter.Net [146.188.7.62]
  7    860 ms    843 ms    843 ms   431.ATM5-0.GW2.NYC5.Alter.Net [137.39.30.141]
  8   1020 ms    919 ms    879 ms   152.ATM2-0.XR1.NYC1.ALTER.NET [146.188.177.246]
  9    873 ms    859 ms    838 ms   295.ATM7-0.XR1.BOS1.ALTER.NET [146.188.176.174]
 10    865 ms    864 ms    863 ms   191.ATM9-0-0.BR1.BOS1.ALTER.NET [146.188.177.9]
 . . . rest deleted . . .
```

The network through which the route between the end-user and www.cisco.com goes is very well designed and run. All router IP addresses map into hostnames, and they even reveal the interfaces on the routers that the packets pass. This information is valuable to the potential intruder who can deduce that there is a router with IP address 146.188.33.161 (hop 4 in the printout) connected to an HSSI link. Usually HSSI is used as a point-to-point interface, making it probable that the neighbor router has an IP address 146.188.33.162. If these two routers exchange EIGRP updates over the HSSI link, the intruder has enough information to disrupt the EIGRP adjacency between them.

NOTE

It's important to note that the "*security by obscurity*" approach (in this case, hiding router names and interfaces) does not work. It only makes the intruder's task slightly more difficult.

As in the previous case study, a number of security loopholes allowed the intruder to disrupt EIGRP routing in the network:

- The remote office router accepted IP packets with source IP address that did not belong to the remote office LAN.

- The remote office router accepted routing protocol packets from interfaces that could not be completely trusted.

- The core router accepted spoofed EIGRP packets.

The remedies for these loopholes include using passive interfaces within the EIGRP process to prevent a router from building neighborship on the subnets that have no other routers, IP packet filters to prevent spoofing attacks at their source, and EIGRP MD5 authentication to stop routers from accepting spoofed packets. It is easy to implement anti-spoofing packet filters on remote office routers in the enterprise networks, but extremely hard to implement them in other scenarios (for example, peering links between Internet service providers). The best countermeasure to EIGRP packet spoofing is therefore the EIGRP MD5 authentication.

EIGRP MD5 Authentication

EIGRP MD5 authentication ensures that routers accept EIGRP packets only from trusted sources. After the MD5 authentication is configured on an interface, every EIGRP packet sent by a router over that interface is signed with an MD5 fingerprint. Every EIGRP packet received over an interface with MD5 authentication configured is checked to verify that the MD5 fingerprint in the packet matches the expected value, making it impossible for the intruder to insert untrusted routers in the network or send bogus packets to the routers.

MD5 is an algorithm described in RFC 1321 that takes a message (EIGRP packet) and generates 128 bits of hash value (called *message digest* or *fingerprint*) with several properties that make MD5 usable in very secure signature implementations:

- Changing a single bit in the original message changes approximately half of the bits in the MD5 fingerprint.

- It's almost impossible to generate another message that yields the same MD5 fingerprint; therefore, forging is very hard.

The MD5 value generated from the EIGRP message packet is appended to the EIGRP packet, and the packet is sent to the EIGRP neighbor. The receiving router can verify the integrity of the packet by recalculating the MD5 value and comparing the result with the MD5 fingerprint in the packet.

This process does not lead to improved security because an intruder can repeat the steps taken by the originating router and generate forged packets with proper signatures. A secret known only to the sending and receiving router must to be introduced to stop the intruder from generating forged, signed packets. The whole process of secure information exchange between EIGRP neighbors can be summarized in the following steps (graphically presented in Figure 15-4):

Step 1   The sending router generates EIGRP information to be sent.

Step 2   MD5 is computed over EIGRP information and the shared secret.

Step 3   The resulting MD5 hash value is appended to the packet and sent to the neighboring router(s). Because the intruder does not know the shared secret, he or she cannot forge the packets.

Step 4   The receiving router computes MD5 over received EIGRP information and the shared secret. If the computed MD5 value matches the MD5 fingerprint appended to the packet, the packet is genuine and is accepted for further processing. Packets that do not pass the MD5 fingerprint check are silently dropped.

Figure 15-4 *EIGRP MD5 Authentication*

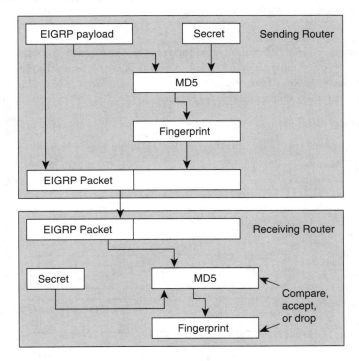

Configuring EIGRP MD5 Authentication

Configuring EIGRP MD5 authentication on the router is a two-step process outlined in Table 15-1. You can enable authentication on individual interfaces and even for individual EIGRP processes when you're running more than one EIGRP process over a single interface.

Table 15-1 *Configuring EIGRP MD5 Authentication on an Interface*

Task	Interface Configuration Command
Specify the shared secret used between adjacent routers reachable over specified interface	**ip authentication key-chain eigrp \<as-number\> \<key-chain-name\>**
Specify the type of authentication used in EIGRP packets (only MD5 is available)	**ip authentication mode eigrp \<as-number\> md5**

Security of EIGRP MD5 authentication relies exclusively on the shared secret, which should be periodically changed. The *key-chain* concept enables the controlled change of the shared secret. A key-chain consists of a set of keys where each key has its own lifetime. An example of a key chain is shown in Figure 15-5.

Figure 15-5 *Sample Key Chain*

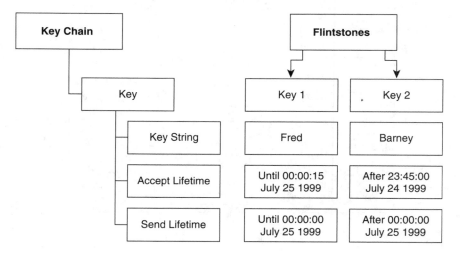

Key chains are defined on the router using the configuration commands in Table 15-2.

Table 15-2 *Configuring a Key Chain*

Task	Global Configuration Command
Define a key chain	**key chain <name>**
Define a key in the key chain	**key <sequence-number>**
Define key value for the specified key	**key-string <value>**
Define the time interval during which the key will be accepted by the router. If you don't specify the time interval, the key is always valid. The earliest acceptable start time is January 1, 1993.	**accept-lifetime <start-time> {<end-time> | infinite | duration <seconds>}**
Define the time interval during which the key will be used by the router to sign the packets. If you don't specify the time interval, the key is always used.	**send-lifetime <start-time> {<end-time> | infinite | duration <seconds>}**

The lifetime of the keys in the key chain normally overlaps to allow seamless key rollover, leading to potentially confusing situations where the router doesn't know which key to use. IOS applies the following rules to avoid potential ambiguities:

- If several keys have an overlapping **send-lifetime**, it uses the key with the lowest sequence number to sign the outgoing EIGRP packets.

- If several keys have overlapping **accept-lifetime**, the incoming packets can be signed with any one of those keys.

Example 1: Using the commands from Table 15-2, you can configure the key chain shown in Figure 15-5 with the IOS configuration commands in Example 15-2.

Example 15-2 *Sample Key-Chain Configuration*

```
key-chain Flintstones
  key 1
  key-string Fred
  accept-lifetime 00:00:00 Jan 1 1993 00:15:00 July 25 1999
  send-lifetime 00:00:00 Jan 1 1993 00:00:00 July 25 1999
  key 2
  key-string Barney
  accept-lifetime 23:45:00 July 24 1999 infinite
  send-lifetime 00:00:00 July 25 1999 infinite
```

Example 2: To configure a very simple authentication scheme with a fixed, unchanging key, use the IOS configuration commands in Example 15-3.

Example 15-3 *Sample Key-Chain Configuration*

```
key-chain SimpleKey
  key 1
    key-string aNiceKey
```

Shortcomings of EIGRP MD5 Authentication

The MD5 authentication of EIGRP information exchange significantly increases the security of the EIGRP routing protocol. However, be aware of the following shortcomings when designing highly secure EIGRP networks:

- EIGRP packets are only authenticated, not encrypted. The information exchange is reliable, but not confidential. The intruder who is able to receive EIGRP packets (for example, by being attached to the LAN interface between the routers) can still gain information about the network topology based on routing information exchange between the routers.

- Shared secrets are manually configured on the routers. No mechanism for automatic key generation or key distribution exists.

- Shared secrets are stored in router configuration in plaintext format. An intruder who accesses router configuration can immediately spoof EIGRP information exchange.

NOTE   The intruder does not have to break into the router to get access to router configuration. (Although that might be the easiest option if he or she gets physical access to a router.) Breaking into the network management station where the router configurations are stored is sometimes easier to do.

Design Issues and Guidelines

Several possible EIGRP MD5 authentication designs are possible, depending on the security level you want to achieve in your network and the potential penetration points you identified during the threat analysis. Only a few parameters influence your design; all of them are covered in this section.

Parameter 1—Scope of an Individual Key

You can use a single key throughout the network (less secure) or you can assign different keys to every subnet (more secure). You can also use different keys for layers of your network with different levels of trustworthiness. For example, you can use one key for the core of your network and another key for the access layer.

The single key approach is secure enough if the probability that an intruder can get your router configuration is negligible. If an intruder can get physical access to any one of your routers or break into your network management station, avoid the single-key approach.

Parameter 2—Key Changes

You can use one key throughout the lifetime of your network (less secure) or you can change the keys on a periodic basis (more secure). Keys that do not change are probably secure enough for networks in which the network manager wants to prevent accidental configuration errors or inadvertent connectivity between test and production networks. For any network with a formal security policy, the key changes would probably be requested by the security policy.

Parameter 3—Key Distribution

You can preinstall the key chains used by the EIGRP MD5 authentication on the router (more secure), or you can change them remotely by using any of the means available for IOS configuration management (less secure). In networks that require a high level of security, you must change the keys on a periodic basis, and the only way to implement periodic key changes is through remote management. Using encryption between the routers and the management station can considerably enhance the security of remote management.

You should be concerned with key distribution issues only if you expect an intruder to be able to tap into your transmission media between the network management station and the managed router. Unless you control the physical media between the two, you can usually assume that an intruder is capable of listening to your management traffic, making encryption deployment mandatory.

With these three parameters in mind, you can design your network with various levels of security. The design can range from a simple network with minimum security where all the routers use a single, unchanging key for EIGRP MD5 authentication to a highly secure design where the routers use different keys on every subnet and the keys change frequently through encrypted management sessions.

Key Rollover Design and Integration with NTP

You can substantially increase the security of EIGRP MD5 authentication by frequently making key changes. The key changes must be well planned and supported by the time synchronization between the routers.

Suppose that you want to change the keys at time t_r. Because all the routers do not have their times perfectly synchronized, the old key should be accepted for some time after t_r (until t_r+t_d), and the new key should be accepted slightly before t_r (starting at t_r-t_d). The time window you need for key rollover depends on the accuracy of the time synchronization between the routers. A few seconds is normally enough for t_d if you use NTP to synchronize the routers to a common clock.

Suppose further that your routers currently use key number N in the key chain *rollover* and that the key was configured to be valid forever.

NOTE   It's arguable whether it's a good practice to configure the current key to be valid indefinitely. On one hand, it ensures that the routers can always exchange data; on the other hand, it probably makes security officers slightly uncomfortable.

The configuration commands you have to send to the routers to prepare for the key rollover are outlined in Example 15-4.

Example 15-4 *Configuration Commands Used to Prepare for Key Rollover*

```
key-chain Rollover
key N
send-lifetime 00:00:00 01 Jan 1993 tᵣ
accept-lifetime 00:00:00 01 Jan 1993 tᵣ+t_d
key N+1
key-string NewKey
send-lifetime tᵣ infinite
accept-lifetime tᵣ-t_d infinite
```

After the time t_r, when the key rollover has already occurred, you should remove the old key from the router configuration using the commands in Example 15-5.

Example 15-5 *Configuration Commands Used to Complete Key Rollover*

```
key-chain Rollover
no key N
```

The key rollover works only if the times on the adjacent routers are synchronized. You can use several mechanisms for time synchronization, but they are beyond the scope of this book. Because NTP is the most commonly used time synchronization mechanism, the commands to configure NTP server on the router that has a built-in real-time clock and to configure secure NTP synchronization with an NTP server are provided in Example 15-6 and Example 15-7.

Example 15-6 *NTP Server Configuration on a Router*

```
ntp master <stratum: use 5 - 15>
ntp authenticate
ntp authentication-key <keyid> md5 <password>
```

Example 15-7 *NTP Client Configuration on a Router*

```
ntp server <server-ip-address> key <keyid>
ntp authenticate
ntp authentication-key <keyid> md5 <password>
ntp trusted-key <keyid>
```

Troubleshooting EIGRP MD5 Authentication

The lack of EIGRP adjacency between adjacent routers normally indicates problems with
EIGRP MD5 authentication. You can verify that the EIGRP MD5 authentication is the
reason for adjacency failure with the EIGRP packet debugging commands displayed in
Example 15-8. The line indicating MD5 authentication problems is highlighted.

Example 15-8 *EIGRP MD5 Authentication Debugging*

```
router#debug ip eigrp packets verbose
EIGRP Packets debugging is on
    (UPDATE, REQUEST, QUERY, REPLY, HELLO, IPXSAP, PROBE, ACK)
router#
EIGRP: received packet with MD5 authentication
EIGRP: Received HELLO on Ethernet0 nbr 10.0.0.1
  AS 1, Flags 0x0, Seq 0/0 idbQ 0/0 iidbQ un/rely 0/0 peerQ un/rely 0/0
EIGRP: ignored packet from 10.0.0.2 opcode = 5 (invalid authentication)
EIGRP: Sending HELLO on Ethernet0
  AS 1, Flags 0x0, Seq 0/0 idbQ 0/0 iidbQ un/rely 0/0
```

Four major reasons for failing adjacency exist:

- MD5 authentication is configured on one router but not on the other. The only way to
  verify whether EIGRP MD5 authentication is configured on an interface is to analyze
  the router configuration.

- Interface configuration refers to a wrong (or nonexistent) key chain. Verify that the
  key chain referred by the **ip authentication key-chain** command exists by using the
  show key chain command. Sample printout from the **show key chain** command can
  be seen in Example 15-9.

Example 15-9 *show key chain Printout*

```
Router# show key chain
Key-chain Flintstones:
    key 1 -- text "Fred"
```

Example 15-9 *show key chain* Printout

```
        accept lifetime (00:00:00 Jan 1 1993) - (00:15:00 July 25 1999) [valid now]
        send lifetime (00:00:00 Jan 1 1993) - (00:00:00 July 25 1999) [valid now]
key 2 -- text "Barney"
        accept lifetime (23:45:00 July 24 1999) - (always valid)
        send lifetime (00:00:00 July 25 1999) - (always valid)
```

NOTE   Key chain names are case sensitive.

- Routers are using different keys. You can verify which key the router is using with the **show key chain** command. Any key where the *accept lifetime* line contains *[valid now]* is accepted by the router and the first key where the *send lifetime* line contains *[valid now]* is used by the router to sign the outgoing packets.

- The routers use key rollover, but the real time on the routers differs. Verify the current time on all the adjacent routers by using the **show clock** command, as shown in Example 15-10.

Example 15-10 *show clock* Printout

```
Router# show clock detail
15:12:03.256 CET SUN Apr 18 1999
Time source is NTP
```

The EIGRP MD5 troubleshooting plan should contain the following steps:

Step 1   Verify that the adjacency is not established due to EIGRP MD5 authentication problems.

Step 2   Verify that the EIGRP MD5 authentication is enabled on all the adjacent routers.

Step 3   Verify that all router configurations refer to the valid key chain.

Step 4   Verify that the key chain definitions match between the routers.

Step 5   Verify that the routers use the same key (or that the key used by any router is accepted by any other router in case of rollover scenarios).

Step 6   Verify that the time is synchronized between the routers if you use key rollover.

Summary

An intruder can effectively use vulnerabilities of interior routing protocols, such as EIGRP or OSPF, to plant Trojan horse servers into your network or to disrupt your core links with a denial-of-service attack. The vulnerability of EIGRP arises from the fact that the routing information exchange is not authenticated and is easy to spoof.

MD5 authentication of EIGRP packets can ensure that the routers accept only packets signed by their trusted peers. The MD5 authentication prevents man-in-the-middle attacks or route spoofing and offers only authenticity, not confidentiality.

The EIGRP MD5 authentication uses shared secret (key) between adjacent routers to generate MD5 fingerprints from EIGRP information and the shared secret. The MD5 fingerprints generated in this way are very hard to forge without knowing the shared secret, leading to a very high level of authenticity.

In a secure network design, you should use different keys that are frequently changed in each IP subnet. Distribute keys in a secure network through a secure protected session.

INDEX

D

J–L

M

Q–R

T

U–V

W–Z

CCIE Professional Development

Cisco LAN Switching

Kennedy Clark, CCIE; Kevin Hamilton, CCIE

1-57870-094-9 • AVAILABLE NOW

This volume provides an in-depth analysis of Cisco LAN switching technologies, architectures, and deployments, including unique coverage of Catalyst network design essentials. Network designs and configuration examples are incorporated throughout to demonstrate the principles and enable easy translation of the material into practice in production networks.

Advanced IP Network Design

Alvaro Retana, CCIE; Don Slice, CCIE; and Russ White, CCIE

1-57870-097-3 • AVAILABLE NOW

Network engineers and managers can use these case studies, which highlight various network design goals, to explore issues including protocol choice, network stability, and growth. This book also includes theoretical discussion on advanced design topics.

Large-Scale IP Network Solutions

Khalid Raza, CCIE; and Mark Turner

1-57870-084-1 • AVAILABLE NOW

Network engineers can find solutions as their IP networks grow in size and complexity. Examine all the major IP protocols in-depth and learn about scalability, migration planning, network management, and security for large-scale networks.

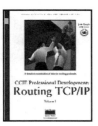

Routing TCP/IP, Volume I

Jeff Doyle, CCIE

1-57870-041-8 • AVAILABLE NOW

This book takes the reader from a basic understanding of routers and routing protocols through a detailed examination of each of the IP interior routing protocols. Learn techniques for designing networks that maximize the efficiency of the protocol being used. Exercises and review questions provide core study for the CCIE Routing and Switching exam.

CISCO SYSTEMS

CISCO PRESS

www.ciscopress.com

Cisco Career Certifications

CCNA Exam Certification Guide
Wendell Odom, CCIE

0-7357-0073-7 • AVAILABLE NOW

This book is a comprehensive study tool for CCNA Exam #640-407 and part of a recommended study program from Cisco Systems. *CCNA Exam Certification Guide* helps you understand and master the exam objectives. Instructor-developed elements and techniques maximize your retention and recall of exam topics, and scenario-based exercises help validate your mastery of the exam objectives.

Advanced Cisco Router Configuration
Cisco Systems, Inc., edited by Laura Chappell

1-57870-074-4 • AVAILABLE NOW

Based on the actual Cisco ACRC course, this book provides a thorough treatment of advanced network deployment issues. Learn to apply effective configuration techniques for solid network implementation and management as you prepare for CCNP and CCDP certifications. This book also includes chapter-ending tests for self-assessment.

Introduction to Cisco Router Configuration
Cisco Systems, Inc., edited by Laura Chappell

1-57870-076-0 • AVAILABLE NOW

Based on the actual Cisco ICRC course, this book presents the foundation knowledge necessary to define Cisco router configurations in multiprotocol environments. Examples and chapter-ending tests build a solid framework for understanding internetworking concepts. Prepare for the ICRC course and CCNA certification while mastering the protocols and technologies for router configuration.

Cisco CCNA Preparation Library
Cisco Systems, Inc., Laura Chappell, and Kevin Downes, CCIE

1-57870-125-2 • AVAILABLE NOW • CD-ROM

This boxed set contains two Cisco Press books—*Introduction to Cisco Router Configuration* and *Internetworking Technologies Handbook,* Second Edition—and the *High-Performance Solutions for Desktop Connectivity* CD.

CISCO SYSTEMS

CISCO PRESS

www.ciscopress.com

Cisco Press Solutions

Enhanced IP Services for Cisco Networks
Donald C. Lee, CCIE

1-57870-106-6 • AVAILABLE NOW

This is a guide to improving your network's capabilities by understanding the new enabling and advanced Cisco IOS services that build more scalable, intelligent, and secure networks. Learn the technical details necessary to deploy Quality of Service, VPN technologies, IPsec, the IOS firewall and IOS Intrusion Detection. These services will allow you to extend the network to new frontiers securely, protect your network from attacks, and increase the sophistication of network services.

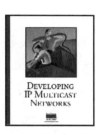

Developing IP Multicast Networks, Volume I
Beau Williamson, CCIE

1-57870-077-9 • AVAILABLE NOW

This book provides a solid foundation of IP multicast concepts and explains how to design and deploy the networks that will support appplications such as audio and video conferencing, distance-learning, and data replication. Includes an in-depth discussion of the PIM protocol used in Cisco routers and detailed coverage of the rules that control the creation and maintenance of Cisco mroute state entries.

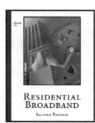

Residential Broadband, Second Edition
George Abe

1-57870-177-5 • AVAILABLE DECEMBER 1999

This book will answer basic questions of residential broadband networks such as: Why do we need high speed networks at home? How will high speed residential services be delivered to the home? How do regulatory or commercial factors affect this technology? Explore such networking topics as xDSL, cable, and wireless.

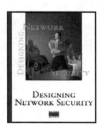

Designing Network Security
Merike Kaeo

1-57870-043-4 • AVAILABLE NOW

Designing Network Security is a practical guide designed to help you understand the fundamentals of securing your corporate infrastructure. This book takes a comprehensive look at underlying security technologies, the process of creating a security policy, and the practical requirements necessary to implement a corporate security policy.

CISCO SYSTEMS

CISCO PRESS

www.ciscopress.com

Cisco Press Solutions

OSPF Network Design Solutions

Thomas M. Thomas II

1-57870-046-9 • AVAILABLE NOW

This comprehensive guide presents a detailed, applied look into the workings of the popular Open Shortest Path First protocol, demonstrating how to dramatically increase network performance and security, and how to most easily maintain large-scale networks. OSPF is thoroughly explained through exhaustive coverage of network design, deployment, management, and troubleshooting.

Top-Down Network Design

Priscilla Oppenheimer

1-57870-069-8 • AVAILABLE NOW

Building reliable, secure, and manageable networks is every network professional's goal. This practical guide teaches you a systematic method for network design that can be applied to campus LANs, remote-access networks, WAN links, and large-scale internetworks. Learn how to analyze business and technical requirements, examine traffic flow and Quality of Service requirements, and select protocols and technologies based on performance goals.

Internetworking SNA with Cisco Solutions

George Sackett and Nancy Sackett

1-57870-083-3 • AVAILABLE NOW

This comprehensive guide presents a practical approach to integrating SNA and TCP/IP networks. It provides readers with an understanding of internetworking terms, networking architectures, protocols, and implementations for internetworking SNA with Cisco routers.

For the latest on Cisco Press resources and Certification and

Training guides, or for information on publishing opportunities, visit

www.ciscopress.com.